Lincoln Christian Coll

P9-DEU-113

# CROMWELL

# BOOKS BY HILAIRE BELLOC

*Historical:*

CROMWELL
CHARLES THE FIRST:
  KING OF ENGLAND
NAPOLEON
RICHELIEU
WOLSEY
CRANMER
JAMES II
JOAN OF ARC
DANTON
MARIE ANTOINETTE
ROBESPIERRE
HISTORY OF ENGLAND
MINIATURES OF FRENCH HISTORY
  ETC.

*Essays:*

CONVERSATION WITH AN ANGEL
SHORT TALKS WITH THE DEAD
HILLS AND THE SEA
THE PATH TO ROME
ON ANYTHING
ON NOTHING
  ETC.

*Novels:*

THE POSTMASTER-GENERAL
BELINDA
THE MISSING MASTERPIECE
SHADOWED
THE HAUNTED HOUSE
THE EMERALD
THE GIRONDIN
THE GREEN OVERCOAT
  ETC.

*General:*

THE CRUISE OF THE NONA
AVRIL
THE FOUR MEN
THE CONTRAST
ESTA PERPETUA
  ETC.

*Poetry:*

VERSES 1910
SONNETS AND VERSES 1923

*Children's Books:*

BAD CHILD'S BOOK OF BEASTS
MORE BEASTS FOR WORSE CHILDREN
A MORAL ALPHABET
CAUTIONARY TALES
  ETC.

*Religious:*

HOW THE REFORMATION HAPPENED
SURVIVALS AND NEW ARRIVALS
EUROPE AND THE FAITH
  ETC.

OLIVER CROMWELL
By Gaspard de Crayer
Versailles

# CROMWELL

## HILAIRE BELLOC

WITH
8 DOUBLETONE ILLUSTRATIONS
AND 12 MAPS

PHILADELPHIA & LONDON
J. B. LIPPINCOTT COMPANY
MCMXXXIV

COPYRIGHT, 1934, BY
HILAIRE BELLOC

MADE IN THE
UNITED STATES OF
AMERICA

FIRST EDITION

# CONTENTS

942.064
B44

32330

# ILLUSTRATIONS

# MAPS

# CROMWELL

THIS book is not another life of Oliver Cromwell; there are dozens too many, the earlier batch a mass of slander, the later a mass of panegyric—all of them myth. My object here is to seek reality; to discover what Cromwell was within; the nature of the man's motives, the quality of his actions as witnesses to the moral truth about himself.

No character lends itself more to myth than does Cromwell's. Violent emotions—not only of affection and detestation but of surprise—are the makers of myth. War in particular produces it; religious enthusiasm notoriously plants, develops and maintains it; patriotism (which is also a religion) does the same.

All these between them had created the huge double myth of Oliver Cromwell. He astonished enormously by coming out of purely civilian life and appearing as a soldier of the first class when he was already in middle age (his forty-third year). He was an extremist during a most violent religious quarrel; his military talents were such that admiration of them was excited to the highest degree, and recognition of those talents served not only to intoxicate those who gloried in his successes, but also those who were his victims. He was national, a man in whom all other Englishmen saw themselves, as it were, glorified or damned. Under his brief rule the power of the nation in the eyes of foreigners stood higher than ever it had done before, or than ever it did for more than a lifetime after.

I say that in the combination of such factors it was not possible but that outrageous myths should arise. Cromwell was the chief factor in the destruction of that which the mass of his fellow-countrymen regarded in his own time as sacred—the national monarchy. His in particular was the will which compassed the death of the sacred Monarch himself. In accomplishing that act he was plainly guilty of plot and subterfuge (as was inevitable) but also during so much warfare he was responsible for wholesale killing, notably in Ireland. Of this he was guilty in the eyes of those who suffered, but it made (and makes) him glorious in the eyes of those who sympathise with his object.

From the day, not two years after his death, when kingship was restored to England amidst the wildest enthusiasm of the people, there ran for something like 150 years a steady stream of hatred directed against his memory. It arose early; it had more than one source. Those who had been Republican during the excitements of the Civil War remembered him as a traitor to their cause; honest men, his contemporaries, who had come across him, men like Huntingdon, had been shocked at his skill in plotting—a skill of which they were incapable and used in a fashion they detested. The crushing taxation without which his armed power would have been impossible roused hatred in the owners of property; memories of confusion and misery and an instinct that a King is the friend of the poor against the rich aroused it in the lower half of the people. And whatever was traditional, loyal, strong-hearted for the past and for the halo surrounding so ancient and so great a Crown was actively repelled by his name. Such forces created the first myth, and Cromwell remained for the bulk of educated Englishmen, and the masses whom they indoctrinated, the Hypocrite and Villain upon the stage of English history. The fantastic figure so put forward in place of the true was a monster of contradictory acts and qualities—all vile. He was of base birth—a thing which in their eyes made his rise appear iniquitous. He had passed a youth of idleness and debauchery (the stories of which do not fit the dates and were not witnessed); he had proceeded to a public career which was one mass of falsehood and guile, wholly designed to serve a most offensive ambition. He was a traitor and a tyrant. He was even a coward. He very nearly murdered the nation as he had murdered its King. He kept no faith. His own child reproached him bitterly with his crimes. The Devil flew away with his soul. It was a last but a feeble satisfaction to know that his body had been dug up and hung in chains in expiation of his enormities.

There was the Oliver Cromwell of one myth, the myth of the eighteenth and early nineteenth centuries. It was so strong that though there was plenty of individual support for his memory and a fairly strong though subdued tradition upon the other side, the phantasm had its way and took on the solidity of an historical truth.

Then came a somewhat rapid revolution in judgment. There arose a contrary current stronger because more profound than the first, and appearing at the time when historical research was beginning to be taken seriously. It was much more than a reaction against the falsehood of the first myth, it was a new contradictory myth, taking the place of the old. It completely dominated the nineteenth century, at any rate after its earlier years, and the impetus of it has reached on into our own time, though the strength of the stream is now happily spent.

According to this second myth Cromwell is a figure over-shadowed by the English God. He is a national hero. The cause he defended was unquestionably just—but it is more than that, it is the very cause of England; and, what is more, the cause of Divine Purpose in action. Cromwell becomes the typical Chief Man of a Superior Race.

The main cause of this revolution was the rise of the new industrial fortunes in England, and the effect of their wealth upon society. But a second allied force was also at work: the effect of time. The new industrial forces were accumulated by men, many (perhaps most) of whom came from that Nonconformist stock of which Cromwell had always been the hero. These were the men who, under the powerful influence of the new French political theories, American experiment, and the successful Revolution in Paris, destroyed the old Tory tradition. But they had not, in their zeal against privilege and the

[ 13 ]

savour of the old world, abandoned their religion. It was strong in them still. They were still full of the Bible, and especially of the Old Testament; their morals were the morals of the Puritans; their restrictions and sanctities identical with those which had ruled in Cromwell's own household and in those of all his world.

While they felt thus there had passed all around them a sort of oblivion worked by the lapse of years and the development of English aristocratic government, which oblivion had left men insensible to the ancient claims of kingship. Those claims had come to sound like nonsense; men had never seen them in action and could not conceive what they might be, acting on their own soil and amid people of their own blood. Quaint foreign survivals of monarchy, all of them decaying, were to be observed at the petty Courts of Italy and Germany or in the much faded grandeur of Spain. There could be no longer a comprehension of sacred kingship: the idea had become ridiculous. It could no longer be conceived how Cromwell had destroyed a thing in his own days most holy. All that for which Cromwell stood and of which his triumph was the climax, the Englishman of the nineteenth century called "constitutional" —whereas it had been in Cromwell's own time purely revolutionary. Government by squires, merchants and lawyers calling themselves the people, power in the hands of their House of Commons, had come to seem for Englishmen the very nature of things; time, the maker of States, had come to make a nineteenth-century England: based upon aristocracy, believing itself to be based upon a thing called "self-government."

There was yet another more obscure but very powerful cause of this "right-about-face" in the attitude of the average Englishman towards this striking figure of Cromwell, standing up so large out of the English past. That obscure but profound force was a new kind of anti-Catholicism which arose in the England of yesterday and is stronger than ever today.

It was not the flaming antagonism mixed with extreme fear

[ 14 ]

as well as open hatred which had been natural to the seventeenth century, it contained far more contempt, and at the same time a power both to forget or ignore its enemy, for it regarded that enemy as now finally defeated. But it was there. You see it at full force in the writings of Carlyle, and thence onwards you see it in the writings of pretty well every accepted and national writer and historian. The nations of the Catholic culture were, in the eyes of nineteenth-century England, declining and decaying societies. And indeed that culture in that time was bitterly divided against itself. Thus the national movement in Italy, Garibaldi and Cavour, could be acclaimed as one more stroke for progress and against the detested tradition. All the stream of events flowed in the same direction, until the time when most of us who are now elderly were already mature. Prussia had conquered France, the Imperial Throne at Vienna had become a mockery, all hope for Ireland seemed lost, Poland could never rise from the dead—and such as still adhered to the Catholic cause seemed romantic eccentrics (we remember how for Carlyle, Newman had "the brains of a rabbit") or pathetic lovers clinging to the dead.

This general spirit, though its effect was but negative, was very strong. It made, for instance, the stories of Drogheda and Wexford less horrible, and the story of Basing House something picturesque rather than tragic. As for the women who had their throats cut and their brains battered out after Naseby, yet another phrase from Carlyle is typical of the man himself and all his succeeding time. He tells us discreetly and without details that "it went hardly with them."

Under the influence of the new myth Cromwell cannot do anything that is not, in some way, right. His strokes of luck become strokes of genius (which is very unjust to his real genius); his blunders become trials and checks, sure to be surmounted. The puritan, whose energy is essentially hysterical, becomes "stern"; if he wallow in blood through nervous instability he is only doing what was normal to the time—or

[ 15 ]

better still, he is but executing justice upon barbarous wretches. When he bullies he becomes "a man not to be trifled with"; when his bullying fails we are asked to wait a bit and see what is coming—for the writer knows well that if we wait long enough success after all is only round the corner.

As for his most conspicuous failure, his inability to govern, his perpetual efforts at getting others to help him and his miserable break-down time after time in such efforts, the comic side of all that affair during the last years before his death is wholly ignored. It is as though one were watching a man attempting to jump a broad ditch, missing by a good three feet, floundering back into the muddy water, climbing back up the muddy bank, taking a second run, missing again, floundering again—a third run, a third miss, a third flounder, and then a fourth repetition of the funny business all over again and actually the preparations for a fifth—and all the while admirers in the field who are clapping their hands and crying "Bravo!" Even the death itself, which is pathetic enough and even solemn amid its incongruity, must be made what it was not—majestic.

All this "Hero Myth" cannot but ultimately belittle Cromwell. The man himself, the true man, had such kinds of strength, such qualities and above all such particular and rare military talent as are warped in our eyes and befogged by this perpetual laudation. The man was compelled, in sheer self-preservation, to get another man out of the way. He did save himself with singular tenacity and yet more remarkable skill; he carried out his plan thoroughly concealing intention, keeping in the background, employing agents privately, pleading doubtfully for the victim in public. He succeeded and Charles Stuart was brought to the scaffold. The plot so achieved is well worth admiring; but one cannot admire it if one is told that Cromwell was alive with an honest good-nature, determined on saving the King all along, and then suddenly receiving an inner light by which he was given divine orders to kill.

To make up the Hero-picture in this point of the killing

of the King and in a dozen others, zealots are compelled to acrobatics quite unworthy of history. Impulse has to be presented as calculation, duplicity as revelation, contemporary authentic documents must be doubted, imaginary motives set down as real.

Finally, this worshipping of Cromwell as something he was *not* hides from us what he *was:* a genius in handling the mounted arm. For *that*, for the command of horse, Cromwell can never be too much praised. Here is a cavalry leader who stands among other cavalry leaders as Milton does among the poets; and yet his exceptional gifts as a tactician must be diminished by pretending that, in a place and time where nothing but the most elementary strategy was conceivable, he was at the same time a subtle and consummate indirect strategist of a much later school.

.　　.　　.　　.　　.　　.

In the presence of these two myths, the first of which, all-powerful in its time, is today nearly forgotten (yet of the two it had the longer run); the second of which is, even today, dying hardly, it is the business of historical judgment to establish the truth on his character. No other object has been pursued in these pages. I have concerned myself almost entirely with what the man was—not with what he did, save in so far as what he did explains him. On this account I have devoted most space to his formation, to the ill-understood effect of the Catholic menace in his day, to the long and careful intrigue whereby he compassed the death of Charles Stuart. I have devoted less to his military actions, which serve only to exemplify his high talent in the field, his lucidity and rapidity of tactical judgment in battle; but also his disabilities in strategy. To the last years in which he was so conspicuous a European figure I have given no more space or detail than is necessary to explain how bewildered he was throughout, how dependent on force for his government, how, therefore, grievously embarrassed for resources and doomed to fail; how incompetent and at sea in foreign affairs. Throughout I would attempt to present the man's mind.

How shall that be done? The task can best be achieved, it would seem, by the envisaging of main points: the social standing of the man, the great wealth of his family, high among the new millionaires, the nature of the intense new religion which possessed him, and this presented not as "Religion" in general but as the particular new and revolutionary religion which in fact it was. To discover his circumstances you must, again, envisage those things in the world around him which made him act in a manner natural to him, strange to us: for instance, the presence of what I have called "The Catholic Menace" to him in 1620-50 most vividly apparent, to us in 1930-40 incomprehensible.

We must see him above all as a soldier, and, to appreciate his supreme talents as a soldier, we must regard the particular actions of the campaigns as so many problems, by the examination of which we can discover the quality of his energy, his courage, his capacity for command, his rapidity of judgment and his magnificently-equipped imagination foreseeing the critical time and point, not indeed strategically, of the campaign, but tactically on the field; his exactitude in striking there and then. We must test the strength of his virtues by special examples; the sincerity with which he adored that God of his, his chastity, the fundamental simplicity of his nature, his lack of ambition—his lack indeed of those capacities which breed ambition. We must also test by examples his excesses of cruelty; we must observe how they were only excited on occasion and against one irritant, the old Religion; we must remember, what the hero-worshippers never do, that he had good-fellowship in him—which is what one might expect from a man natively a soldier. And, at the close of his life, we must appreciate in its fullness that main cause of his indecision, the torturing need of money sufficient to support a military power

but for which he and all his precarious and undesired achievement would fail—as fail they did in the end.

If we but see him thus in the light of realities, of things he
really said and did, of the actual society in which he moved,
we get a figure in the round and of a piece: the figure of one
who is national, the more national today because the faction
to which he belonged has ceased to be a faction and, while
losing its fierce doctrines, has spread their spiritual effect
throughout the people: one inconsequent as all men are inconsequent, but of a simpler and therefore more united sort than
most: one who has given glory to his country through the
triumphant exercise of an excelling military talent: one who
could not use that talent save under conditions of increasing
financial strain which broke him: one who, under such a strain,
was condemned to increasing vacillation, and one who died
worn out, having accomplished nothing permanent, not even
the destruction of the Irish people.

Oʟɪᴠᴇʀ Wɪʟʟɪᴀᴍs—universally known as "Cromwell"—was the cadet of a family grown suddenly opulent in a religious revolution. Till past his fortieth year he lived obscurely the life of his class; marrying early into another landed family, administering local government, sitting in Parliament for his constituency like any other squire.

Not till his forty-third year, a civil war having broken out, did he discover an unsuspected talent—he appeared as an exceptional leader of cavalry, a soldier of genius. The first engagement proved his quality. Within twenty months he had decided in person, at the head of his horsemen, the main action of the war; less than a year later the final victory. He planned the death of the King he had conquered. He ravaged Ireland, occupied Scotland, and thenceforward ruled these islands with unquestioned, though reluctant, power; commanding the best-trained forces in Europe and those of longest service by land and sea. At the height of his fame and its unwelcome burden, not yet sixty, he died.

What kind of man, and that man moved by what accidents, produced so strange an episode? To answer these two questions is the task of any who would attempt to comprehend Cromwell.

. . . . . . .

There arose nineteen centuries ago an institution round which, from that day to this, the story of Europe has turned. It called itself "The Church," it rapidly developed a strong organisation, and within a lifetime of its founding the greatest of historians had branded it, "The Enemy of the Human Race." For indeed this mark was stamped upon it; that it should be hated (but also loved) beyond any other thing.

It grew yearly in numbers, in strength, in the vivid definition

of its own personality, which it had from the beginning proclaimed to be Divine. It fiercely suppressed dissidence within
its own boundaries. It challenged the general society around
it, suffered the intense hostility thereof, but overcame and absorbed it. Thenceforward our civilisation, baptised under the
name of "Christendom," survived amid incessant most varied
and recurrent perils, each seemingly invincible. It maintained
itself against domestic rebellion and foreign assault, still so
loved, still so hated: poisoned, disrupted from within by the
Arian, the Manichean; assieged and pressed hard from without
by hordes in arms. The heathen and barbarian from the north
and east broke against it for five hundred years; from the east
also and from the south an enthusiasm from the desert, inspired
by the memory of Mohammed, swept forward intent upon
its destruction and mastered half its territories, hither Asia,
North Africa and Spain.

This mortal duel was still in progress when, the last of many
internal disruptions closely threatening the Church with death,
upsprang the earthquake of the Reformation. To this last the
origins, the nature and the career of Cromwell belong.

Two strains of influence proceeded therefrom: one was
temporal, external, concerned with wealth, family fortunes and
social station, which mould by pressure from without the nature of a man. The other, far more important, was an influence
directly affecting the soul and therefore by action from within
making a man's whole self. Both combined to produce Oliver:
the new wealth and the new religion. I will take first the influence of wealth.

In that cataclysm of the Reformation the distribution of
wealth and land in half Europe (but especially in England),
the social structure thereof, was first shaken to pieces, next
transformed. Thence arose a class of men holding newly acquired wealth, which class came to dominate all English society.
Vast estates grew up, as it were, in a night from the sacking

of Church endowment. Among these were the possessions of those from whom Oliver, his traditions and his very self derived. It behoves us therefore to grasp this revolution in the control of English land and to mark how, therefrom, the great Williams fortune suddenly arose.

A LIFETIME before Oliver's birth there was settled as a publican in Putney, a short way up river from London, one Morgan Ap-Williams, a Welshman from Glamorgan. He seems to have been born in some small village a couple of miles north of Cardiff. He traded also here in Putney as a fuller, and a blacksmith's forge was attached to the inn.

This Williams had for neighbour another publican, Cromwell or Crumwell by name, of whose children one, Margaret, married the son of Williams, while the other, Thomas, her brother, set off on vagabond adventures.

Young Mrs. Williams bore her husband a son who was christened Richard and grew up in his father's public house, while his uncle Thomas was lost somewhere abroad. He had run wild, got locked up, quarrelled with his drunken father, and at last went overseas to enlist for hire as a soldier in the wars. Speculators would form armed bands of such and let them out at a price to the Princes of Europe in their quarrels.

But Thomas Cromwell was destined to greater things than a precarious daily wage and death from the pike of another enlisted vagabond. From what opportunities we know not, perhaps a bag of coins in the sack of a farmstead, perhaps from a first few pence lent by the week to a comrade, he learnt the beginnings of money-lending: many great men have started so. He had method and application. After adventures in the Netherlands he found at last employment with the greater moneylenders of Italy. He returns to England with some capital, and new clients fall into his debt.

It was the moment when Cardinal Wolsey ruled the State, and, having heard of the man's capacity, and substance, he offered him a post suitable to so much cunning, industry and acquaintance with affairs. Thomas Cromwell, a man of Wolsey's own age, managed the Cardinal's business and did well at it. One part of it was the investigation and taking over of certain small monasteries whose revenues the Pope had allowed to be used for the founding of Wolsey's new college at Oxford. The experience served him.

Thus was he established, a solid, equable, reserved moneylender, well on in his forties, with sapient little pig's eyes set deep in a fat face, when his progress was disturbed, as was all England, by an adventure of his master's master, the King. Henry VIII of England had been caught by Anne Boleyn, who would be satisfied with nothing less than the throne. The putting away of Catherine, the reigning Queen, must be obtained from the Pope. Wolsey failed to obtain it, was disgraced, and died just in time to save himself from Anne's vengeance. Thomas was loyal to the fallen Cardinal, but had the boldness and address to reach the King, for he had experience of men, especially in their weakness, and he knew that Henry, having lost one guide, would need another. He was the author, by suggestion, of all that followed.

Religious revolution had been roaring in the Germanies for a dozen years with Luther riding, distracted, the crest of its wave and the noise and heat of it felt over all Christendom around before Cromwell had got hold of the reins in England. Under his direction the King of England broke with the central spiritual power of Europe and became his own Pope over four million souls. In doctrine, in Liturgy, in all Church things save that one symbol of unity Henry, like his subjects, was unchanged. The new exaltations were horrible to him and to the English people, having a foreign, newfangled air ill-suited to their temperament. But in England, as everywhere else, there was universal discontent with the Church machine, its accumulation of legal fees, fines, dues; and the ceaseless pressure of its Courts on private men, the vastness of its endowments abused and prostituted. The clerics were less corrupt here than in any other province of Europe, but they were corrupt enough. Their wealth, the incomes of sees and livings of every kind, of hospitals and colleges and schools—all Church corporations—lay now defenceless, isolated from Christendom. And the German merchant cities and princes had already set the example of spoliation. The estates of the religious houses which stood by the hundred large and small all over the land had been long watched with especial envy. There was grave laxity in their discipline and vices, which rumour exaggerated. Their inhabitants, halved in numbers through a general decay, enjoyed the full revenue of earlier and better times. Upon them Thomas Cromwell would begin his great experiment, and institute it by first attacking the lesser and weaker units: he proposed to enrich his sovereign vastly and himself. He had become the King's Vicegerent in religion, all-powerful over the English Church when his scheme was launched.

It began with the sending out of agents to draw up as black reports as they could upon the morals of the smaller houses—those with a revenue of under £5,000 a year. The year of this economic revolution which inaugurated modern England should be memorable to all Englishmen: 1536. The lands and goods of these lesser religious houses were first to be seized. Such an attack upon old-established things raised a fierce popular rebellion which nearly overset the Throne; but it was betrayed and crushed with horrible cruelty, and, as certain Abbots of the great monasteries had joined it, Cromwell made them go the way of the lesser houses. The drive lasted four years. By 1540 the last of the monasteries had gone. Their dues from land and stock—perhaps a fifth of English plough and pasture—with herds and stock, the proceeds of the furniture, books, gold and silver of the Altar, rich cloths and jewels, the moneys in their chests, their great buildings, had all passed to the King's Treasury.

But not to the King's Treasury alone. The agents of the huge confiscation kept their share, Thomas Cromwell at their head.

By gift from the Crown, commission, concealment, tricks of conveyance, purchase at half-price, great parcels of the robbery fell at a stroke into the hands of those who served the King and the King's Vicegerent in "the Things of Religion." They arose in a moment out of nothing into enormous fortunes—and with them Richard Williams.

Thomas Cromwell, when this last and chief work of his life began, had for some years kept at his side as a dependant his sister's child, now grown to manhood and serviceable. Uncle Thomas set up nephew Richard with the rest as agent, bully and spy, to further the precipitate and tremendous business of those four years.

Richard Williams was assiduous in the affair, reporting his success in coercion, serving Thomas Cromwell eagerly and reaping as blood relation and lieutenant a prodigious reward. It came at once. In grants at easy charges, with exchanges, etc., he leapt into millions. Already in the second year of the plundering he had received estates in five counties of East England and its neighbourhood, in Huntingdon, Cambridge, Bedford, Rutland and as far off as Northamptonshire. Next he got the Cistercian Abbey of Saltrey in Huntingdon and its great buildings and rents assessed at from three to four thousand pounds a year, later the Priory of the Augustinians of Our Lady, with four to five thousand a year assessment and the houses; and yet another still larger body of wealth in that countryside, the great house of St. Neots—some £6,000 a year assessment and more. Later was added some unknown part of the Franciscan estates at Stamford.

But the biggest fish in the net was the famous abbey of Ramsay, also East Anglian and of the Fenland. Its riches were famous and had become proverbial throughout England. In rents alone it was assessed at just on £50,000 a year, and we know that the official assessments were far below the real value. Richard Williams did not get *all* that land, though he got the splendid buildings and all their dependencies and gear, but he had the first claims on it. He had had his eye on it from the beginning of his foraging up and down these East Anglian parts for Uncle Thomas Cromwell, saying in a letter, "now we have done with Ramsay," whose Abbot he finds well cowed, "we go on to Peterburgh." Peterborough still stands to show what these splendours were, and of its revenue only a third was seized.

Richard Williams got much more than all this. The items are but such as research has separately discovered, for there is no full list. Apart from this sweep of Abbey lands he had the wardship of two castles upon the Welsh Borders, salary upon salary accumulated in his hands, the stewardship of Royal manors, the headship of the infantry in the King's next expedition abroad, etc. He was already possessed of a great heiress as wife, the daughter of the Lord Mayor of London. And a marriage into the Lord Mayor's family had been, alone, the making of many a house. With Williams it was but an important increment, so huge was his new fortune from Church lands. Within five years of his leaving his father's public house and business in Putney he was established among the new millionaires of the religious revolution; within seven years his immense fortune was at its full; within four years more he was dead.

Richard Williams had early tacked his famous uncle's name on to his own. He thought it of advantage—and it flattered his benefactor, the master of England—to call himself "Richard Cromwell": but as in those days a false name was not accepted at will, he had to sign his true name in grave matters, and "Cromwell, alias Williams" appears not only as his own sign-manual but as that of his descendants. He had been knighted, and men had been taught to call him "Sir Richard Cromwell" when he died, a few months before the King, in the autumn of 1546.

Of a dozen places he might have chosen out of the booty as the seat of his great new family he pitched upon Hinchinbrooke.* It was a comfortable nunnery of no great size, its revenue hardly worth mentioning in the flood of his other properties, but it was most convenient and with unlimited wealth at his disposal he could turn it into whatever he wished. It stood just outside and dominating an important town, the chief of its county, Huntingdon, a larger place then than it later became. Hinchinbrooke had also double main communication by water and land, for the Great North Road from London to York and Scotland passed close by, and the river Ouse bounded its park. It was also central to the main portion of Williams's numerous estates, scattered over five counties around. Cambridge was but fifteen miles away, St. Neots an hour's slow ride, and Ramsay (on the ruins of which he raised a summer residence) an hour's fast one.

But the point of Hinchinbrooke which counted most in the story of the "Cromwell" family was its relation to the capital. London, now the permanent centre of government, was within an easy day's posting by one of the few main roads, well kept up, under sixty miles: not so near as to be in the immediate grasp of Whitehall, near enough to be in full touch with affairs and news. And from Huntingdon town action could radiate east and north to Bedford, Cambridge, Ely, the Fens—it stood at the gates of half-isolated East Anglia.

Sir Richard, dying, left an heir, Henry, a minor, to succeed him at Hinchinbrooke, and his fortune to use or spend. He spent it largely when he came of age, famous for his wealth, and very famous for display, in the course of a fairly long life. He played to the full the part of a great new Reformation family in its second generation. He was generous, too, and not restrained. There were two illegitimate daughters put down to him, of whom modern historians do not speak, fearing to mention Oliver Cromwell's bastard aunts as though these were a shame to *him*. In the same way, we hear little of a cousin who

* The name *was*, of course, but also still *is* variously spelt and the various spellings fiercely defended by purists. I follow the one-inch Ordnance.

was hanged for murder. Yet that also is in no way derogatory to Oliver himself.

Sir Henry's reign at Hinchinbrooke corresponded exactly with that of Elizabeth; he sat in one of the first Parliaments of the reign, he entertained the Queen royally under his roof before she had been on the throne five years, he was sheriff of the County over and over again. He died (in January, 1603) only a few weeks before the Queen. With him the new designation "Cromwell" and the new gorgeousness of riches took root. Putney was forgotten. Sir Harry Cromwell of Hinchinbrooke stood resplendent among the rest of an England transformed—Russells and Wriothesleys and all the other names of which, less than a lifetime before, no one had ever heard.

Henry Cromwell had married into further great wealth, of course, the daughter of yet another Lord Mayor of London, and the great House was filled with children—ten of them—through whose marriages the Williams family were to be connected right and left with the landed class that was soon to govern England. One daughter married into the Whalleys of Kirton, whose ascent to sudden fortune out of Church lands had been exactly parallel to the Williams ascent. Another married the head of the Ingoldsbys; another Sir Francis Barrington; another the squire of Wittingham where the twin hills stand alone above the Thames. But the finest of all those daughter-marriages was Elizabeth's. She captured—or rather there was captured for her—one of the greatest fortunes in that fortunate world, William Hampden of Great Hampden, head of the millionaire Buckinghamshire family.

Of the sons who grew up under that roof the second, Robert, is the first we must mark; for though the elder brother would have Hinchinbrooke and most of the wealth, it was Robert who was the father of so much fame.

When Robert was grown a man and it was time for him to marry—some half a dozen years after the Armada—he was given his portion of the monastic property (rifled forty years before); it was the land of the Augustinians of Huntingdon, and for house a large place in the town which had once been the Hospital of St. John, looted with the rest. The Augustinian rents—the portion segregated for him—were some £3,000 a year, the portion of a younger son in so rich a family. He married into yet another bulk of what had been directly and indirectly Church property under the Stewards of Ely, and he further supplemented his income with a brewing business.

This Steward marriage is important to any understanding of Oliver. Elizabeth Steward, his mother, was wealthy, as all the women were whom the numerous rich Williamses married, but it was the particular character of her wealth and its origin that we must notice.

When Richard Williams was riding round England bullying, threatening and cajoling the heads of religious houses in the service of his all-powerful uncle, he had to deal, among others, with Ely. Now the Prior of Ely was a certain Richard Steward. It had been feared that he would make difficulties about yielding to the spoilers, but he proved open to the golden argument. When the monks were dispersed and much of their great revenue used to establish a new cathedral, Richard Steward was made Dean of it with a fat salary, which he is said to have spent charitably enough. He procured for his nephew William Steward the lucrative post of tithe and revenue farmer to the chapter. William Steward had a son and daughter, the great-niece and great-nephew of the original renegade Prior. The son, called Henry, became that Sir Thomas Steward who inherited his father's accumulation and his lucrative office as well. The daughter, called Elizabeth, was this wife of Robert and mother of Oliver. After an early marriage into another family of the same wealthy kind her first husband and one child died, and she married Robert when she was over thirty, in 1591.

The son takes most from the mother, as the daughter from the father. Were it not so the two sexes would long ago have become unintelligible to each other; and the chief moral inheritance of Oliver was presumably from this woman who bore him close upon her fortieth year. Of her we know little, and it is a pity, for her nature could explain his own. At any rate we see in that parentage a maternal strain similar to his father's, another fortune sprung as the Williams fortune had sprung from the lost lands of the old religion. The Cromwells and the Stewards were of one kind. She lived on to an extreme old age, not dying till shortly before Oliver's own death and when he was at the height of his power.

Robert Cromwell, then, living on an income of perhaps four or five thousand a year all told, at the gate of his father's Mansion and Park, brought up his children in that air: so we have at Hinchinbrooke, the "Golden Knight," now growing old, and near him his eldest son, the heir, and Robert established in the town, all making as it were one household. The other brothers marrying as he had done into the new wealth of the Religious Revolution, or the old wealth suddenly increased by it, went off, each as he married, to his own household. They did all that their new class did, as squires in Parliament like the rest, adventuring capital overseas, as sheriffs, as everything that the rich then were. Through these marriages there arose in those few years a whole class of wealthy landowners all hand in hand with the great Williams (alias "Cromwell") fortune, and the Hampdens the richest of them all.

So things stood, when there was born to Robert a boy, on April the 25th, 1599.

The first impressions of the child were those of splendour. He was four years old when the new King, James Stuart, came down the Great North Road to within the last stages before the capital and was received at Hinchinbrooke with magnificence. The eldest son had but lately succeeded to his father's immense fortune; that father had already been famous for the unequalled pageantry with which he had received his contemporary and Queen, Elizabeth. The heir was determined to continue the tradition. The uncle, godfather and namesake of the little boy—for the name Oliver had been given him after the head of the family—shone with the display of his wealth on that occasion, and James so well remembered the unaccustomed grandeur that he returned more than once in the coming years to Huntingdon, that he might taste again the glories of a fortune poured out in his honour at Hinchinbrooke. There is a tradition that when little Prince Charles, the puny, seemingly crippled second son of the new King was brought down some months later to the Court from Scotland, the two children met. It is likely enough. The Royal baby—much of an age with Oliver—came down that same Great North Road which his father had followed, and Hinchinbrooke was always eager to show how rich it was, and to play the host to Sovereigns and their kin.

So the lad grew, all penetrated with the greatness and income of the Cromwells, and himself in the comfort of some thousands a year and the largest house in the town which his uncle's estates and revenues overshadowed. He was lapped around and nourished in the air of those great squires to whose class he belonged, and who were so soon to take over the kingdom. He knew nothing else. His father's ample income was increased by the successful venture in brewing, and Oliver in his early teens was the more conscious of his position from the fact that he was an only son. Another boy, born four years before him, had died; all the other living children, older and younger than himself, were daughters. So in all the formative years of his early life was Oliver framed by the influence of very great position based upon the ever-present air of apparently endless wealth in those of his blood. A score of great county families his close relatives, a Lord Chief Justice his cousin, his father and his father's brothers conspicuous in the usual national occupations of rich men—summoned to Westminster and sheriffs, that is, governors (as sheriffs then were) of the countryside for a hundred miles. In all things was he moulded externally into his rank and had it the more deeply impressed upon him from his early independence. For he was not eighteen when his father died, leaving him, while still an undergraduate hurriedly recalled from Cambridge, the head of his branch of the family.

Yet, though he could not think of himself save as one of that new governing class to which he already belonged, its wealth was not of principal effect upon him. Much more was it his peculiar temperament, and that intensely affected by a new religion, which were to make the man.

JEAN CAUVIN,* a young Frenchman, a Picard from Noyon, north-east of Paris, published in 1536 a certain book. He was but twenty-five years old when he finished the manuscript and barely twenty-six when he passed the last proofs.

Jean called his book "The Institute" (that is, "the scheme," "the rule," "the fixed affirmation")—"The Institute of the Christian Religion"; a Latin book; "*Institutio Christiana.*" And he set at its head the cry, "I come not to bring peace but a sword."

That book launched a new religion, wherewith the burning but unchanging will, the tenacity, zeal and ceaseless predication of its author clove Europe to the heart and came near to transforming the world. See the man Calvin as the origin of what follows, for, of the millions whom the new religion inflamed and filled was Oliver.

No Calvin, no Cromwell. You shall not comprehend the mind of Cromwell, nor any of the innumerable minds who have known themselves, from that day till yesterday, to be Elect of God, until you have felt the fierce blast from that

* "Calvin" is the archaic form of the French surname "Cauvin," "al" becoming "au" in the development of the French language from Latin. The older form was still occasionally used in the sixteenth century, though Calvin himself and his father and neighbours said "Cauvin." The general use of the form "Calvin" today is due to three things:

(1) The Latin form of the name "Calvinus." Latin was the universal language of religious controversy.

(2) "Calvin" is easily pronounced as a native word by German, Dutch, Scotch and English disciples, the original French nasal "Cauvin" is not.

(3) The form "Calvin" therefore masks and helps to render forgotten the essentially French character of the man. Since the failure of Calvin and his disciples to impress the new religion on French culture, this culture has come to seem alien to those formed by Calvin's mind, and they prefer to think Calvinism native to Geneva, where it took root. Yet French it is in everything, in its logic, its hardness, its universality.

furnace which Jean Cauvin of Noyon in Picardy kindled.

In 1536, then, the Book appeared. It was the very year that saw the launching of the Church loot in England. The same year wherein arose the great fortune of the Williams family, arose also the influence which was to possess and make their most famous son. How did the Book and he who wrote it come to be?

Formless as a confusion of waves in flood, the religious revolt, long surging, had broken the dykes at last. The distant rumour of it reached Noyon when little Jean Cauvin was a child of eight years old: the far noise of it away to the eastward, and Luther's name now first heard above the clamour.

As the boy grew into his teens the thing touched him not at all. The wealthy household of his father was all mixed with the priests of the ancient Catholic cathedral town; it stood in the midst of them, for that father, Gerard Cauvin, was lawyer to the Bishop and Chapter; his fortune was drawn from the administration of their large properties, the defence of their pleas. Church rents and dues were his science and his livelihood; in these also he invested his rapidly increasing surplus wealth. He provided for his sons by buying them Church revenues. Thus this young Jean had a parish living bought for him among other clerical emoluments, which, in the corruption of the time, changed hands like stocks and shares.

The lad could not, of course, say Mass, nor had he any need to become a priest, nor was he trained for one. A priest was hired after the custom of the day to say the Parish Mass in Jean Cauvin's place, while Gerard Cauvin drew the income of the living for his boy, who was designed for the law, to prosper in it like his father. So Jean was sent off to the schools in Paris with an ample allowance, there to study for his preliminary degree.

While he was in Paris, he being then just eighteen, there came sudden ill news from Noyon, from home. The father, Gerard Cauvin, had been accused of embezzlement. The Cathedral authorities had demanded his accounts and he had refused to render them. He was thrice summoned, still refused, and was excommunicated.

Calvin returned to Noyon in a fever to find this bad money-quarrel at its height, his father forbidden the sacraments, his own income and that of his brother threatened with interdiction. There was open war between the Cauvin family and the Church on which they had so prosperously lived. The father was still stubborn in his refusal to show his accounts and meet the charge of embezzlement, the sacraments were still refused that household. It seemed outcast. Under such a shock Calvin returned to his now embittered studies, wherein he took refuge; he lost himself in that intense intellectual labour and discovery which, with certain very young men at the opening of life, occupies all their being. By such a path was he led to engage in the new religious disputes which were now raging throughout the learned world.

He was a man now. His tall lean figure, somewhat bent, always in black, moved rapidly among its fellows. His health already threatened to break, but he paid no heed to that; continuous toil did but anneal his now overpowering will, and his intelligence of steel was hardened to creative effort.

He passed to the University of Bourges to complete his mastership of Arts in the Law. His father died, still excommunicated and denied burial in consecrated land. He now associated—at first somewhat, then mainly, soon wholly—with those who were in confused but violent rebellion against the ancient religion. He prayed with them in their secret "Suppers of the Lord"—which were the negation of the Mass. He preached the Word. And all the while, thus young, he worked enormously at his growing Book.

Here was he in the midst of a white-hot upheaval. It had begun in the Germanies when he was but a little boy and heedless of such things. It had filled special men with a prodigious enthusiasm, strongest among the scholars of the Uni-

versities, in France, in England, in Italy. But it had remained
negative, vivified only by a hatred of the Thing and Personality to be attacked, the Enemy—that ancient Church which
centred in the Mass, was framed in the Priesthood and was
bound in one by the Papacy. For the rest, the early tempest of
the Reformation was an assault of many eddying opinions,
"formless as a confusion of waves in flood."

Calvin himself was to give it form, and to create a new
Thing, strong to destroy the old. His Book appeared. He was
launched upon his awful task.

He, that young man, had heard—as all had heard who had
mixed in these wild disputes—the advocates of Grace who
denied the value of man's works, and so disarmed the Priests
in their penances and sacramental aids. But the idea was vague.
He evoked a new Spirit. He struck suddenly at the root of
Catholicism, which root is the doctrine of the Human Will:
that it is free and must work through a free intelligence, man
being in the image of God.

Indeed the ancient Religion of Europe may be called an
exercise in the Will; and to destroy reliance upon the human
will, to expose it for an illusion, is to drain the blood from
Catholicism, so that it must fail and faint away. The Catholic
must earn beatitude—but what if beatitude cannot be earned?
A doubt on that palsies the Faith at its heart. Calvin sought
with passion and with proof to annihilate the Human Will.
He proclaimed One Will alone in the Universe, the dreadful Will of God.

From the beginning of his generations twin terrors have
overshadowed the mind of man, like poisonous ivies inter-
twined: Evil and Doom. Their menaces increase with age. To
give to Evil at least an equality with Good and therefore to
stand in awe thereof was what our fathers of old called "The
Manichean taint"; it is this which pervades throughout all
human history the mood today called "Puritanism," and puts
it in conflict with beauty and with joy. But Calvin did more

than revive the ancient Manichean obsession; he transcended it. He left no rivalry of Good and Evil. Our intolerable sufferings, our despairs, final and eternal, lay within that One Will of the Omnipotent: the Immutable Decrees of God. Under the pressure of a coherent system, rigid with hammered logic, Calvin drove such convictions home. God alone acted, and all we are was but the operation of unalterable fates at work from all eternity.

It could not be other for those who heard his message; the finite could have no place against the Infinite; the Creature was not "less than" the Creator; he was nothing: the Creator was all. In Catholicism a man may damn himself by the deliberate choice of evil. But Calvin could prove to you that a man chooses not at all. He does not damn himself but *is* damned; he is no one in the matter, save that he goes through the necessary motions of the part assigned to him. And seeing what men were—evil—damned must the multitude of them certainly be. The young man saw this truth with fiery eyes. He had taken "The Fall" from those Scriptures which, after the revolt against a teaching Church, remained the only basis of belief. He had selected what he found in his immense reading of the Fathers to emphasise the prevision of God, suppressing what equally emphasised our freedom—thus did he forge his iron creed.

The race of man was accurst. It had fallen not from a supernatural to a natural state (as Catholics did vainly pretend), but to a diabolic one, and was native to Hell. Such as might be excepted owed their strange good fortune to no act of their own, but solely to the merits of a Divine Saviour which merits were, by a lawyer's fiction, "imputed" to the elect.

Calvin's Book which, I say, so nearly changed the whole European world and did change one half of it, is intolerably dull to the modern reader, even if he be in the tradition of its author. It is really more interesting to those who are in opposition to him—for them at least it presents an astonishing thesis. But even those who think it dull should do violence to themselves and read it. They will find that it is essentially the book of an advocate, a lawyer. He holds a brief (from God) against the old religion. He argues against it with a mass of selected instances which show, for a young man of twenty-six, the most astonishing research. There is a prodigious bulk of quotation, and the business of all of it is to upset the pretensions of the Catholic Church and especially those of its organized hierarchy, and the ritual whereby it is bound together—all its fundamental practice. Hence the attack on images, hence the more essential attack upon the Sacrament of the Altar. Calvin had no scruple to use the advocate's method of selection and special pleading. He was not seeking the truth. He had the truth already. But he also had burning desire to drive it into the public conscience. To convince. Therefore he picks out everything that can be said in favour of his case, leaving out all that can be said against it—as might any hack lawyer pleading for money today. But such was the genius of the man that he sets alight the whole affair, and from the dull argumentation and precedents there rises up the flame of a new religion. It is as though while he merely pleaded, merely argued, he had worked himself into a vision.

Not that any eloquence thereby appears in the book, nor, as it seems, was the man himself eloquent though he was a rising preacher. But he was on fire, and the fire was communicated. Hardly had he thought of one good point to make against the enemy—that ancient religion of Europe which had broken up his family and condemned his father to ignoble burial—when there is suggested to him some positive doctrine arising from his negative effort. Because he is attacking the Catholic Church he must do all he can against the hierarchy and the sacramental idea. There must be no bishops, no priesthood, no relation between the material instrument and the inward spiritual thing. But even so, an enthusiasm of his own is aroused in those whom he influences. The sacrament is but

[ 39 ]

bread, yet in that memorial service he introduces vision. Images are idols, but his disciples are worked upon to make in their own minds other images most vivid, and to be shaken by these. That overwhelming God of Calvin's was seen with the eyes of the spirit, an enormous figure, holy by definition, but more terrible than holy, and wreaking angry vengeance against those who rebelled against Him. He was that Jehovah, compeer of Chemosh and of Moloch. He was the necessary instrument of doom, more fearful for being Personal, with a personality more inexorable than Fate because it was inhabited by an infinitely active consciousness, and because necessity lay not in a dead sequence of mere cause and effect but in the drive of that One inexorable will. To this towering Thing—enormously alive—was all mankind subjected. By This was all mankind thrust down—a negligible victim, but a victim horribly suffering. By This also were certain exceptions picked out from the welter of the fore-doomed; and these were the Elect, the Saints, the chosen of God who repose under His protection and are commissioned to wreak vengeance upon His enemies, with eternal beatitude for their end.

Now here we have the key to what is otherwise inexplicable. How could such a doctrine inspire enthusiasm? That it did so we know. Men went wild over it. Some of them actually, and in the presence of an admiring audience, foamed at the mouth in the excitement of their vision! In part no doubt that attraction was the attraction towards anything supernal, the trembling adoration of that which is revered as immeasurably great. So men may worship the sudden view of a mountain, the sudden revelation of shining virtue or a supreme sacrifice.

But there was more than this. The enthusiasm could not have been fed indefinitely upon mere adoration of immensity. It was as the *chosen* of that Immensity that they retained their zeal. They were the Saints, and those whom they opposed were the reprobate of God. *That* was the driving power: *that* was the steam in the machine.

[ 40 ]

How did they know that they were thus exceptional amid the doomed race of men? By a singular experience, known even to this day as "Conversion." By this is not meant, in their vocabulary, a change from a false opinion to a true one, not the perception of a just reasoning, or even of an unsuspected and eternal beauty—but a man's sudden inward conviction that he has been picked out for the special favour of Him Who had made all things, and Who has condemned the greater part of His fellows to Hell.

It is difficult today to appreciate the vitality of such a creed, the heat, the white heat at which it worked in its first devotees. There are few left; of those few most are today in Scotland, and of those in Scotland most are in the barren isles and mountains, far away. But you will never understand the seventeenth century in England unless you know that a very large body of Englishmen—not the mass of Englishmen indeed, but a large minority, especially of the merchants and gentry, but also many among the artisans—were by, say, 1630 filled with these emotions and that others not carried away by them were influenced.

The new religion had worked through the French language and culture. It was allied with the older and vaguer German Protestant movement—a movement based on emotion indeed, but innocent of "Conversion" and of orgy, mainly concerned with a confused protest against officialism in worship, and a reaction against the old Organised Church with its Roman centre. The prophet of the new religion being a Frenchman, its first and hottest focus was in French-speaking Geneva, which is still in some fashion its Holy City. It worked strongly in Southern France also, and thence throughout French territory, especially in the ports. It was lively in the Netherlands, allying itself there with the revolt against Spanish taxation. It affected the German Palatinate. It had run through Scotland like a forest fire in the time of Cromwell's father. It came late to England, as so many revolutionary ideas from the Continent come late to the southern half of this island. It interested but a small number in the days of Cromwell's father, though its adherents were mainly to be found in the hierarchy of the new Establishment. But in Cromwell's own generation it had spread widely. It had arrived, and once arrived, the powerful English imagination got hold of it and filled it with vitality.

So much for the spirit of the thing: but what of its body? The business of that body was to kill another body, the Catholic Church, an organisation. Therefore it must itself be organised, if it were to conquer; for loosely bound forces can never do that. There must be a new Church to kill the old Church, and the new Church must be universal as the old one had been. It was *this* that Calvin saw, *this* which distinguished him from all the other reformers, and makes him not only so much the superior of his German Lutheran colleagues in their attack upon that ancient creed of Europe, but of a different kind from them. It was this also which has made his effort endure so long.

Priests were forbidden: but an army must have officers, therefore the new Church must have such. These, called in the new language "ministers," were to be elected by their troops—but once elected they must be exactly obeyed. Herein we see Calvin at the origin of yet another modern thing (he was the father of I know not how many things developed since his time) the Parliamentary theory, which is now, under the strain of experiment, breaking down: the theory that the elected man has a special authority and that the electors, though they had certainly not intended the strange result, must submit. The new Church was designed to destroy clericalism—and of necessity erected a stricter clericalism of its own.

And we may note in passing how, since all Europe was now a battlefield, there arose upon the other side an order itself thoroughly military, the Society of Jesus. On both sides the spiritual war was waged by a spiritual soldiery, disciplined and embrigaded.

In the same spirit of discipline the taboos of the new religion must be most rigid. Sabbatarianism had been lively enough in the Middle Ages: under the spirit of Calvin it went to the utmost limits. The sanctity and authority of Holy Writ, the Word of God, had run through the Christian centuries; under the spirit of Calvin it was segregated and made an absolute model, with no compensating humour and no relaxation, no parabolic use, no remembrance of other principles which should modify the application of biblical examples. So with the moral sanctions in matters of sex: so also with the moral sanctions in pretty well every other relation of human life. The new religion selected its own, but having selected them, enforced them with blind violence.

They of the old religion said, "By their insistence these people (from their very insistence called Puritans) worship the truth, but have isolated a part of it, disturbed the full balance of it and thereby poisoned human life." But they of the new religion answered, "You of the old compromise and shift: you have failed to maintain the standards, and therefore you are manifestly reprobate. You have made your pact with evil."

The effects of the new religion we all know well enough: they run through history, they are apparent in the characters of individuals, they have almost become commonplace. At the root of them all is the isolation of the soul. Overshadowing the world which the new religion started lay a level cloud of gloom. The toppling enormity of God in the vision of these devotees was such that even the gratitude of His Elect was second to the detestation they held for the Reprobate.

Such were the immediate effects: the secondary effects were in the long run of more social importance. The isolation of the soul destroyed the corporate economic effort of man, and thus gave the opportunity for the loot of all corporate property. Such loot became the mark of the time; and side by side with it the new religion introduced the doctrine of competition, the fruits of which we are now enjoying, and the permission of Usury, which is also today completing its course.

That the new religion also produced a distaste for joy and ease and beauty—having in it the Manichean inheritance—is a commonplace. But we must also insist upon what became perhaps, in practice, the most important of all these results, the admiration of unchecked greed. The pursuit of bare wealth remained, of temporal activities, the only thing worth while. Good works had no value. Holy poverty was a contradiction in terms. Men did not therefore say "holy wealth" but they soon came to think it.

Lastly this new religion produced, and necessarily produced, the conception of a Chosen Race. This derived in part from the election of converted individuals who as "the Saints" enjoyed "indefectability"; once a saint, always a saint—the decrees of God are immutable. The Chosen Race proceeding from the Chosen Souls was supported of course by a steeping of oneself in the Scriptures—taken no longer, as the old religion took them, for a prefigurement of the Incarnation and a leading up to it, but for a model and a guide to daily conduct and an inspiration. To the Puritan, Abraham setting out to murder poor Isaac was not a prefiguring symbol of the sacrifice on Calvary, but a lesson in family life. To the Puritan the curse of Meroz worked as efficiently as of old. To the Puritan the Jewish Sabbath—oddly advanced by twenty-four hours—was absolute. The same rule applies to the massacre of all those unfortunate small tribes with the odd Asiatic names; they became household words to those who were Puritan among the English; they were identified with Papists. They were, it will be remembered, exterminated by the order of Jehovah at the hands of His Chosen.

This conception of superiority proceeding from the new religion of Calvin involved a determination to impose one's will upon others, more especially if they should be weaker than oneself. It was a spirit intensely combative, but one which detested chivalry: men inspired by the new religion would not fight for the fun of fighting. They could fight magnificently, but they could not conceive, any more than could the heroes of the Old Testament, that appetite for fighting odds which is the essence of the chivalric temper. Hence they have always failed in finally coercing those who have made a sufficient resistance.

Such was the new religion. And it is of the very first importance to remember that, unlike the religion which it set out to destroy, it produced a great "penumbra" as it were, a margin of those influenced by its spirit in varying degrees yet rejecting its organisation.

Of Catholicism this had never been true: the Ancient Church had from the time of the Apostles onwards denounced and excluded that within it which was not of it. You were of the Faith, or of the Enemies of the Faith. The process of excision went on uninterruptedly throughout the centuries and continues today, and heresy, in the eyes of the orthodox, is not a mere difference but a poison.

Now with Calvinism it was not so. The strict organisation of the new Church whose business it was to destroy the old might be, and was, rejected by multitudes who none the less felt the full effect of the Calvinist spirit. For let it be remembered that Calvin had arisen on a foundation of revolt against organisation. He was the greatest by far (and not only greater in scale but greater in quality) of all the Reformers, and his mastering intelligence had seen the necessity of a strict machine. But the tide flowing under him was a tide of reaction against authority; therefore you have the paradox throughout the generations in which Calvin had a greater and greater influence, that the most part of those subjected to it refused the Presbyterian pattern, the limits of the framework. Hence the Independents, hence the Evangelical Sects and hence Oliver Cromwell himself. Calvin demanded a universal and strictly organised religion. His more devoted followers repeated his commands and attempted to carry them out. That was the whole spirit of the Covenant and of the effort to enforce it in England during the civil war. But there is that in Puritanism which prevents such unity, and even as the effect of Calvin spread his strict organisation dissolved.

.    .    .    .    .    .    .

We must see Cromwell then—from youth—surrounded with this air of Conversion, of Election, of Reprobation. We must see him ever in the presence of Calvin's God: caught by the enthusiasm of Calvin in manhood, wholly filled with new religion during the active vigour of his life. It is this, side by side with his descent from the New Millionaires and, of more effect than that descent, which moulds him and drives him.

CHARACTER grows from circumstance acting on that which is within. What circumstance, in the formative years and in early manhood, acted upon what inward material here, in this cadet of a great but new fortune?

First, of course, the new religion. We shall see it at work. He will suffer Conversion in his agonies. He will wrestle with God. He will be of the Elect. Beyond that, certain things favourable and unfavourable: an early and happy marriage saving from nervous ruin a very young man who still suffered for years from that horror of darkness where the soul is abandoned and evil calls from the abyss—and the pretty modern name for that is "depression." Next a bitter humiliation, never forgotten: the loss of the house that had made his family great. Next a good life in the fields, on a horse and with his beasts; the delight in children; some consideration of friends; the whole remote and obscure. Luckily for him an ample income, plenty of backing. Then common entry into public life such as comes to scores of his kind. Underneath all this, quite concealed from his own soul and all around it, was a soldier made for soldiering: fitted throughout with all the capacities for that trade. Only when that trade was, by an accident of life, thrust upon him, did he know what he was. It was a special dispensation. Henceforward he felt himself guided everywhere by the direct intervention of heaven almost to the end—but not quite to the end.

The years of Cromwell's youth and early manhood, up to his twenty-ninth year when he first entered public life, have no interest to general history: they have the highest particular interest in the question how such a man came to be.

His worshippers, who have collected every scrap of information and tradition available, have discovered very little about him; but that little has at least one value: it is consonant with what followed and therefore explains the man.

Here we must remember an historical principle which the men of the nineteenth century nearly always lacked when they spoke of Cromwell, as had those of the eighteenth century and later seventeenth before them. The principle is that we must accept evidence neither helped nor hindered by affection or hate. It was inevitable that a man who had had so extraordinary a part thrust upon him for such a few concentrated years should become a Demi-God or a Demon in the national story. For the hundred odd years and more during which he was the national Bad Man any wisp of tradition, any fragment of evidence which made him ridiculous or wicked was eagerly seized and established—and plenty of guess-work followed upon the same lines. After the turnover between the end of the eighteenth century and 1830, the influence of the new Nonconformist mercantile fortunes of the Whig policy in triumphant defence against Rousseau, it was the opposite; nothing that was remembered, nothing that was proved—of the few things that are remembered or proved upon those early years of Cromwell—was accepted if it were derogatory to him; or, if accepted, it was explained, often absurdly, in his favour.

Carlyle does not (of course) even attempt to weigh the evidence; but it is unfortunately the same with men better balanced than Carlyle. They follow each other throughout the period immediately before our own in a long string of denials, refusing any story, tradition or even known fact which did not conform to their imaginary picture of one whom they had now set up to worship—just as he had been set up by their fathers to be condemned. When the fact was too prominent and too well attested to be thus passed over it was given a favourable interpretation at all costs.

But Cromwell remains the same man, whether he be made to play the one exaggerated part or the other, and the right

[ 48 ]

way to treat the very meagre evidence upon the earlier years—
from his birth in 1599 to his presence in the Long Parliament
of 1641—is to judge it by its agreement with the mass of things
we know of him in later life, that is, from 1641 to his death
in 1658. These last years were less than one third of the whole
—17 out of 59—but if we find the mature acts consonant with
the acts or moods of youth on which there is even only vague
tradition we are justified in accepting that tradition, whether
it proceed from an enemy or a friend.

The traditions and statements, certain or half certain, help
us to understand that character, for they belong to the formative period of his development. After the Parliament of 1628,
when he was already a man approaching thirty, that character
can develop no longer; his life changed and the curve of
his career developed out of all knowledge—but the man himself was fixed before his thirtieth year, as very nearly all men
are.

We have seen what his childhood was, brought up in close
intimacy with the great house at the head of which stood his
uncle, living under the shadow of that wealth and growing
up in the principal family of the town which it dominated.

The first thing to note about that childhood and the ado-
lescence which followed it is the intense nervousness of temperament apparent in them. That also was a characteristic
which followed Cromwell to the end.

I use the word "nervousness" with some hesitation, for it is
ambiguous and might convey a false impression of timidity. I
use it in the sense of a mind at tension, a gift of visual imagination which may fall suddenly into an extreme, an inability to
repose, mortal fears, a liability to sudden anger, and a source
of energy.

There is here a very marked contrast between the two chief
military figures in modern English history—Cromwell himself
and Marlborough. Marlborough was the most stolid of men.
Save for the passion Sarah Jennings inspired—an emotion which

completely mastered him—he was the most indifferent of men. Cromwell was all the other way. The violence of his emotions is apparent from the beginning to the end; it fastens upon him in the matter of religion as it would upon a similar man today in the matter of patriotism or of some political or economic creed —Communism for instance. It shows itself in floods of tears which he cannot restrain even at awkward moments and into which he falls quite naturally even when he is exciting himself by an argument which he himself knows to be insincere. It is a very great error to think such characters lacking in tenacity. It is an even worse error to think them lacking in judgment. There is no necessary connection between violence of feeling and instability, nor any between such violence and confusion of thought. They are often found in combination but they do not grow from a common root.

This leading mark in the Protector's spirit, half morbid, and nourished by what was defective in the material part of him, runs through all his life. As a child he sees a great shadow opening the curtains of his bed, and is convinced that the vision communicates to him great things upon his future. For such an extravagance his father had him whipped; without result, for he remained convinced that the apparition was real, and he could not keep the memory of it to himself.

He had, as he grew older, alternative fits of horseplay and despair. Fantasies upon, or beyond, the borders of what is sane haunted him in his early manhood. Of one of these manias we have certain and curious record though not a sufficient description of its character. We only know that it had something to do with the Town Cross of Huntingdon, and that he saw in or about that inanimate object horrors beyond this world. The medical profession catalogued him in early manhood under the term "*melancholicus*," which meant, in the technical language of the day, what we call today in a similar case, "melancholia." And to that diagnosis of "*melancholicus*" there was added the adverb "*valde*" ("very") to emphasise it; he was looked upon as a very bad case. A modern critic would see illusion also in his confidence that repeated revelations were granted to him throughout his life; while the other symptom, the terrors, also reappear at the end—as naturally they would when the strength of the body began to fail. It is all of a piece with his exceeding anxiety in the matter of Government, leading to bewilderment and exasperation. This I say must be put first because it conditions all the rest. That intensity of nervous structure is allied to the rapidity of his decisions in the field, to the clarity of his vision and is the main source of his drive.

But we must also note, side by side with this nervous character, what is very rare in that connection—an absence of extravagance in sensual appetite or, at least, of indulgence therein during the main part of his career. Such a temperament may have led him to debauch in early youth—he seems to accuse himself of that and there are traditions of it—but whether it did or not he was of a plain straightforward conduct in these affairs throughout all the significant years of his life; there was never a vibrant man of eminent public activity so simply devoted to his home and so certainly satisfied with his marriage. He gave example of what is meant, in any sane and just definition, by the word chastity.

There is not a sign of extravagance or irregularity from the day of his early marriage at twenty-two to his death close on sixty, nor do his innumerable enemies record anything of the kind. There are indeed two belated stories of natural children. One, a girl, the mother of that Mrs. Hartopp who lived in the eighteenth century, the other a son. The first can be easily proved a confusion between the supposed bastard and Cromwell's legitimate daughter, Bridget. The other is no more than a silly imaginary romance—and a dull one—brought out in France. To estimate Oliver we must bear continually in mind this sobriety of sex in alliance with such fervour of fancy and exaltation of nerves.

Closely mixed with and proceeding from that exaltation of

nerves in him must be noted once more his consuming religion. Not that it comes next in importance—it is first in importance by far, the chief element in Cromwell's character. That high potential of emotion which would, as I have said, under other circumstances have been directed to some other object was, in this early seventeenth century and in the particular case of Cromwell himself, directed to transcendental doctrine and worship.

Now in that family of Williams-Cromwell it was certain that the religious interest would be anti-Catholic; and what that meant in the first years after 1600 when Oliver was a child and his character beginning to form will be the better understood a few pages later, when there will be presented the great strength and menace—as it seemed to families like this—of Catholicism in England. Since the emotion would be anti-Catholic it would certainly be of the new religion. Things had inclined that way since the foundation of the family sixty years before Oliver's birth. The inclination had remained an inclination only when, in the days of Oliver's own father, Puritanism had begun to affect some few but in Oliver's own day it affected a multitude of whom he was one.

A family founded on the loot of the old religion was not necessarily opposed to it; many were not; for instance, the senior branch of the Paulets. But those thus benefited tended to be opposed to it and any individuals naturally inclined to anti-Catholicism were certainly confirmed in their attitude by inherited interests of this kind.

The foreign influence of Calvin, which had become infused throughout the Protestant world (and by which indeed the whole of that world had been informed and strengthened) spread at first but slowly in England, more slowly than did conformity with the new establishment which the Cecils had framed and of which Elizabeth had been the unwilling figurehead. Much the greater part of Englishmen were already indifferent to the Papacy long before Cromwell was born; an increasing minority were actively hostile to it and were more ready (not only the hostile minority but the indifferent majority) to accept the outward practice, at least, of a national Church, with a national liturgy expressed in the national vernacular. That great majority which at the beginning of Elizabeth's reign had regretted in varying degrees the religion of its fathers lost its traditions gradually as the years proceeded; but the essential spirit of Calvin had appeared in a minority only during the years 1560-80, and those few increased at first very slowly.

Towards the end of the sixteenth century, however, a younger generation was beginning to grow up which, in its need for strong religious feeling, filled the void with the doctrines and the certitudes, still more with the enthusiasm which radiated from Geneva. The clergy of the new Church establishment after 1560, in their higher ranks at least, were preponderantly upon that side; those below the Episcopacy were recruited, as the older generation died out, from men often in active sympathy with the new religion and hardly ever strongly opposed to its influence. Such were soon to be called "Puritan." Their prime convictions, strongly and, of their nature, often passionately held (Election, Conversion and the rest) inspired a growing minority of laymen as well, and after the turn of the century, in the years when little Oliver was beginning to receive those impressions which make a character for life, that Calvinist influence was running strongly through a large minority of the squires, as also through many merchants of the towns and the more substantial artizans. It even already had some hold, though only here and there upon patches of the village people, especially near the coasts in the east and south where foreign influences were strongest. It was particularly powerful in London.

Its presence among the greater landowners of the Williams-Cromwell type did not yet mean that it commanded a majority among them, let alone their class as a whole, but a larger and larger number of squires were attracted by Puritanism as the years 1600-1625 proceeded. The Church organisation of Calvinism was not an issue, there was as yet no talk of constituting that in England; but within the Establishment itself Puritanism and the Calvinist ideal grew. It affected the practising and sincere members of the Establishment till they formed a large body. Perhaps before 1630 nearly half the educated men were leaning in this direction. And there was among them a growing extreme wing wholly Calvinist in tone and speech, though with no thought of setting up the strict Presbyterian system; for the squires were wholly mixed up with the established parochial system of which they were the patrons and not, as yet, opposed to Episcopacy; indeed the episcopate had long been itself, in general, Calvinistic in its direction—and especially at Canterbury—since William Cecil had set up his new Church.

Young Cromwell in early boyhood received this Calvinist or Puritan spirit, in part no doubt from his parents, in part from the group of townsmen in Huntingdon with whom they were connected; but especially from the man whose natural place it was to give him his first training—Doctor Beard. This Beard was at the head of the Grammar School at Huntingdon; he was a Puritan Churchman, not without learning and with a reputation which extended far. He had written books upon his side of the controversy, notably one upon the common theme that the Pope was anti-Christ; he was a man engrossed in such things.

Beard's influence upon Cromwell was strong and continuous, and Oliver's interest in him long survived boyhood; it was apparent years after in middle life when Beard was an elderly man, and continued till his death. But there was another influence of great moment—of how great moment we know not by direct testimony but by its effect—and that was the appearance, as Cromwell was reaching puberty when the most vivid impressions are received, of what has ever since been known as the "English Bible."

The Authorised Version was but the last of some few vernacular renderings upon the Protestant side; the rhythms of its most famous rhetoric came from a lifetime earlier; its diction was already somewhat archaic—and the more impressive—so that it established itself during the course of a very few years as a verbal inspiration and literal authority throughout all that section of Englishmen for whom it was designed. It was destined at long last—by the end of the eighteenth century—to give its colour to the whole nation. It was as the Mohammedans say of the Koran, "The Book." Of all the cases in which the power of The Word has shown itself in the formation of societies this is perhaps the chief. Its high phrases acted like the music of armies; men drank of it and were set on fire.

Now that Book was first at work, I say, raising its earliest ferment in Oliver, just during those years when great verse or great rhythmic rhetoric most strongly seizes and stamps itself upon a mind. The new English Bible would have reached the household at Huntingdon when he was between thirteen and fourteen; he had it in his ears week by week and most probably daily, year after year, all through his early manhood. The influence was so violent that it produced in him (as in thousands of his contemporaries and scores of his social equals) that special vocabulary which seems to us grotesque but which soon became to them native. The strange names of half-savage Orientals, the metaphors drawn from the climate of Syria or the life of the desert, the characters of little highland tribes in Syria—three thousand miles away from England in distance, three thousand years in time—became in that group so thoroughly adopted that to this day men think of them as English. As for Oliver, the thing possessed him and spoke through his lips his whole life long.

Though a character is formed by thirty, though Cromwell was all this, the man on fire with the new Scripture and the man reading it in an atmosphere of Election and Conversion, yet the effect continued to develop in him. It was perhaps at its height shortly before he appears fully upon the stage, some four years before the outbreak of the Civil War, when he was nearly forty.

Here enters an element negative but all-important, too often missed, even omitted—the corresponding fear and hatred of the Catholic Church, and, consequently, the immediate readiness to act with every violence against it. To appreciate that capital matter we must see what the strength of Catholicism was in the eyes of such men during the years of Oliver's boyhood and of his earlier manhood, and on, until there were given him the weapons with which he could directly attempt the destruction of such an enemy. But this factor, which I have called "The Catholic Menace" is so essential to the understanding of the time, and of Oliver himself, that I will leave it to a separate division.

Already half formed by such influences, there came upon Cromwell two things which matured him.

The first was his father's death, which took place early in his nineteenth year, while he was still a freshman at Cambridge of just over a year's standing. Most of the large income was left for his mother to manage, but he was now the head of the younger branch, and soon to have considerable interests in his own hands.

The second, three years after, was his early marriage, which moderated his dangers of temperament. That marriage was serenely successful. The high career to come owes to Mrs. Oliver a debt which history has not paid because it remains so silent upon her, as she also was silent, preferring her home. History should be written in the recollection of such women, for they are creative as the talked-of women are not.

It was such a marriage as the Williamses all made; one into their own wealthy world. She was the daughter of a rich and knighted London merchant called "Bourcher" or "Bourchier"; and the family of Oliver's millionaire uncle-by-marriage, the Hampdens, seems to have made the match. Her first four

RICHARD, THE PROTECTOR, SON OF OLIVER
MARY, THIRD DAUGHTER
OLIVER CROMWELL
MRS. ELIZABETH CROMWELL, WIFE OF OLIVER
ELIZABETH, SECOND DAUGHTER
HENRY, YOUNGEST SON

# MINIATURES OF THE CROMWELL FAMILY
IN THE COLLECTION OF THE DUKE OF BUCCLEUCH

children were born to him while he still lived in that largest of the Huntingdon homes, himself the most prominent of the younger townsmen. For seven years he thus lived on his paternal land; they were not years in which he had peace—it was at their close, not their beginning, that his worst morbidities were noticed. But they were years in which his home and his wife kept him sane.

It was a simple, exactly consonant marriage with a woman of his own rank; it was fruitful, giving him a number of children to whom, as to his wife, he was devoted. That marriage, then, was the saving of Oliver.

It did not give him good equilibrium, it did not furnish him with full ballast, he was subject to violence, impulse and superstition all his life; but it calmed him sufficiently, and it gave him a certain background of happiness—as great a measure of that as a man of such temper could have. He had in his home a foundation all his life, and this is the more certain because his home obtrudes so little on to the outward story of his life. The strongest emotion in that very emotional man was his intense love of his children, of his family, his roof. Of most laymen who did great things while the Christian tradition of marriage still endured, it seems true that they were either very happily married or very unhappily, and that an inward state so nurtured provided them with reserves of power, or goaded them to external effort. For Cromwell his good marriage was a spiritual fortune.

Cromwell had another strong affection which puts him in the tradition of famous Englishmen—patriotism. But this was so much interwoven in his case (as in most others) with self-sufficiency that it is only half affection, the other half being something which you may call, according to your mood, vanity or pride. Such men see their country in themselves, and themselves in their country. And if to this natural emotion there be added a sense of divine election, which extends to both the nation and the man, then the nation is as naturally

"The Chosen Race" just as the man himself is "The Chosen Individual."

In the particular case of Cromwell, under the influence of that religion in him, there was a further selection, whereby his own sort in Protestantism were also specially chosen. But it must be remarked that, within the general boundaries of Protestant feeling, Cromwell was not fanatical, still less exclusive. His demand for independence in Protestant worship, his instinctive dislike of a fixed and still more of an imposed Protestant liturgy were abiding and obviously sincere. It was on this account (though the explanation may seem paradoxical) that he repeatedly showed sympathy with men who preferred organisation in their evangelical worship, so long as it was *they* who chose such organisation and so long as there was no forcing of it upon others. But all this toleration was granted, of course, only under the condition that the tolerated accept the main tenets of his own creed—the nullity of man's good works; the infallible witness of the English Bible as interpreted by the reader thereof; the ethical code which the Puritan takes for granted, not only in its commandments but in the order of precedence which he gives to its commandments. Cromwell cannot but believe that all men agree with him in their hearts and that therefore men with a different code or a different emphasis are, in proportion to their difference, liars and the enemies of God.

Seeing the false character that has been erected of Cromwell in order to glorify him spiritually, the sort of hagiography with which he has been surrounded, especially by men of the last generation, the errors in this laudation must be exposed. There are to be found among his actions, treasons, betrayals, falsehoods, acts of abominable cruelty, and false pretensions of motive. There are also certainly to be found acts, such as the pursuit of the King to his death, which it is difficult not to call crimes, because their motive is personal. But these do not make him black. They do not form one whole body of evil intention which would make us call him (as did Clarendon, who watched him closely) a bad man. The test is that whenever Oliver does something evil it is the yielding to a special temptation. The sin or turpitude is not part of a whole system of conduct springing from an evil root.

I have spoken and shall have frequent occasion to speak of the accusation of ambition brought against him. If there is one thing certain about the moral character of Cromwell, to the man who reads fully upon him and remembers his reading impartially, it is that he was not ambitious. Such a verdict would have sounded nonsense even to those who read widely a hundred years ago: Lingard, who must perpetually be quoted as the founder of modern English history, the forgotten quarry from which all the mid-nineteenth century historians dug their material, makes ambition the key to Cromwell's character.

It was not so. He lived to be over forty-five without making any effort at fame or power; and no man ever develops the desire for them long after youth has passed.

An immense fame came to him—he was not at all certain how—and almost unchecked personal power. Therefore was it taken for granted that he had sought both. As for fame, he takes no trouble to record his very remarkable achievements or to have them recorded; in his own accounts he frequently passes them by, and the man is plainly so absorbed in other emotions, principally religious, that there is no room for anything of the kind. As to power, it ought to be evident that he actually dreaded it, that its exercise was for him a task, and a task uncongenial. He had never been trained to exercise it in all the years of his formation; there is no complaint from any victim of it in all those years; and they are years, remember, prolonged far beyond the ordinary in the story of famous men —they reach right into middle age.

If ever Shakespeare's phrase of greatness being "thrust upon" a man applied, it applies to Cromwell's political domination. As for glory, the great concomitant and attraction of power, he did not know what it meant. And if it could have been explained to him it would have seemed to him folly. He could never hear the music of it, nor were his surroundings such as to give him the least conception of that emotion. Someone had to govern a distracted and exhausted England. The only instrument to hand was military, and Cromwell's only experience of getting things done was getting them done as a soldier. He had been contented enough before he was compelled to control, he would have remained contented all his life—and much more contented—if he had never been compelled to order anything beyond his own household.

To return to that early married life of his at Huntingdon. He remains secluded but in his natural place, the chief man in the town, the nephew of the great personage at Hinchinbrooke, under whose wing he could live proudly and by whose reflected light he shines.

At the end of that seclusion, when he was just twenty-eight, fell the blow which both affected his character and illustrates it. You shall not understand Cromwell until you have understood what that blow was and the effect it had upon him.

Hinchinbrooke, the glory of the Cromwells, had to be sold —and, as it were, forcibly sold.

The wealthiest families among those many who rose suddenly upon the ruins of the old religion had fates of two kinds. Some kept their money and therefore increased it until they became the governing names of England; of these the chief type is the Russells—small gentlemen before the plunder of the Church, multimillionaires after it, increasing in wealth and therefore in power with each generation until they became the leaders of their class in its destruction of the monarchy during Cromwell's own day. Others spent their money lavishly, and thereby somewhat began to impoverish themselves; and having started on that slope slid down it, though gradually: of these last a sufficient example is the Williams-Cromwell family. Had they maintained and increased their original huge stock, given in a lump to their ancestor Richard Williams at the very beginning of the great turnover, they would have stood a lifetime later (as the Russells did) in the first places of England. It is not to their discredit that they preferred to accumulation, enjoyment, show, and the facile pleasures of generosity.

On this account the Williams-Cromwell fortune gradually decays, just as the Russell fortune, its contemporary, increases. Thus it is that we have Dukes of Bedford flourishing on the ruins of the monarchy after the destruction of the Stuarts, while there is no Duke of Huntingdon, no Lord Ramsay for an eldest son, no Lords and Ladies Bill and Molly Cromwell (or Williams-Cromwell)—though in the destruction of the monarchy a Williams-Cromwell was himself a principal agent.

This careless handling of great wealth, a chief mark of the Williams blood, was discovered in more than one of its descendants. Being the immensely wealthy family they were, they were necessarily allied, as we have seen, to wealthy families of the same sort all over the place, and Cromwell had for cousins, connections and in-laws a little mob of the well-to-do, rich squires and rich lawyers and the rest. But none of those descended from the original, suddenly fortunate Richard Williams seems to have attached himself to the worship of wealth with that fervour which secures permanent millions.

Oliver himself is an excellent example of this better side of the family spirit, in which there is not much other to praise. He felt with his class; he was well-to-do all his life; he was as glad as is any man to receive accession of wealth; but he never devoted himself to it—and he is perhaps the only master of men in the seventeenth century of whom that can be said. The statesmen and soldiers of that day, having an opportunity for peculation, jobs and the rest, availed themselves of that opportunity universally. Gustavus Adolphus bargains like a fishwife with the French Government for his five barrels of gold; and Sully, that much overpraised stand-by of Navarre, blackmailed Navarre's widow, the Queen Regent, shamefully; threatening to levy war unless she handed over to him a further fortune. Wallenstein, grasped like a robber, Richelieu, and after him Mazarin, the one embarrassed in youth, the other sprung from the poorest class, left the largest fortunes of their time. Cromwell, almost alone among the men who had all advantage to their hand, remained by habit in the class to which he was born; accepting large gratuities only when they were open gifts from the State, neither marrying his daughters nor establishing his sons in as great a way as he might have done. Even had there been no Restoration it is doubtful whether the family would have been conspicuous for very great wealth.

Living in our own day, when the stability of property has disappeared, such a family would have been quickly ruined. As it was, their decay was slow; but already in less than a century after the first foundation of that great heap of gold it was visibly diminished. They had had the fun of startling first Elizabeth and then James with the magnificence of their hospitality; they had thrown away money broadcast in the very streets of Ramsay; and now they must begin to pay the price.

In 1627 the elder Oliver, Sir Oliver Cromwell of Hinchinbrooke, though no further off than grandson from the original Richard, woke up in a cleft stick. He had had to borrow to find ready cash, and there was no way out of it but to sell something. Hinchinbrooke, to one who had lived in its reflected glory all his life like the younger Oliver as chief citizen in Huntingdon town, as the cadet of his kinsman in the great house just outside the borough, was the symbol of the family position: and the passing of it out of the hands of the family was a wound ever to be remembered.

It must not be imagined that this sale of Hinchinbrooke meant the ruin of the Williams-Cromwells, nor anything like it. They still retained the better part of their great income. The other possessions of the family were untouched; it had only been necessary to sell under the pressure of money-debts, probably carrying (after the rate of the day) interest at eight per cent. Further, old Sir Henry, their grandfather, had generously provided for his own. But Hinchinbrooke was a symbol; it was there that what it was hoped would become one of the great families of England had taken root, and the loss of the house was a deep humiliation. Moreover, the necessity for actual cash must have been pretty sharp, since the sum obtainable at apparently short notice was not more than what we should call £20,000 today, at the most, perhaps, what we should call £25,000.

Now the man who had thus supplanted the Cromwells at Hinchinbrooke in the month of June, 1627, was a certain Sidney Montagu.

Who were the Montagus?

In the last days of an entirely Catholic England there had lived in Northamptonshire a certain Thomas; a gentleman, but on no great scale. He was the lord of only two manors. He was called indifferently Mountagu or Montagu, and claimed some connection with that great family of the *Mons Acutus*, feudal Earls of Salisbury of whom the ancestor was that Drogo the Norman who had come over with William the Conqueror. He founded the Montagus and had taken his reward in dues upon lands in Somerset. There, after centuries, many generations from the original invader, the house of Montacute still recalls his name. It is like enough (though not certain) that the claim to Drogo descent was justified; but whether it were or not, this Thomas Montagu with his two manors in Northamptonshire was of quite the smaller fry among the gentry, and died in the very year when the flood of the Reformation was first let loose over Europe (1517). It was not he but his son, and his second son at that, who made the fortunes of the family.

This second son was called Edward, and since at first he had not the prospects of his elder brother he must make his way in the law. To that profession he owed some part of the great wealth that was coming to him, but much more did he owe it to the religious revolution by which he was to profit hugely—as were the Williamses to profit, and so many more. His first piece of good fortune was the death of his elder brother without an heir, and Edward Montagu in the first few years after his father died, began to push his way into the King's service.

He snatched money at every chance that came his way; accumulating and adding to his original rents, serving on many commissions, and in particular doing the King's business in assessing the great fortune of Wolsey, when the King decided to sweep that wealth into his net. His were the pickings, therefore, and into his purse dropped those percentages and fees and the much larger private oddments which went with work of this kind. Edward Montagu was already (by the time the great Cardinal died disgraced and ruined) a rich man— and he increased his fortune very considerably upon the ruins of that fallen glory, so that, in a few months, he could even entertain Henry himself, and Catherine, the imperilled Queen, with splendour.

But though he spent thus grandly for his master and benefactor the King, he never wasted money: and all was spent with a purpose. Four years later came the rising of the people against the first destruction of the monasteries, and it gave Edward Montagu another opportunity. He became Commissioner to the Commissariat for the army which suppressed the rebellion and butchered men up and down the north country. This post brought him every sort of profit. Then, immediately after, in the general flood of loot, when the monastic lands began pouring into the coffers of the spoilers, he was among the first of them. Like Richard Williams, much on the same scale and much in the same part of East England, he got hold of the Abbey lands right and left, and was already set up to do the King's work in this crisis as Lord Chief Justice of the King's Bench.

He continued actively the work which earned him such enormous payments; he was principal agent in the killing of Catherine Howard in 1541. Right up to Henry's death he was still labouring in the good cause, for he was one of those commissioned by the dying King to bully a confession out of the Duke of Norfolk and procure *his* death.

It was as Lord Chief Justice (no longer of the King's Bench but of the Common Pleas) that he supported Dudley's plan for the usurpation of the throne by Dudley's son in the person of that son's child-wife, Lady Jane Grey; Edward Montagu did so with hesitation, terrified of the consequences—and might under Mary have lost that huge accumulation of gold which the Reformation had brought him. As it was, he lay in peril; but he and his vast fortune outlived the danger; he did not die until William Cecil had been in power and Elizabeth upon the throne seven years, and by that time the Montagus were thoroughly secure. He lived to see, five years before his death, his eldest-born grandson Edward—who should be the heir to all this and in due time given the first peerage of the family— put into the House of Lords as a buttress of Cecil's new religious establishment, the Reformed Church of England.

This eldest grandson of the old millionaire had sundry brothers, of whom note two in particular: Henry, who was also born in his grandfather's lifetime, and Sidney.

As with the Williamses, the great fortune built upon the ruins of the old religion could provide amply for its younger sons. Henry Montagu, taking to the law like his grandfather, rose rapidly, was Lord Chief Justice in his turn, distinguished himself by the condemnation of Raleigh, turned Lord High Treasurer, a post which he bought at a high price, but one which procured him a revenue many times that price. He bought Kimbolton Castle on the southern edge of Huntingdonshire, within an hour's ride of Hinchinbrooke, and because long ago

Kimbolton had belonged to the great family of Mandeville
he desired to adopt that name, so he entered the peerage under
that title, "Kimbolton," and was later made Earl—Earl of Manchester, the first of that name. He served his King, Charles I,
faithfully enough, as he had served his father James, though
he was strongly on the Puritan side and of the stuff of which
later the Rebellion was made; but when he came to die (in
November, 1642) that Rebellion had only begun.

Brother Sidney, the youngest of the three, was a member
of Parliament as all the members of the family had been as
a matter of course, and member (also as a matter of course)
for the *Shire* of Huntingdon. He also prospered in the law,
adding by it to the large portion of the family estate which
he had inherited; he was a Master of Requests at the moment
when the too generous or too lavish Sir Oliver Cromwell had
found himself compelled to turn Hinchinbrooke quickly into
cash.

So here we have the three Montagus, grandsons of the old
Reformation millionaire, contemporaries of Sir Oliver Cromwell, the grandson of the Williams Reformation millionaire;
and Sidney Montagu, descended from a line more avaricious
and more determined to accumulate, had bought out the
Williams-Cromwells from Hinchinbrooke.

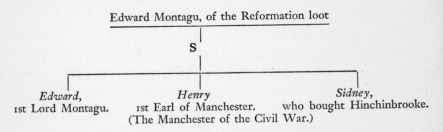

Edward Montagu, of the Reformation loot

S

| Edward, | Henry | Sidney, |
|---|---|---|
| 1st Lord Montagu. | 1st Earl of Manchester. | who bought Hinchinbrooke. |
| | (The Manchester of the Civil War.) | |

We must bear all these well in mind, for Sir Oliver's nephew
who was to be the Protector never forgot that first blow delivered in his youth, the loss of the ancestral home. He put all
three brothers into one basket as despoilers of his family.

Of these rich men, one, Sir Sidney Montagu, the Master of Requests, a lawyer in the traditions of his family, was now master of the roof and acres which Oliver had known and revered all his youth. Oliver himself was still the chief citizen in Huntingdon, the fame and influence of his family remained and would only slowly fade—but its solid basis in the place had gone. Henceforward there was feud between Oliver in his reserved, violent mind, and the Montagu blood. We shall see the earlier and later action of this: the earlier in Oliver's passionate attacks upon the Montagu's influence in the Fen Country, where the Cromwells used to be supreme; the later, upon a larger scale and more persistent, in the hounding out of Manchester from the command of the Parliamentary army.

We see Cromwell, then, capable of a strong personal quarrel and a long retention of the animosity it had aroused. He became the permanent enemy of Manchester, because Manchester was a Montagu. And the greater joy must he have had when Manchester's nephew, the son of the very man who had purchased Hinchinbrooke, fell into a youthful hero-worship of himself, Cromwell, as a soldier. That indeed was a fine revenge for the loss of the great house!

This power of deep-rooted antagonism goes with Oliver's other qualities; it goes with that harsh, loud voice, and with that extravagant manner of his in his frequent fits of indignation.

Such emotions, so strong and so natural, do not diminish Cromwell in moral stature or in our estimate of the scale on which he was built. There is indeed a certain ideal man who remains impassive, through virtue, in spite of insult and in spite of loss and in spite of humiliation: but nine times out of ten when men do not resent insult, humiliation and loss it is through some lack of substance in them, a flabbiness which is often obviously cowardice. To praise a man for not being vindictive is to praise him for worse qualities than a natural desire for vengeance, unless indeed he is one who has reached such holiness that he does indeed habitually forgive. Certainly no one could pretend this of Oliver, nor of most active men.

Now let us turn to the most debated (and debatable) point in the whole affair; one upon which our judgment must chiefly depend in our estimate of the man between good and evil. It is this: What of his integrity? Had he the fundamental defect of insincerity, which poisons all character and which, when it be pushed to the extreme of hypocrisy, renders the whole man vile?

He lied, of course. All men lie. And men engaged in public intrigue cannot but lie, and that lengthily and often. But upon what did his falsehoods turn, what was their frequency, what was their occasion, and what their nature? *That* is what we must examine if we are to judge him rightly.

It is an all-important question in our enquiry. For, just as Cromwell was universally accused of ambition, so he was accused of hypocrisy. Now ambition is a defect but hypocrisy an abomination.

I think we shall conclude that Cromwell's falsehoods, even when connected and prolonged, were not rooted in his character but peculiar to the special circumstances of the moment; and I think we may certainly conclude that he was free from that fundamental lie which is hypocrisy.

Today we blame Cromwell for drawing a picture of himself as the humble middle-class fellow. This is the absurd description which has been used by hundreds of modern writers, who make out their hero everything that he was not, and particularly mask or ignore the fact that he was born and bred of a great family in the very heart of the Reformation millionaires. But we must remember that there is an element of convention in such things: we have all of us heard a rich man describe his palace as "my place in Blankshire," or even "my little place in Blankshire": and we must remember that when Oliver used those words about himself he was talking to men who knew all about him and were not taken in (as modern people are taken in) by the portrait of the rough farmer-grazier-petty-brewer, scraping along on a few hundreds a year.

The list of his dissimulations is a long one, and that of his specific departures from the truth (in so many words), though not so long, presents many concrete examples of lying. Yet, when we look into all these, we still find each of them particular to an occasion. Remark that there was no lying from him until necessity appeared, nor any after necessity had passed.

The largest bulk of dissimulation and the one to which all his critics have turned is the long chain of false acts and words, plotting, hiding and the rest, by which he compassed the death of Charles Stuart. It was this which made him for a hundred and fifty years the victim of misrepresentation. He was set forth as plotting the King's death for the sake of supplanting him: of lying, for the sake of power. In reality he was only aiming at what most men will aim at, self-preservation: he saw much more clearly than did others that Charles's survival would mean the death of the revolution sooner or later, including the death of Oliver himself. Therefore did he plan the King's destruction, not from ambition.

The distinction is important; for if power were Oliver's aim in killing Charles, that would make him out much baser than he was, and what is of even greater moment, it would make him more permanently false; it would make his whole life a falsehood from the moment when he first begins to intrigue against his military superiors, or against the Parliament. As a fact it is all the other way. Nothing is more remarkable in Oliver's lapses from sincerity than the way in which they correspond to an immediate occasion, and are dropped when the occasion is over. He lied when he told the King he had not sent Joyce to Holmby House, and the King answered him pretty plainly that he was not to be believed. But Cromwell had here a clear motive. He still intended to treat the King better than the Parliament had treated him, and it was urgent that the King should not come into the custody of the Army under the impression that he was in the hands of enemies, otherwise he could not have been used as a bargaining asset against the politicians—and to use Charles as a bargaining asset against the politicians was Cromwell's whole motive in carrying him off from Holmby House.

Cromwell lied when he told the Parliament that he would never support the Army against them, but that also was a necessary occasion. Had he not done so, he could not have worked his plan. He lied when he professed to abhor the very idea of Charles's being put to death. But the same test applies to that also. If he wrote the anonymous letter preceding Charles's flight from Hampton Court (and we shall see that this was believed by the one contemporary who had the best opportunity of judging, Whalley's own chaplain) he acted yet another lie and a decisive one.

We may say that in the whole business, from the sending of Joyce to Holmby House right down to the trial of the King in Westminster Hall, Cromwell was concealing outwardly what he was feeling and intending inwardly. But a man who manœuvres against others must be thus secret, and must preserve his secret, or he cannot act. It does not follow that his whole character is affected because he pursues what he believes to be a necessary plan. And the same is true of his rather transparent protest when he is offered the supreme power. He said that he had not heard of the plan to make him Protector three days before it was published. Considering that the Little Parliament was led to its dissolution by those who were notoriously Cromwell's creatures in that Assembly, that those who differed from them and met afterwards were silenced by the use of force, and that the whole of the elaborate scheme for a Protectorate was revealed suddenly, immediately after that action was taken, this play-acting of having known nothing about it all will deceive no one. Oliver knew very well that they were going to offer him the Protectorship, he knew very

well that the Little Parliament would dissolve itself at the insti-
gation of his own emissaries. But then, he also knew that politically the thing had to be done, that Government could not be
carried on with the aid of such an instrument as the Little
Parliament: he acted from necessity and certainly not from
the desire for power.

And the same is true of his performance after the second
battle of Newbury, from the first accusations against Manchester to the plea for the Self-Denying Ordinance. In his bitterness at the unsuccessful result of Newbury and under the
impulse of the long-treasured Montagu quarrel he gave what
was almost certainly false testimony: for he pretended that
Manchester had not attacked at Shaw House until after darkness had set in, and is there at issue with every other contemporary witness. But when he said that Montagu was fighting
slackly because he did not at heart wish to destroy the King,
he was telling if not the truth, at any rate what he believed to
be the truth. That is exactly what Cromwell did believe about
Montagu.

Later when he was met by Montagu's vigorous reply and
the publication of so many of his own sayings which shook
his position, then he backed out and said that he could not
accuse Manchester of half-heartedness in attacking the King,
but only of incompetence. Such a retractation was false; Oliver
continued to think Montagu half-hearted, and when he said
he did not, he lied for the sake of taking refuge from the storm
which Montagu's accusations against him had aroused.

In another department altogether, where soldiers are more
disposed to abandon truth than other men, he is singularly
blameless. Never for the sake of propaganda nor for the sake
of deceiving the enemy, and not often—and then from an over-
excited imagination or from a particular quarrel—did he give
a false picture of a general action. Here are two examples:
what he said about Marston Moor and what he said about
Naseby. Let us look at them.

[ 71 ]

The action of Marston Moor will be dealt with in its own place. Here, in order to appreciate Oliver's falsehood on that occasion, we need only a word on it. At Marston Moor the allied armies, the Parliamentarian and the Scottish, defeated elsewhere, gained a great success on the left wing, and this success decided the battle. On this wing Cromwell commanded the horse and was supported by David Leslie with three Scottish regiments. The proportion of Scottish to English—that is, of David Leslie's command to Cromwell's—was twenty-two to forty-eight; in other words, David Leslie commanded all but one-third of the combined force. The Scotch were in reserve. At the beginning of the action Cromwell's horsemen were thrown back by the fury of Rupert's charge, including as it did a body of Irishmen. Cromwell himself was slightly wounded. Just at the critical moment when it looked as though his horse were broken, David Leslie came round by the right with the reserve (close on half as numerous as the whole of Cromwell's own body) and charged home against the exposed flank of Rupert's cavalry. This turned the tide, and the result was a final victory the details of which will be followed later on.

Of all this, and that the decisive effect of the Scottish charge in flank extricated the wounded Cromwell from the threat of disaster, we are certain. It is also certain that Leslie took over the command while Cromwell himself was disabled, but we do not know for how long a time he did so. Cromwell was also certainly present at the end of the business, when the Royalist horse were routed. And it was Cromwell who rode round the rear of the field during the last stages of the battle and in alliance with Leslie achieved the decision.

Now these things being so, let us see how Cromwell describes them. He says in his letter to Valentine Walton (written on the third day after the battle, Friday the 5th of July, 1644):

"Truly England and the Church of God hath had a great favour from the Lord, in this great Victory given unto us, such as the like never was since this War began. It had all the evidences of an absolute Victory obtained by the Lord's blessing upon the Godly party principally. We never charged but we routed the enemy. The Left Wing, which I commanded, being our own horse, saving a few Scots in our rear, beat all the Prince's horse. God made them as stubble to our swords. We charged their regiments of foot with our horse, and routed all we charged. The particulars I cannot relate now; but I believe, of twenty the Prince hath not four thousand left. Give glory, all the glory, to God."

Yes, the glory to God, by all means: but what about David Leslie?

It is certainly a very shocking thing to read such stuff from the pen of a man who has been just saved in life and fortunes by a comrade in arms, who treats the decisive action of that man as negligible and makes out the important thing as being, "what I commanded," and "our own horse"—save "a few Scots in our rear." But we must remember that Cromwell hated the Scotch and the Scottish alliance, that he was affected by the heat of an action in which he had been wounded, and that in a man fresh from such excitement the lapse is natural though despicable.

The second example again shows a contrast between reality and Cromwell's picture that is even more startling.

To begin with the facts. Cromwell stood on the plateau of Naseby with 3,600 sabres, awaiting the arrival uphill against him of 2,000 or less under Langdale, the Royalist commander. In Cromwell's counter-charge downhill he overthrew this inferior force, and so decided the battle. Further, the nucleus of his command was drawn from the New Model, trained and professional. Now this is how he describes the appearance of Langdale's 2,000 or less against his 3,600; coming uphill against his downhill, and in personnel and training notoriously the inferiors of his own command.

"I can say this of Naseby, that when I saw the enemy drawn up and marching in gallant order towards us, and we a company of poor ignorant men, to seek how to order our battle . . . I could not but smile out to God in praises, in assurance of victory, because God could by things that are not bring to nought things that are, of which I had great assurance; and God did it."

This is blatant. To talk of the Parliamentary army at Naseby and in particular of Cromwell's own command, some of them from the New Model, after some months of its exercise, as "a company of poor ignorant men"; to say that they were at a loss how to draw up their order of battle, when they had drawn it up at leisure and with full experience, in perfect shape—and to leave the impression that the on-comers were so manifestly stronger and superior, when they were as a fact inferior and not much more than half his own men, is a falsehood the quality of which would be spoilt if one were to pile up adjectives on it. It is much stiffer than the *suppresio veri* in the letter to Walton after Marston.

Now I repeat, our interest in these two documents is to discover the motive which prompted them. The ordinary motive for falsehood in military documents is either political, to support civilian opinion in favour of the soldier; or military, and if military one of three kinds: Either to enhance the writer's reputation as a general, or to strengthen the morale of his own troops, or (most common and most legitimate) to deceive the enemy.* In the first of the documents we have just been exam-

---

* Napoleon, the greatest of soldiers, excelled in military falsehood, as in every other military function. Marlborough was perhaps the most truthful, almost contemptuously so, though he also liked to heighten in a word or two the inferiority of a colleague. There are examples of great commanders deliberately telling the truth: it was Turenne, I think (but I am trusting to memory), who told a young enemy officer exactly what he was going to do, released him that he might tell his own general, who would certainly believe that it was a ruse and that the French commander intended the opposite of what he had confided. Moreover, Napoleon himself before Austerlitz had the main lines of his plan read out openly at the head of his battalions. He told the truth to give them confidence. As a rule, then, the motives of your military falsehood are clear enough when you know them, but here they are not so easy to discover.

ining there may have been an element of personal vanity—a dislike of admitting how much the writer owed to David Leslie and the detested Scotch—though why fifty per cent. of your force coming to help you in flank should be called "a few," and these not decisive in flank but useless because in rear, is less easy to determine. But the element of personal vanity even if it were present must have been slight. Cromwell was not a vain man; he was a devoted, enthusiastic man. He was as he believed the instrument of his implacable God, and if he continually exalted that instrument and held his tongue about other inferior instruments who appear to have been pretty useful, it was probably more because he was thinking of himself in his capacity as Captain of the Lord of Sabbaoth— which he had been told meant "Hosts"—than for lesser reasons.

I think something of the same cause or motive is to be discovered in the second document as well. He was guilty of this enormity about the position at Naseby—of this fantastic picture of a mighty host coming against him, his superior in every way, and he helpless in front of it but for Divine aid— because he was enthusiastic in praise of that aid. He was singing the praises not of Oliver but of Jehovah whom Oliver served. It was enthusiasm that led him into these extravagances.

Here then would seem to be the best explanation, as it is also perhaps, for many, an excuse. Those who may deplore Cromwell's wanderings from the truth in these examples may be strengthened by remembering the many, many thousand enormous lies which stand to the credit of I know not how many good and gallant men on both sides of the recent Great War. For indeed there is something so exalted about the noble trade of arms that it pushes men over the edge of reality into a world of romance.

It is we who deserve to be called hypocrites if we pretend that these acts on the part of Cromwell, even his long scheming for the ruin of the King, diminish the essential integrity of his character. That character is in general candid and transparent. His deepest emotions are publicly admitted, he does not deny himself straightforward explosions of anger; there is nothing about him of that permanent restraint which is necessary to the man habitually false. He scrupled not to use stratagem, but he is not poisoned by the hateful "second-nature" deception which you get in sly and calculating men. That outburst of his to the poor dregs of the Long Parliament just before turning them out is a perfect orgy of truth-telling. After all those years of supporting the alliance of Marten, what a blast of fresh air to expose his debauchery! After all those years of putting up with Vane, from the very early day when that empty conceited fellow had brought out his very doubtful evidence against Strafford, to this day twelve years after when he protested against Cromwell's manners, he had borne with Sir Harry Vane. What a glorious burst of truth there is in the famous words, "Oh, Sir Harry Vane! Sir Harry Vane! The Lord deliver me from Sir Harry Vane!" Such almost physical reliefs are not the mark of an untruthful man.

Nothing could be more sincere than his external religion. It corresponded exactly to the most intense of his internal emotions in this matter. Never did there breathe a man less anxious to conceal his burning heart in that affair. One may even say that there is humility in his perpetual display of it. I know but one single anecdote by which could be defended an opposite opinion. That is the story of his aside, after a piece of talk unusually Hebraic even for those times, that one had to speak in that sort of jargon to people of that kind. This again was only an explosion of irritation, and explosions of irritation are the mark of a sincere man. One can get tired even of one's own habitual vocabulary, and when one hears it in the mouths of others one can react against it.

Moreover a character of general integrity and even simplicity is consonant with the element of good-fellowship in Cromwell, to which there is ample testimony. He would carouse, he would play practical jokes. He is very much himself in the story I have related in another, shorter sketch of him, when he made poor Thurloe get into a coach in Hyde Park after a good dinner in the open, himself climbed up on the box, and drove the horses so violently that he was thrown. And what is pleasanter than his calling for tobacco pipes when he would discuss grave affairs of State? Sincerity is consonant also with his courage in action and against mutiny, and with that other, inherited, trait of his, a carelessness about money. There is no contradiction between that carelessness and his occasional anxiety for payment. Men who are careless about money often get into a tight place and become angry or imprudent under the strain. But such anger or imprudence does not go with covetousness. It does go with a temper generally sincere.

He was of this sort then, I think, at that moment when, approaching his thirtieth year, mature and completed, he comes for the first time, very slightly, under the public notice of his fellow men.

No one guessed—no one could dream, he himself cannot have remotely imagined it—that there lurked under all this a special supreme gift, a unique genius for cavalry.

.    .    .    .    .    .    .    .

Lastly, we owe it not only in justice to Cromwell, but still more to that comprehension of him which is our task, to notice his mildness in all that was not impulse. Where Catholicism was concerned he saw red, as we know; but even during the continual plots against his life, even in the face of the most violent vituperation, he was still possessed of this spirit. He had, as the phrase goes, "no enemies to the Left"; but it was not only the extremists on the left, republican, side but his opponents from the right whom he so treated. There was death, of course, for those who plotted against him; that was inevitable; but such executions were not numerous; and as for personal insults he accepted them easily enough. If he was to retain authority at all he had to imprison that brave, just and quite impracticable man Lilburn; but he went no further. And when the fanatical preachers at Blackfriars called him "Anti-Christ" and "The Beast," would have it that he was "666," said he had "drunk of the Cup of Iniquity" and hobnobbed with "Her that is Dressed in Scarlet," he bore it all well enough and no harm ultimately came to the lunatics who thus raved. They had the more excuse because their language differed only in degree from the idiom which he himself would have used, and from the extravagant Biblical rant common at the time upon the Puritan side.

It remains for an understanding of Cromwell's Character and Circumstance to appreciate that he and his lived their whole public lives under the apprehension of renewed Catholic power: of a threat to the very life and survival of all they so passionately upheld.

This dread of a renewed Catholic influence came from three things:

1. The great numbers of Catholic-minded men surviving even so late as 1640-50. They remembered the traditional religion of the English, universal in the memory of those elders to whom Cromwell had talked in youth, the memory whereto the conservative instincts of many Englishmen vaguely turned.

2. The fact that there was a large neutral mass which might well be increasingly influenced by the Catholics if once their religion was tolerated. Active Protestantism was not the religion of Englishmen in that day. It was rather the religion of a faction, large, but still only a faction, "the poor despised Saints."

3. The fact that a great reaction towards Catholicism had been going on throughout Europe all during Cromwell's youth and early manhood; had nearly been completely victorious, to the destruction of the small remaining Protestant powers, and might yet triumph.

Whoever reads even superficially of the great Civil War in England is curious to note a phrase apparently grotesque which repeatedly meets his eye: "The Papist Army," "The Papist Camp," and so on.

Before Naseby the soldiers of the rebellion have pointed out to them the group round the King on the opposing hill—

they are told it is a "Papist" army—they are told that the Royal Army is being grouped round "The Mass."

When Newcastle's forces, two years before, were threatening Lincolnshire and perhaps a march on London, they also were called "The Papist Army." You get the phrase from the beginning to the end of the struggle.

It produces on us today an effect merely absurd. How on earth (we ask) could these masses of Englishmen be regarded —in 1643 and 1645—as Catholic? It is true that individual Catholics had been allowed to join the Royalist forces, but surely (says the modern reader) they could not have been numerous enough to affect the character of the whole?

Yet an explanation of these remarkable and reiterated sentences must be found, and it is not far to seek. Those who used these phrases exaggerated, as enthusiasts always exaggerate; they were giving to their opponents the vilest nicknames they knew in order to excite opposition to those opponents and to justify their own angers. They extended to the whole body a term that only applied to a part of it, just as your heated Tory of a generation ago would talk of all advanced opinion as "Socialist." But this Puritan catchword "The Papist Army" was not, as it seems to most readers today, mere nonsense. It was understood by those to whom it was addressed. It had in *that day* a strong meaning. Why? *Because the number of Catholic-minded Englishmen in the mid-seventeenth century was very large.*

How large will be discussed in a moment; but the initial point to seize, without which the past is incomprehensible, as are especially the character of Oliver himself and all his actions, is that the English of that day had so large a proportion still attached in varying degrees to the Catholic tradition that they might in the early part of the period have decided the character of England. The toleration of Catholicism in the earlier half of the seventeenth century would have decided great numbers to declare themselves openly, and a much increased

organised body of Catholics would have influenced the neutrals. Even in a later part of the century—1660-1680—the Catholics furnished an important fraction, at issue with the rest of
the nation, dividing its unity and attracting converts freely.

In other words, we have to recognise "The Catholic Menace," as it appeared to Cromwell and all those with whom he
stood, and indeed to whatever in England belonged to the
non-Catholic group of religious tendencies. The time was, as I
have said, essentially one of conflict between two religions,
and if we underestimate the force of the lesser and defeated
party we get a thoroughly wrong impression of the whole
affair.

Yet the truth is difficult indeed for a modern Englishman
to grasp. "Reading History backwards," thinking of the past
in terms of the present, is so natural that for most men it is
impossible to avoid it. The Catholic-minded Englishman today
is, with very few exceptions, definitely enrolled under the
Catholic organisation; the practice of his religion is open; being
a member of a very small minority he is as a rule intent on
emphasising his special position. The whole Catholic body in
England forms little more than a twentieth of the population.
The bulk of the petty total is Irish by descent or connection,
and the whole spirit of it is felt to be un-English. To everyone
outside its own small body the Catholic Church in England
is a sect, and an anti-national sect, of which most men hope to
be tolerant because they are persuaded that religious toleration
is politically good, but which repels them when they are
brought into personal contact with it. Catholicism is remembered historically as something which did harm to the English
people in the past, was only powerful in what are thought to
be half-barbarous ages, uncritical, ignorant and unused to the
exercise of reason. Later—in the story of the sixteenth and
seventeenth centuries—Catholicism is associated with peril of
invasion from abroad. It is thought of as the sullen and secret
ally of England's enemies in those times, or, at the best, as

admitting the support of those enemies. It is a restricted, exceptional group, attracting indeed some few brilliant, unstable minds but with difficulty maintained by a special and jealously guarded system of education. It is above all alien, it is foreign, it has nothing to do with the great stream of national tradition; and is indeed of a kind so separate as to seem hostile. The Catholic Church in England is looked back upon by the modern Englishman as though it had always been the same small and foreign body it is today. It takes no place in the mental picture a modern Englishman makes to himself of his ancestors during and since the reign of Elizabeth.

Such a conception of Catholicism in England fills the mind of the reader even when he is dealing with the wholly different conditions of 300 years ago, for the England of the Civil Wars and the Commonwealth seems to him of a like substance with his own.

Such is the domestic aspect of Catholicism in England now; but what was its aspect in 1620-40? What was it to the men then most active in public life, the contemporaries of Cromwell? It was the original religion of their people, an ancestral, powerful, rooted thing, of which they were the desperate opponents. They were struggling to maintain the success of an enthusiastic revolution which, in their eyes, might be the saving of Christendom and especially of England herself, but which was still very new. The recent past was still with them, and that past had been Catholic. Their fathers had known the Mass; their fathers had been born in an England which had taken the whole Catholic scheme as a matter of course. The tradition of Catholicism was still widespread, as was affection for the memory of it, and all about them were fellow subjects who in their hearts desired its return. So strong was that remaining momentum of the old national religion that numbers avowed it at the risk of liberty and fortune, that very many more, less able to stand out because less courageous, heartily wished them well and looked to some ultimate restoration of the Faith.

As to the aspect of Catholicism in the foreign relations of England today, it is somewhat as follows:

In the Englishman's general view of our civilisation today the Catholic culture outside England is seen to be failing, it has been largely abandoned in the countries which it once dominated, the Protestant countries appear as the more advanced, more wealthy and powerful—and increasingly so. What is called "The New World," the English white Dominions and the United States, are all anti-Catholic in origin and tradition. A Catholic minority is present among them much larger than that in England, but it is still only a minority, in some places at most a quarter, in others less than a tenth. It is on the whole much poorer in proportion than the average of the non-Catholic world around it, it does not give the tone. In all these communities, amounting in the aggregate to more than half the western European culture, the Catholic Church, though not negligible, is subordinate. Further, the great problems of our time would seem in the eyes of Englishmen to be economic; and they are specially concerned with the industrialised part of civilisation, where the violent issue is between the controller of capital and the wage-earners, and where in this quarrel the factor of religion is forgotten.

In general, then, the modern Englishman, even if he be of wide instruction, travel and experience, even if he has a considerable knowledge of the historical past, thinks of the Catholic Church, its presence and influence in the world, in such terms as these.

Now the conditions of Cromwell's lifetime were quite other. In his day the only great issue before men at home or abroad was the conflict between the Catholic tradition and the new influence of the Reformation. At home and abroad this was the one question, and it appeared to all men a question of life and death. Half Europe had been fiercely fighting in wars of hitherto unknown cruelty, first in France and then in Germany to decide the issue. To those in the Catholic tradition their ultimate success in the struggle all over Europe and in each country meant the salvaging of civilisation; their defeat meant its destruction. To their opponents the survival of Catholicism, let alone its victory, meant the failure of all that by which it was hoped to restore the world, to save it from putrescence. The battle was still raging at full heat when Cromwell was born, within a lifetime of the first Protestant movements. He came less than sixty years after the dissolution of the English monasteries on which the great fortune of his family had arisen, less than forty years after the beginning of the official Protestant experiment under Elizabeth.

All over Christendom the reaction against the first overwhelming onrush of the Reformation had been in active progress during most of the lifetime of Oliver's parents. In those days England was not nearly so much cut off from Europe as she is now; the general affairs of Christendom and especially the fate of religion throughout the West were of common interest and discussion here. The French Wars of Religion, of which so much had been hoped, had ended in a compromise which was upon the whole a Catholic victory, and that a France which had come within an ace of being conquered by Calvinism. Paris had compelled Henry of Bourbon, the legitimate King and head of the Calvinist faction, to accept the Mass. That victory of the Catholic counter-offensive had been won half a dozen years before Oliver was born. The Spanish Crown had not recovered its old sovereignty over the seven Northern Provinces of the Netherlands, but it was thoroughly and firmly re-established in the nine Southern ones, the Belgian Provinces, which had at first been just as much in rebellion as the Northern, or Dutch group. The Jesuit effort had reached its greatest intensity during the generation of Oliver's parents; with the aid of the Franciscans it had recovered Southern Germany and Poland. The whole of continental Europe was passing through a victorious reaction which looked as though it might well enough proceed to complete victory. The presages of such a victory were "in the air" of Europe; the tide of enthusiasm for religious revolution was receding; the ancient things returned.

In England, therefore, the Protestant cause felt, during all the years when Oliver's character was being formed, that it was holding a defensive outpost, as it were. It was privileged to be secured by the sea, but was still in grave anxiety for the future.

But this Protestant Cause, of which the English Puritans now felt themselves to be the especial champions in Europe, was far from being identical with England. Many were indifferent to it; and there was present throughout the country that large body of sympathisers with the old religion (gathering round a nucleus of avowed Catholics) which made the Protestant future of England doubtful. If England were not made wholly Protestant how should the other, smaller Protestant bodies abroad be saved?

To examine the conditions of Oliver's time, then, we must clearly grasp the quality as well as the quantity of the Catholic element in his England. As for the *quality* of it, I have suggested it in the phrase, "The Catholic-minded minority." When we say that Catholicism in England during, say, the years 1630-50, was of such and such weight, we do not refer to a body of men frequenting Mass and the Catholic sacraments, affirming a violent contrast between themselves and their fellow-citizens in liturgy, and the rest of it. For one thing, save for a very small number the practice of the Catholic religion was physically impossible. A wealthy man might precariously entertain a priest, and more or less surreptitiously carry on the services of his chapel; in London a man might—usually at some risk—appear in the very few and small buildings where the Ambassadors of Catholic Powers were permitted their weekly worship; but everywhere else, whatever the family tradition might be, there was no Mass to hear.

Neither do we merely mean, when we are talking of the numbers, those who refused to attend the services of the established Church. Such recusants were necessarily few, for to stand out in this fashion required a peculiar temper, a fixed intensity of feeling; still less do we mean the handful who were willing to sacrifice the bulk of their fortunes if they were rich or to risk their small savings if they were poor by deliberately accepting the position of "recusant." We do not even mean the very much larger body which in private would with greater or less reluctance call themselves Catholic, or be pointed out as such by their contemporaries—how large that body was we shall see, but it was incomparably larger than the tiny group who submitted to heroic sacrifice. To those who would, at a push, admit Catholicism must be added a very large number of Englishmen who may be called "Catholic-minded." These sympathised with their more positive fellows. They retained in their households long-lived traditions of an older, and what still seemed to them a better, time, and they would not have found the restoration of free Catholic worship uncongenial.

It was this very large "fringe" as it were, of Catholicism in England, which appeared to the anti-Catholic Englishman of Cromwell's time as a mortal peril. This "fringe" would, were Catholics once armed, or should Government ever make an alliance with them, pass almost at once from sympathy to activity, and a very large really Catholic body would be present, ready to extend its boundaries and to annex larger and larger sections of the great neutral mass which is always to be found in the centre of society, indifferent to the more conscious opposed feelings of the right and left.

Now what were the numbers?

There are no statistics save the capricious and insignificant returns of recusants. But there are three methods by which we can approach the problem. I will present these three methods in their order, from the least to the most cogent. The three combined will, I think, give pause to those who would reject certain estimates, on first hearing, as fantastic. The first method consists in judging the general ground of the whole position, by the use of our common sense, and by considering similar occasions in other countries and in the past. We must ask ourselves at what rate and in what fashion the decline of a national religion would presumably progress, and the substitution of its opposite be attained. Secondly, we have the method of memoir, biography and anecdote: the impression gathered in our reading of the omnipresence of Catholics and of the Catholic-minded in the generation of Charles I and the Protector. They are met with everywhere. Thirdly, there is the method of contemporary statistical statement: the very striking successive estimates, made by friends and enemies alike, of the proportion held by the Catholic body at various stages of its slow decline.

As to the first method: the conclusion of history on the way in which one mood of a community declines and another takes its place is universal—there is no exception from it, and there can be none, for it is in the nature of things. The new mood begins enthusiastically in a small number. They gradually convince increasing numbers. These are often at the outset opposed and persecuted, though such opposition has very different periods of duration; sometimes it is brief, sometimes extended for centuries. The nature and rapidity with which the new revolutionary doctrines spread is very greatly affected by the degree of support they receive from the organised government of society. When or after the Government appears on their side their battle is usually won; but the progress may still be slow. What makes for rapidity in such a transformation is the presence of one or more prophetic souls aflame to communicate their faith to the crowd. In such cases the transformation may be widespread and rapid: the Reformation in Scotland is an example of this. But when the support of the new worship is merely official, as it was in England, that new worship will be long indeed in taking root.

Again, men brought up in childhood and youth to one set of ideas do not, in the absence of any great enthusiasm, easily discard those ideas. The ideas may grow dim and the disuse of the practice attaching to them may weaken them further, but they give their colour to society until the generation so trained has passed; if there has been an effort to maintain them in family life, those traditions will carry well on through two lifetimes.

On the other hand, once the revolutionary movement is set going, if there is no breach in its continuity and particularly if it has the organization of Government behind it, the old original mood will not only decline in intensity, but regularly and progressively in the number of its adherents. Moreover to the forces of Government there must be added the education which Government supervises and influences, and the literature which proceeds from such education.

Now, following these lines, mark the business of Catholicism in England. Round about 1560, the first months of William Cecil's power (it was he more than any other individual who launched the new official change of religion), England was Catholic. All that generation which grew to manhood and lived to old age while Elizabeth was on the throne and in the first years of James, that is, during the fifty-two years dominated by William Cecil and his son, had been brought up (save for a very small minority) in the Catholic practice. A man, born in 1540, trained in Catholicism—and boys were so trained in the vast mass of English households— would have been twenty when the new establishment began. He would be sixty-three when Elizabeth died and still no more than seventy-two when the last of the two Cecils, who had conducted the change, died. Such men, in the bulk, retained the influences of their youth. Those influences faded of course;

they were abandoned by more and more as time went on, but during all that time the lapse of Catholic influence upon the mind, though progressive, was slow.

The change was the slower because the policy of the Cecils was all for "gradualness." It had to be, or they would have provoked rebellion.

For the first few years there was no prohibition on the Catholic side against attending the established worship, and on the Government side pressure was at first very gradually applied. After that there came in new factors. No schoolmaster could teach Catholicism definitely; the older priests occupying cures in the Established Church were dying out; the old hierarchy, long dispossessed, disappeared; at last by, say, the year of the Armada, though an active Catholic tradition was kept up by a minority only it remained a large minority. What the general tone of society then was we know amply from such documents as Shakespeare's plays. The phraseology and the state of mind are Catholic. Attachment to the Papacy, though it became a test to distinguish Catholic and anti-Catholic, was by no means widely spread, but Catholic morals, expressions, traditions were everywhere.

It is the next generation that sees the turn of the tide. In the last years of James I and the first years of his son Charles, say, from 1615-30, the Calvinist attitude, the seed of which had been sown in the previous lifetime, attained vigour. It had largely affected the Established Church through a succession of Calvinist Prelates under Calvinist direction from Canterbury. Cecil's man, Parker, at the origin, had been all on that side. Abbot at the end of the process is in the same tradition. All that body of Protestant thought which is in varying degrees detached from and even opposed to Calvinism, had become by 1615-30 clearly anti-Catholic. The nation was still divided, but the Catholic-minded part of it was now subject to the social influence, universally exercised, of its opponent.

Moreover, those who adhered to the ancient tradition were

not united; not even such of them as were clear in their minds upon the full authority of the Catholic Church. In the minority, and it was not a very large one, which was prepared to suffer for Catholicism, and to proclaim it openly, there was strong dissension upon the claims of the Papacy, and a large body were for accepting a modified Oath of Allegiance. Nationalism was beginning to be what it has since so strikingly and permanently become, the "religion of the English." This mood affected even the most convinced and clear-cut Catholics; in the very wide margin between those on the extreme right wing who proclaimed their ancient religion openly and those on the extreme left wing who felt no more than a vague and dying sympathy for what they remembered of their father's traditions, the latter were of course absorbed into the ambient atmosphere. Yet even in them general "Catholic-mindedness" remained. It was now kept alive by reaction against the growing and formidable Puritan body.

This Puritan body was certainly not the majority of the nation by, say, 1630, nor even by 1642 at the outbreak of the Civil War. Puritanism was accepted as an ally by the great taxpayers in their discontents, by all who suffered the political ferment of the time, and this alliance tended to colour the whole movement of rebellion against the Crown, but England as a whole was not Puritan. Rather were the Puritans a very large vehement and cohesive party, not commanding a majority.

There followed what does not immediately concern the period of Oliver Cromwell; a third generation, in the second half of the seventeenth century, in which the area of Catholic-minded England still dwindles, but remains a considerable fraction of the population, of what probable size we shall see in a moment. What ended the Catholic influence for good and all, and ended it late, was the revolution of 1688-89. It is only after this date that a really rapid decline of Catholic feeling in England begins. The Catholic body grows separated from the rest of its fellow-citizens, it shrivels, it fossilises in its isolation, it shrinks to insignificance; less than a hundred years after the fall of the Stuarts Catholicism in England is a tiny insignificant thing. You find it in the affectionate allusions of such a man as Dr. Johnson alluded to as "the old religion"; but even he and such as he—rare enough—had by this time long repudiated that "old religion" and stood in very definite opposition to it.

In general then we may say that the process of Catholic decline in England was the very gradual thing one would expect in a society where the new religion, though enthusiastically held by its votaries, threw up no prophet, such as John Knox had been in Scotland at the very origin of the affair. For the better part of a lifetime, Protestantism in England created no widespread fervours; and, though supported by Government, was so supported for political, not doctrinal reasons.

Now let us turn to the second method of estimating Catholic numbers in Cromwell's day; the general impression gathered in our reading of the Catholic or Catholic-minded population. Individual examples meet one at every turn throughout the generation of Charles Stuart and the Protector. Most of those mentioned come, of course, from the small wealthy stratum of society and among its more conspicuous members, for nine times out of ten it is only these who appear upon the stage of history. But take a few names at random.

At the head of the great English families, typical of all that gave its tone to England, were the Howards. They are under attainder in Oliver's day; there is no Duke of Norfolk. The Earl of Arundel (as the chief of the house then was) not only does not practise Catholicism but is offended by the action of a nephew who becomes a Dominican. Still, that nephew *does* become a Dominican.

No one stands out more strongly on the Puritan side for his religious conviction than Manchester. Yet Manchester's brother is a Catholic, and a prominent one, dying at the head of a great religious house abroad. The two rivals, Bristol and Buckingham, are neither of them to be found professing Catholicism, at least not openly; though Bristol may have been reconciled before he died. But they are both steeped in surroundings of Catholic influence, Buckingham's mother and Buckingham's wife—Bristol's sympathies.

No one is more clearly opposed to Catholicism than the head of the Percys, Northumberland; he affirms his Puritan sympathies so strongly that he betrays the King's fleet, of which he was the head, to the Parliament. But this head of the Percys had been brought up during James's reign in a household intensely Catholic; his father one may call passionately devoted to Catholicism, and Northumberland's own sister was another example in point. The immensely wealthy head of the Paulets, Winchester, is flamboyantly Catholic.

Nor is it a matter of great families only. The survival of Catholicism in the great families is remarkable because they were specially tempted to abandon the ancestral tradition; it was they who suffered most in pocket and position by showing a conservative attachment to it. But you get the same thing in the middle classes.

The example of the Miltons is notorious. The Milton of the preceding generation had fiercely disinherited his son for conforming to the official worship; the poet actively opposed his grandfather's faith, but the poet's brother was as sincerely Catholic as the poet himself was Protestant and was willing to sacrifice his career at the Bar and his chance of sitting on the Bench to the steadfastness of his creed.

That Milton's brother should be a Catholic will be, for most people, a striking example of what I mean. Even more striking perhaps is the presence of Fauconberg in Cromwell's own family. The Lords Fauconberg were Belasyses, famous for their tenacity on the Catholic side of the nation. The first peer, who lived on into the time of the Protectorate, was conspicuous for his Catholicism; his son John was a Royalist officer most prominent in the King's cause, fighting in all the main battles from Edgehill to Naseby and affirming his Catholicism all his life. Thomas Belasyse, the first peer's grandson and heir, born in 1627, was steeped in that tradition. Catholicism was in the air he breathed and for which his name stood during all his early years. Well, at thirty we find him marrying Cromwell's daughter. It is true that he had abandoned his religion, or he could hardly have looked so high, for he made that marriage just when Cromwell was at the very height of his power. It would be difficult to regard his change of creed as proceeding from any spiritual motive, for he was a rat by nature, he went over to the Stuarts lock, stock and barrel at the Restoration, and then when he was over sixty was one of the most eager traitors and all for the usurpation of William III. He had his reward, for the Dutchman made him an Earl, who had hitherto been but a Baron. But it is not the contemptible character of Fauconberg which concerns us so much as his connection with the Cromwell household. To find such a man in that household, coming from such origins and having such connections, vividly shows what Catholicism was in England at that time.

Or look at another family which is identified in our minds with the anti-Catholic side of the nation—the family of Rich. It was founded of course on the usual big bag of monastic loot, Church land robbed from all over Essex. Richard Rich, the first peer, none the less held strongly to the older tradition in religion; his inclination to Catholicism was notorious, his son (who married and perhaps ill-treated the shameless sister of Elizabeth's Essex) played fast and loose. His son again, the original peer's grandson, Robert, Lord Rich, became that Warwick who was a byword for Puritan sympathies and the head of the fleet which Northumberland had already betrayed to the Revolution. Well, this Warwick, whose name is for all of us a symbol of extreme anti-Catholic feeling, the first cousin of the incompetent Essex, the Parliamentary General, has one son who married one of Cromwell's daughters. But another much more remarkable son, Henry, became Lord Holland, in the service of Buckingham; he worked like a slave for the toleration of Catholics, he negotiated the secret clause with that object in the marriage treaty with France. He was not steadfastly loyal to the King, for he was a man of intense personal animosities when he thought himself slighted; but after all it was he who helped to raise the second Civil War, and suffered death on that account.

Take the name of Russell, in the following lifetime. Here again is a name which is identified with the whole anti-Catholic story. The Bedford of the Civil Wars is the very chief of the Puritan group which was undermining the King, and the family of which he was the head had stood during a hundred years for the destruction of the ancient faith. Yet you find with that family, with Bedford's household, exactly what you find with Cromwell—his daughter marries a Catholic. And what is more that Catholic does not turn renegade, as one might expect; on the contrary, he is a sincere convert and even a violent one; while Russell's third son, John, is as violent a Royalist, conspired under the Protectorate and lived to command the Guards under Charles II after the Restoration.

You have, as a sort of typical case, the case of the Digbys. The wealthiest of them is prominent in the Gunpowder Plot, and suffers death on that account. His son Kenelm, is fast and loose with Catholicism all his life, but, in that time of come and go, mainly on the Catholic side; promising Laud that he is sincerely Protestant and then conspicuous abroad as a Catholic, ending no one could say which. This is the Digby of whom men talked most; it was his relative who became Lord Bristol and was the Ambassador in Madrid with whom Buckingham quarrelled, of whom we have seen that he never openly professed Catholicism, but was always accused of it and worked continually for toleration. His son again was that strong and convinced convert who had married into the Russells—and remark that in the very middle of the seventeenth century conflict he had as a young man insisted on his dislike of Catholicism and had had a hot controversy on the matter with his cousin Kenelm, wherein Kenelm had maintained the Catholic side. After that controversy, Digby suddenlv appears himself strongly and convincedly Catholic.

What name is most conspicuous upon the anti-Catholic side? Without a doubt the name of Cecil, for it was William Cecil who by his genius set up the new state of affairs. He was the true father of the Church of England. And who carries on the tradition more strongly than his son and successor, Salisbury, that dwarf of genius, with his humpback and enormous head? Well, what of the later generation of Salisburys? The Salisbury of the lifetime after the Civil Wars, the grandson of the great Salisbury who nourished and exposed the Gunpowder Plot and was the captain-general of English Protestantism, appears as a Catholic—and what is more, so does his son after him.

There is one further piece of very strong evidence. It concerns the *minimum* number of known Catholic priests in England alone during the eleven years of Charles's personal government, just when the anti-Catholic feeling of men such as Cromwell was being nourished to its climax.

In a society where by the open laws of the country a Catholic priest was a criminal to be hunted down and condemned to a most horrible death, the numbers of them were over 800—perhaps if every one had been known, nearer a thousand.

This is as though in modern England the *leaders and organisers* of a proscribed and criminal body, large in itself and held to be a mortal peril to the State, were 10,000 in number—and yet were strangely allowed to live undisturbed. More than half the total were regular priests; there were a hundred Benedictine monks and a hundred and sixty Jesuits, of other religions between forty and fifty. We have this on Panzani's report: and when was this great number of priests noted? Why, in the very heart of the time when men like Cromwell throughout the country were reaching the highest point of exasperation, in the middle of those eleven years during which Charles I was ruling as a free monarch.

Sporadic instances of this kind, if they were all we had to go upon, might mean little or much according to the way in which one comes across them; to the man who reads widely of the period and is at first astonished to discover how perpetually he stumbles upon Catholic names, their number and universal distribution are most impressive. The man who only sees a chance list of them haphazard, such as is put down here, will be less impressed.

But now turn to the third and more cogent method, that of contemporary estimates. In the absence of any census or indeed of almost any statistics in the general departments of social life, personal estimates are all we have available. They are of course exceedingly rough, they are biassed, they must fall wide of the mark, as all such general guesses do, moreover they are not carefully undertaken with the special object of getting as near as possible to an exact number, they are chance allusions in letters, conversations and speeches. Moreover they are few. But they are sufficient to fix our judgment within certain wide limits. We begin with the first testimony of this kind, Paget's declaration—a strong particular statement made at the moment when it was first attempted to abolish the Mass in the parish churches of England. Not a dozen years before an enthusiastic supporter of the Protestant ideas coming in from the Continent, an official who stood in the very heart of the Government (he dealt with all the papers concerning home affairs and was therefore in by far the best position to judge) and his whole fortunes based upon the overthrow of Catholicism, Paget estimated the adherents of Protestantism in his time—Edward VI—at less than one Englishman in twelve. This was not fifty years before Oliver was born, and we must remember that so high an estimate as one-twelfth was possibly exaggerated, because Paget was immediately impressed by London, where the Reformation had advanced much further than elsewhere. England as a whole was a mass of small agricultural villages, and certainly in these the proportion of one inhabitant in twelve or even perhaps of one in fifty did not hold.

Was this very small minority of anti-Catholics increased during the Marian persecution? The thing is generally affirmed and it may be so, particularly in London. It may be that the violence of persecution—and in the capital which counted for so much in all public affairs the persecution was permanently before the eyes of the people for nearly four years—there may have been a certain accession to the anti-Catholic ranks by way of reaction. There was certainly a tradition of it and that tradition must be noted; though what ultimately and very slowly became the conquering side naturally exaggerated the effect of their martyrs. It must be remarked that there is no record of strong and general public feeling, not even a small collection of documents to illustrate it, such as are associated with that undoubtedly most unpopular thing, the Spanish marriage.

Anyhow, no one will deny that in the first ten years of Elizabeth's reign we are dealing with an England that is Catholic as a whole. Just as they end, comes the grave political change due to the imprisonment of Mary, Queen of Scots, and with it the opportunity for active persecution under the excuse of repressing treason. Without a doubt in the thirty years and more of this pressure the anti-Catholic body increased largely.

Be that as it may, we start with Paget's estimate of eleven-twelfths Catholic in feeling in 1549, a proportion which is slowly, but only slowly, diminishing in the twenty years that follow.

The next estimates we have are those of the Catholic exiles who organised the belated but vigorous resistance to Cecil's terror in England while he was preparing and accomplishing the killing of Mary Stuart. They judged that towards the end of Elizabeth's reign and in the first few months after it, preceding the Gunpowder Plot, say in the period 1590-1606, "half England was Catholic." That is the repeated statement you see cropping up in their arguments and efforts. Sometimes they put it higher.

Now here we must discount a tendency familiar in all such estimates of a losing cause among those who have suffered exile for it. Such men naturally tend to exaggerate. If they intended to convey that half England was still strongly Catholic and in active opposition to the other half, their picture is false. But we are not considering active opposition; we are considering the mass of "central" people who vary from warm sympathisers with Catholicism to the many who are almost indifferent.

No one can do more than guess vaguely at the sentiments of the great mass of neutral or nearly neutral, lukewarm, people during quarrels of this kind. But though it may be somewhat of an exaggeration, the general impression that not much less than half England was still in sympathy with the old tradition up to the Gunpowder Plot is not unreasonable. Men associated the personality of Elizabeth with the repression of the national tradition in Religion. They were wrong, as people are nearly always wrong about the real forces that govern them; the ceaseless pressure, attempting to crush out Catholicism, was exercised not by Elizabeth Tudor but by the Cecils, father and son. *That dynasty* was continuous and long outlived Elizabeth. However, the false impression of Elizabeth's responsibility being established in the populace, we know that when Elizabeth died in 1603 there was expected of the new reign a general toleration; a sort of interim; an eirenicon, such as had begun to be familiar to the European mind through the compromise in the French religious quarrel a few years before, and the see-saw balance still precariously maintained among the Germans, whereby as yet the two factions there had been prevented by Imperial policy from flying at each other's throats.

The origins of the Gunpowder Plot are obscure; some of

[ 98 ]

its members certainly acted under the impression that the initiative was theirs: contemporary Catholics laid that initiative
to Cecil. Whatever be the truth, it is certain that Cecil nourished the plot and was able to expose it at just the right moment
for his objects. The exposure of it had a profound effect upon
opinion; and it is from this moment (1605-6) that the centre
of gravity definitely shifts over and that not only the wealth
and the direction of England but the numerical majority
among Englishmen becomes increasingly anti-Catholic.

Fifteen years later we get another estimate of great interest.
It is that put forth openly in the House of Commons by a
man high in public affairs and belonging to a connection where
all official reports were heard and discussed. Phelips, the powerful owner of Montacute House in Somerset, and one of the
most prominent men in the early struggles between the Crown
and the greater tax-payers in Parliament, complained in 1621
of the leniency shown to Catholics and presumed that if it
were continued *their numbers would soon amount to half the
King's subjects in Great Britain.*

Now here again we must discount exaggeration. Phelips
desired to produce an effect, he wanted to arouse his audience,
and he would therefore naturally make as much as he could
of the peril. He did not say the Catholic numbers actually *were*
half, but that they *soon* might *become* half. He was not talking nonsense, which it was not his character to do, and which
would have been silly and a waste of time at such a moment.
He was not a mob orator; he was making a deliberate statement
from his official place. Whether at the moment the whole body
of whom he was thinking, counting the least definite, the most
tenuous, sympathisers with the old national tradition in religion, were still more than a third cannot be affirmed—but it
is fairly safe to say that they must at least have been a third.
A public man talking of the danger of the spread of ideas—
say a public man today talking of the danger of the spread of
Communism—would not say that we should in a short time

have half the English people Communist. It would be nonsense, and he would be making a fool of himself. But if he said that short of such and such measures we should soon have half the English people voting Labour, it would mean that he had in mind an existing very large minority. So it was with Phelips.

We get another estimate about twenty years later again, in connection with the Civil Wars. It is that of a careful compiler, well acquainted with those in the landed classes who admitted their Catholicism, and he sat down to write of them for posterity. He tells us that, of the officers who were killed in the service of King Charles during the Civil Wars, two-fifths were Catholic—some 200 out of 500.

Now here we have a lower limit of considerable value. The estimate is dealing not with the whole body of Catholic-minded men and women, including that very broad margin which fades away into pure indifference, but with such of the squires as openly professed their Catholicism and were willing to suffer for such profession. Among other things they had to suffer the indignity, keenly felt at that time by men of gentle birth, of being forbidden to bear arms. Charles I, in his need for cadres for his army, had lifted that ban, permitted the recruitment of Catholics and granted the gentry among them commissions.

Now at the height of the Civil War the numerical strength of the two parties was fairly even, and the wealthier class, the protesting tax-payers, were fairly well divided. At first, of course, a majority of squires were against the King and his high taxation, but when it came to the grave decision of armed rebellion you may fairly put the division on *that* point among the gentry at about half and half. It is true that on the revolutionary side there were a number of commercial men—the whole weight of the City of London for instance—who were not then included among the gentry; but it is not an unjust general judgment that, taking the officers of the two sides as a whole, the losses in gentry were not much greater on the one side than the other. The mortality of the Catholic officers cannot have been greater than among the run of their colleagues. At this rate the general estimate of two-fifths of Charles's losses in officers being Catholics who openly admitted their religion and had suffered for it, we get for the landed classes the large proportion of one-fifth as Catholic in, say, 1642-1646.

That proportion would apply not only to the squires but to their tenants. In the England of that day the squire *was* the village; not to the same extent perhaps as he was in the nineteenth century, but still in the main. There were many more freeholders than in Victorian England; the fee-farm tenant was a freeholder, but he also took his tone from the lord of the manor. We know, for instance, how in Lancashire, when Catholicism had dwindled to insignificance, such squires as retained the old religion were followed by their tenants, and this was the general rule throughout agricultural England.

But if you have one-fifth openly adhering to the old tradition and suffering for it, the number of those privately retaining some sympathy for their fathers' religion cannot have been much less. There was presumably no longer, so late as 1642-45, a full two-fifths of England closely or distantly attached to what had been not so long ago the general religion of the whole people; they were perhaps even less than two-sixths—one-third. Their numbers were dwindling; they had had twenty years and more to dwindle between the estimate of Phelips and the estimate of the Catholic officers fallen in Charles's army; but we may safely say that they were still a good deal more than a quarter.

In this we are confirmed by two very important and more definite pieces of statistic, which appear from twenty to thirty years later again. These help us to fix the rate of decline—to plot the curve of it, so to speak—and they confirm the conception that, less than a third, no doubt, but, still, more than a quarter was the numerical weight behind "The Catholic Menace" during the Civil Wars.

[ 101 ]

Lincoln Christian College

We can confirm the "curve of Catholic decline" by following it on after Cromwell's day. There are three more estimates. That of the Catholics who left London and Westminster rather than deny their religion in 1678; Louis XIV's remonstrances to James II against his efforts at religious toleration in 1688; and the almost contemporary figure of the Justices of the Peace who were prepared to follow James's policy. The first gives us one-eighth for the citizens of London who preferred the loss of their business and their own exile to denial of their creed. Thirty thousand left out of a total population—excluding the outer districts in the Bills of Mortality—of under 250,000. Louis—knowing little of the circumstance and arguing desperately to prevent James from exasperating Protestant opinion, yet puts the open Catholics as high as one-tenth and the magistrates sounded for their support work out at one-eighth—so do the House of Lords.

Put all this together and you get a rational and consistent rate of decline in Catholic numbers which fall, as to the overt Catholics, from eleven-twelfths in 1549-60, to perhaps one-third in 1620-30, after half a lifetime of persecution, to one-fifth in 1640-50, to one-eighth in 1670-90. And at each date we must allow for nearly as many again in sympathy though not prepared to suffer for it. Take the curve in the decade of the Civil Wars—1642-51—the moment of Cromwell's greatest inflammation against the old religion, and you see him dreading the influence of a party in England, which, first and last, was perhaps less than a third but certainly more than a quarter of the whole people.

This was a proportion still capable of reversing that anti-Catholic ascendancy which had increasingly given its directing tone to the nation since Cromwell himself had been a child, and since, at the critical moment of the Gunpowder Plot, the moral centre of England had shifted definitely to the Protestant side. Such a large proportion of traditionalists had working for them the fact that all the forces of Europe were making more and more towards a Catholic victory—at a time when such a victory would have meant the decline and ultimate extinction of the small Protestant groups in Scandinavia and the Northern Germanies, Great Britain and the Northern Netherlands.

There had come a critical moment, the test, when Cromwell himself was already in his early twenties, a young man married and established and following the news of the world. This was the ignominious defeat of the Calvinist Count Palatine, son-in-law of James I, King of England. Cromwell had been in his twenty-sixth year when the last effort of the English Crown at retrieving that disaster failed in its turn.

None knew with certitude during the years of Cromwell's public career whether the final defeat of Protestantism upon the Continent might not appear. The Dutch Calvinist Government was not safe, it had to keep in restraint a very large Catholic minority; the treaties which at last recognised it were not signed until the end of the English Civil Wars.

We, looking backwards, can fix the year of King Charles's death as the final turning-point after which the religious quarrel in Europe definitely settled into two camps—after which it appears certain that the much greater area and the much greater wealth, the far larger population of the Catholics, could not achieve the destruction of their opponents. Also we live in a time all the recent memories of which are those of anti-Catholic triumph; the success of the Protestant culture, its vast growth in numbers and economic power—Prussia, England and the United States.

But up to the very end of Cromwell's lifetime and long after, indeed to well after the turn of the century, no man could be certain of these things as we are certain of them today. Of the vast anti-Catholic expansion in numbers and strength there could be of course no conception, but even of a drawn battle between what was then so much the weaker party and the stronger forces of the old Church there was no certitude. When Cromwell died he died envisaging an England in peril from what he and a determining number of his fellow-English-men regarded as the forces of Death and Hell. The England that was to be and of which they were themselves the creators was at stake.

That Catholicism in Europe did not decisively win its battle was due to Richelieu's action in hiring the services and the genius of Gustavus Adolphus. Let the reader remember how late this came—the famous hour in which the power of Catholicism under the Hapsburgs of Vienna and Madrid was checked did not strike till the victories of Gustavus Adolphus in 1631. All Cromwell's own judgment of public affairs, formed as he grew to manhood and up to his fortieth year, was of a beleaguered and imperilled Protestant force in Europe. He lived to witness the Catholic rising in Ireland. He lived in active consciousness of the Catholic numbers in his own country.

That is what we mean when we say that to understand Cromwell we must see him continually faced by the Catholic Menace.

CROMWELL was a soldier, a cavalry soldier, a genius at handling cavalry tactically and in the field. Whether he showed high strategical ability may be doubted, or rather may be denied; the Civil War in England gave little opportunity for any display of strategy, save of the elementary sort that must appear in any conflict. Moreover, grand strategy had hardly been revived in the seventeenth century abroad, let alone in Britain. But in tactics, cavalry tactics, he was supreme. That was his point; that is his chief meaning in history.

He was not a religious enthusiast, a leader of men and all that, who happened to take on the profession of arms—he was rather a cavalry commander who happened also to be a Puritan. Had fate made him a Papist cavalier or an atheist gambler accustomed to the saddle it would have been just the same— his prime quality would have remained that of the cavalry leader.

There were any number of enthusiasts all around, thousands upon thousands. There were any number of men who wrestled with the Lord in prayer and all the rest of it. There were scores at least possessed of nervous energy of his own intense sort. But no other man of those about him could make and bring to success in action a troop, a regiment, a mass of mounted Englishmen as Cromwell could. In cavalry work, for which Englishmen are as well fitted as any men in the world, he was supreme.

Cromwell, therefore, until he appears as a soldier, is a soldier out of place. You do not get him functioning, it is not really Cromwell himself, until he is "forming and informing," making his armed cavalry, filling it with his own spirit and leading it as he so marvellously did.

That other great talent of his, the talent for intrigue when intrigue was necessary (which was so specially shown in his shepherding of Charles Stuart to his doom) was all part of the same group of talents which made him the cavalry leader. Rapidity, lucidity, restraint, judgment of the exact moment—these are the things that make a master of horse; and these are also the qualities which appear in the plans he makes for saving himself and his cause at the expense of the King's life; these are the gifts that brought his plan to a successful issue.

The private life of Cromwell ends with the shock of the Hinchinbrooke sale, in 1627. In the first days of the next year, on the 23rd of January, 1628, he was nominated at a meeting of the townsmen of Huntingdon to go to Westminster as one of the members for the town. Thenceforward he is to be found in a more or less public position. That he should be in Parliament like any other of the rich landed class is not of great importance to understanding him, but we note that on this day his career has begun. For twelve years, until his second election to Parliament and his third election immediately afterwards as a member of the Long Parliament, he remains in a sort of half obscurity. He is more talked of than he was, he is known, he does in the last two years (1640-41) a certain amount of Parliamentary work; but he is not conspicuous.

Then, with early 1642, the change comes. Civil war is at hand, he raises a troop of which he is Captain, he takes military action in his own district of Cambridgeshire; he becomes a soldier. From that moment (but not before that moment) the real life of Oliver Cromwell begins, and we begin to judge him by seeing him in action and fulfilling himself.

This interval of fourteen years during which he was a soldier out of place and during the first twelve of which he remained in obscurity may be briefly dealt with. These years are known to us only in fragmentary form, but such brief glimpses as we have of them fit in with the rest we know of the man. They are the years in which his family is growing up around him, in which his preoccupation with religion intensifies, and in which, without his being very conscious of what was coming, the structure of his fate is cast.

I have said that our initial date is the 23rd of January, 1628. His name had appeared among those of the principal burgesses in Huntingdon for the return of members in the earlier Parliaments of Charles I; he was now himself chosen. The old identification of the Williams-Cromwell family with the town, the overshadowing influence of the Hinchinbrooke connection secured his return. And side by side with him was sent up to Westminster one of the new Hinchinbrooke people, a Montagu, the third son of Manchester. He appeared at Westminster with all the other squires on Monday, the 17th of March, and it is to be noted that during the few months of that assembly such small part as he plays he plays only in connection with religion.

It was the moment when the revolutionaries, of whom Pym was the very able leader, had determined to add to their political effort the driving power of the new Puritan excitement, and, of these allies, where Pym was the creative mind, Elliot was the rhetorician. When the idea first occurred there was something odd about it. The wealthy landed tax-payers had for their half-conscious ultimate object the supplanting of the monarchy by themselves as an aristocracy, and for their immediate object their own relief from the new financial pressure put upon them. The zeal of Puritanism was not directly connected with such objects: how, then, could the Puritan zealots be roped in to reinforce the original political and financial attack on kingship? It was the aim of the attack to destroy the authority of Charles. But that end would be hard to attain in spite of the impoverishment of the Crown, because all men lived under the conception of the King as the natural leader of the English people, the rightful authority, the one power to whom all owed loyalty and obedience.

Against an established position of that kind, to overset it,

[ 107 ]

more was needed than the cunning of the lawyers, more even than the holding up of supply and the statement of the new revolutionary principles. There was needed some inward fire, without which no revolution can succeed. Such a fire has often been provided by patriotism; often by following a rival for the throne; but always by some flaming loyalty with which to meet the natural attachment men have to the government they have always known. Pym saw, and those who followed him agreed, that the taking into their camp of the Puritan enthusiasm was just what was needed.

Now of this moral force Cromwell, though as yet hardly known, was an excellent example. All his interest, in that Parliament and long afterwards, lies not with any political problem but with the establishment in England of the Kingdom of the Lord, the destruction of all that savoured of the thousand-year-old English religious tradition, the triumph of that force which Calvin had unloosed upon the world.

It was on the 11th of February, 1629, that Cromwell's voice was first heard; a voice vulgarly harsh and loud, compelling attention especially from those to whom it was vulgarly offensive—and that voice was raised upon a matter of religion alone. The excited but determined words were spoken upon the one thing that moved him—the peril of Popery. Beard, that old schoolmaster of his who was also in Huntingdon (one of the new "lecturers" as they were called, that is, lay-preachers as it were, endowed by the Puritans and set up in rivalry to the Established Church) had told his pupil the dreadful story which Oliver now must relate to the House; how Alabaster had preached "flat Popery" at Paul's Cross, and how the Bishop of Winchester had condoned the act and supported the evil thing. The House was in Committee of Religion and John Pym was in the Chair.

This testimony from Doctor Beard, a man publicly known —much better known then than his pupil Oliver Cromwell was—exactly suited the present tactics of the revolutionaries.

For Beard's name had influence; already for three years men had read his powerful dissertation showing the Pope of Rome to be anti-Christ and proving the thesis in two separate ways. It had been dedicated to Williams, the Bishop of Lincoln (later of York), who was, it seems, a sort of distant cousin to the Williams-Cromwells; and the dedication gave Beard further fame, for Williams was the counterweight to Laud; Williams was toying with Puritanism, Bishop though he was. He was not sincere; his motives were those of personal ambition and a personal quarrel (and let it be remembered that he it was who by the advice he gave the King compassed the death of the great Strafford); but whatever his motives, his name had its effect and helped Beard's fame. The allusion to Beard as a friend and the bringing in by him of Beard into the debate thrust Cromwell a trifle forward; but he took no pleasure in the slight incident. He showed no desire to be prominent in the discussions of Parliament. The trade did not suit him, and all the while this young man, not yet thirty, was under the heavy burden of his black thoughts, his native nervous taint and his depression. It was during this same session that Cromwell had fallen into that melancholy which we have noted. It was during his presence in London for the Parliament that he had left it so strong upon him as to make him seek the physicians.

During that sharp struggle of the year, fought, as it were, over the body of Buckingham, Cromwell does nothing more. He goes back to Huntingdon to brood over his odd visions, which still hold him, and over his soreness against the Montagu name. He found himself on his return richer than when he had started. An uncle of his had died leaving him further property in the town itself and another nineteen acres just outside it; and in the next year after this first revolutionary Parliament had been disbanded, he was a Justice of the Peace for Huntingdon.

Now Cromwell thus returned from Parliament, and

awakened to the quarrels of the time and angry over the family misfortunes, found occasion to increase his unsatisfied mood. He had spoken vainly against the new constitution or Charter which had been arranged for the Town and gave special power to the Mayor and nominated Aldermen; he was summoned, therefore, before the Privy Council to account for his action, but nothing came of it: he had been summoned before them in the December of that year (1630) and he went home still as much in money and consideration as he had left, and still busied with the main issue of religion. He was particularly anxious for the continuation of the Puritan "lectureship." His old and revered master Beard whom the Puritans had chosen for it died; and Laud was now beginning that policy of unity in the English Church which he prosecuted so vigorously as long as the King was master in his own house: that is, from the abortive Parliament of 1628 which had just been dismissed, to the elections of 1640.

It is singular that Laud's grievance against these Puritan lectureships all up and down the country (but especially in the south-east) was founded upon the power they gave to laymen to summon or dismiss, to be the creators of the clergy of the parish. It is difficult to understand the indignation of the regular Churchmen on these lines. That they should have objected to the more extreme Puritan laymen preaching side by side with, and in antagonism to, the regular ministration of the Church of England clergy may be understood easily enough —but that they should have maintained that laymen should not nominate to such posts was inexcusable considering that the whole clerical system of England was under patronage and control of laymen from the King downwards, and that its whole point consisted in lay control.

Meanwhile the strain of seeing the Montagus displaying their increasing wealth under the roof which had covered him in childhood was more than Oliver could bear. He sold some part of his lands, notably that which had been (before the

Reformation loot) the endowment of the Augustinian Friars. It brought in about £12,000 in our money. He thus got rid as well as he could of the Huntingdon connection with its Montagu memories. His mother went on living in the great house; he himself took some grazing lands five miles down the river near St. Ives, stocking them with this new accession of capital.

He managed his land not too successfully apparently. There is no proof of his having done anything in the way of resisting that long and prosperous kingly government which now seemed to be established in England for ever. In 1636, eight years after his first return to Westminster, yet another accession of fortune came to him. His mother's brother, Sir Thomas Steward, who farmed the tithes of Ely Cathedral and in general got the pickings from the management of the ecclesiastical estates, died and left the advantages of those positions to his nephew. It is possible or probable that Cromwell, true to the spendthrift inheritance of his blood, had been embarrassed. There is no very definite evidence but a likely story of yet another quarrel with that same uncle, and even some attempt to get the old man out of the way by having him declared mentally unfit to carry on his duties. Anyhow, Cromwell, already somewhat enriched by one uncle, had his income added to by another. In that same year in which he stepped into Steward's shoes, acquiring the gathering of the rents and tithes and the management of more land, he moved to Ely, where his family remained settled for eleven years, and in Ely he acquired some considerable local power.

There are strong traditions of his occasional embarrassment and one rather worthless story of his having contemplated emigration during some one rather more difficult year; there is no real basis for that tale nor good corroboration of it.

But what did appear at the end of this period of his life, at the beginning of his fortieth year, was a blow which affected him deeply. His eldest son, whom men liked, who was pious, simple and quiet, died in Felstead—at the house of his grand-father, Cromwell's father-in-law, Bourcher, the wealthy City knight. At that moment Cromwell was tempted to suicide. He gives a clear and very touching account of what he suffered, though he kept it hidden for many years longer. He testifies to the power of Scripture in him, saying that "it saved his life." He read the words of St. Paul (he calls him "Paul" of course), tells us that he relied upon, and was made secure by, "Christ strengthening him."

To those same years belongs a singular document, also vio-lently sincere, wherein he speaks at great length of his "con-version"—though this typically Calvinist "experience" must have happened long before. He denounces himself for the enor-mity of his early sins; he testifies, after the fashion of the new religion, to a change of heart; he is a brand snatched from the burning.

For the rest, he does nothing. He does not follow the lead of his powerful cousin John Hampden. Had the King not had to face the Scotch rebellion, Oliver would have continued to collect rents, his own and others, to live his prosperous life at home, steeped in the emotion of his religion, of that family life to which he was so much attached, the wife on whom he relied and his surviving children.

But a new struggle in the north changed all. The costs and disappointments of the Scottish War, the consequent urgent necessity for exceptional revenue, were together wearing down the King; he would soon be compelled to summon the rich landowners to Parliament again. There seems to be little doubt that Oliver desired to be returned again. He canvassed and was canvassed for in his candidature for the coming inevitable Parliament. There was a good deal of petty local activity around him, of which confused tradition has remained. He had himself made a freeman of Cambridge. Huntingdon he had shaken off, there was no more Cromwell influence there; but he had supported the Russells, and Bedford, their head, against the King during the money-quarrel over the drainage of the Fens, and that had given him a party and a following in Cambridge. In this setting forward again, vague and contradictory as the stories are, there is at least one delightful name —a supporter of Cromwell's candidature is called Wildbore, and though we cannot disentangle what happened, the name at least deserves to be remembered. Anyhow, in the October of 1640 the returns were made, and the Burgesses of Cambridge, perhaps after some debate, and, according to one account by a very narrow majority (possibly only a majority of one in a day when voting of that sort was uncommon and voting as we have it unknown) set him down for Westminster at their meeting. He and John Lowry were to go up to the Commons from Cambridge. As for Huntingdon, it was now wholly in the pocket of the Montagus; two of that family came up side by side to that same Parliament, and what a bitterness for Oliver to find them there! As for the Shire, yet another Montagu was to speak for it in the same Assembly, and with him was Oliver's own brother-in-law, Walton.

There is a contrast between the soldier and the man fitted for what is grimly called today "public life"; that is the man called politician or courtier, according to the regime, Monarchic or Parliamentary, under which he lives. Cromwell, though he did not yet know it, was a soldier; that was his trade and character, soldiering was his native calling, it was what he could do. Therefore the other activities, those of the courtier or the politician, did not fit into his pattern.

For let it be considered how this "public life" works in the two essentials of action and responsibility. The soldier must necessarily practice direct action, and he must be openly responsible for such action. The military machine would break down at once if each man from Corporal to Commander-in-Chief were not known to be responsible for this or that duty and open to the consequences of right or wrong activity in his function.

[ 113 ]

Further the soldier is, from the nature of his trade at one and the same time subordinate and in command.

With the courtier or the politician it is just the other way; the whole point of their trade is the avoidance of responsibility. The individual is to get as much as he can in the way of glory or occupation or (much the most important) money without showing his hand. If he shows his hand too much he is doomed, for he lives in a perpetual turmoil of competition against his fellows.

His action must never be direct; he must always be one of a committee, a unit lost in numbers; he must suggest, influence, bide his time, work by elimination. Direct action—which is violence—is the one thing especially odious to assemblies or courts.

All this does not mean that the soldier is incapable of intrigue, God knows, or that his trade unfits him for it. All tactics and strategy involve a plan to be carried out, rapidly changeable or adaptable and yet concealed from the enemy. But the soldier's intrigue, whether for self-advancement or self-preservation, is of a direct and simple sort, it attaches to one issue, it is not universal with him. Napoleon intrigued first for command and later for power; Cromwell intrigued first from the desire to exercise that function which he had discovered in himself, from the desire to be doing the trade for which he was born, later under the necessity of preserving himself, later still under the necessity of maintaining some sort of government. But neither Cromwell's intrigues nor Napoleon's nor Cæsar's, nor those of any other man eminently and by nature a soldier are of the ambient unceasing sort which comes at last to pervade the whole of the character in the courtier and the politician. The soldier has not a prime interest in intrigue against colleagues, nor is he under a necessity of living by such intrigue. It is not the air he breathes; on the contrary, it is exceptional to the main activities of his life.

Therefore from the moment Cromwell enters the Long

Parliament on his election of the 9th of November, 1640 (the preceding Short Parliament hardly counts in relation to his career) you find him of a marked sort indeed and beginning to be conspicuous in the assembly, but not consonant to the air of an assembly, and bound sooner or later as soldiering grows upon him to abandon the assembly for the soldiering. Indeed, one of the first things we get from him now is a piece of violence in committee. It was provoked by his now ancient and deep-rooted quarrel with the name of Montagu. The family of Montagu had had assigned to them in the person of Manchester, their head, certain lands granted out of the Queen's property in the Fens. They proceeded to enclose, and therefore to get to loggerheads with the small free-holders. Cromwell in the committee appointed (with Hyde in the Chair) to inquire into the affair, launched out against Manchester as though he were engaged in a personal fight. His conduct was shocking to a man of Hyde's legal descent and talents and sense of decorum; assemblies could not carry on if shouting and brawling of this kind were allowed.

Next let us remember that, save on one occasion, everything Cromwell does in the brief year and a half between the first gathering of that revolutionary Parliament and the mustering of forces for war, is directly connected with religion or with arms. With the political theory growing among the squires and their lawyers he has less to do, though he does move one resolution (which came to nothing) in favour of annual Parliaments. But the rest is always either that preoccupation with worship which was his driving power or something connected with armament for the coming fight. He speaks strongly in favour of the petition against the Episcopacy and stands by the "root and branch" policy of 1641. He moves against the Bishops having the right to vote against their own exclusion from the Upper House, and it is at this moment when his religion, always passionate, is becoming inflamed, that there arrives the news of the rebellion and massacres in Ireland.

Now in a study of character, which is all this book pretends to be, we have on that subject another of those critical points whereby Oliver's morals are to be judged. What he did in Ireland when he had power there we shall see in due time, and what he did was directly connected with the shock which, in common with the mass of Englishmen, he received when that first news of the rebellion in Ireland came. In judging him we must ask ourselves three determining questions: (1) Did he believe the enormous exaggerations which ran like wildfire through England? (2) Was he ignorant of the Irish case for rebellion? (3) If so, was he indifferent to that case: did he think it gave the Irish no excuse?

You have here a problem like that which confronts lawyers when they have to distinguish between murder and man-slaughter. Eight years later Cromwell set out to work on Ire-land what her foes call execution and her friends murder— the slaughter of the nation as a nation, and above all the de-struction of that religion by which the Irish race lives. Did he believe that his victim had been guilty of all the enormities attributed to her? Was he ignorant of the provocation which that victim had received? Was he, supposing he were aware of that provocation, indifferent to it, unable to treat it as an excuse?

The fairest answer that can be made to these three points would seem to be as follows:

First: Cromwell presumably believed more or less and in a sort of inflamed way (not in a cold or accurate fashion), the general myth current in England upon the Irish rebellion. In reality the native Irish had risen against those who had thrust them off their own soil and had taken their land from them— who were alien invaders, enemies of their religion and of all they held holy. In their vengeance they had driven the usurpers out, often with great cruelty, and were accountable for some 2,000 deaths, most of them due to exposure, the rest to direct violence. The excited imagination of the anti-Papists in England put forward figures of fantastic extent. One estimate multiplies the true numbers a hundredfold, and in general there was present to the mind of contemporaries in England a lurid and horrible picture of general massacre and destruction. It was "war-mentality" with a vengeance.

Cromwell cannot but have been, in the main, deceived by these huge exaggerations. He was a fairly well-educated man but not a travelled one, nor one who had mixed with many circles, even in England; he did not come across people from the other side of the barricade; he had no special means of judging; he would naturally follow the tide, and we must in justice to him conclude that even if he did not swallow the story whole, as the more ignorant or fanatical of the populace (especially in London) did, the false picture in its main outlines was well fixed in his mind. Catholic Ireland suggested to him from 1641 onwards torture, massacre, fiendish cruelty, and all these upon such a scale as Christendom had—he believed —never known.

Next we must decide upon whether he was acquainted with the provocation: almost certainly, yes. The mass of Englishmen above a certain level, possibly the greater majority of Englishmen (in those days when a larger proportion of the population by far followed the main lines of public affairs than is the case today), knew that there had been what was called "The Plantation of Ireland." They knew that the Irish people had been dispossessed of their land, and that ruthless war had been waged for now a long lifetime against the nationhood of Ireland and her religion. They may not have appreciated the proportions of the robbery, they may not have been awake to the fact that already rather more than half the land of Ireland had been seized for the use of aliens in religion and blood and renegades: but they knew that the thing had been on a large scale and they saw nothing strange in that. Therefore that second count must be answered in the affirmative: Cromwell knew what the provocation had been. He also knew that the provocation had been not only one of robbery but of prolonged and continual cruelty, treacherous massacre—and all the rest.

But what about the third point, which is really the crux of the moral problem? Did he regard the provocation as a palliation of the cruelty that took place in revenge of wrongs so recent and so glaring? Here I think the answer can be simply given in the negative. Cromwell would quite certainly deny any moral basis for such vengeance, or any right in the rebels to attempt to retake their own goods. Above all would he deny their right to re-establish "idolatry."

Much the greater part of modern men and especially modern Englishmen, save when they are blinded by some public crisis, would admit at once not only the fact of such provocation, but its value in a greater or less degree as explaining the vengeance taken by the rebels. To an impartial view indeed it is obvious; and most men can be fairly impartial about events some centuries old, even though the religious duel underlying the whole affair be still in progress. Moreover for most modern men that religious duel does not appear on the surface; it is still the true motive power at work, but it is not apparent now as it was then. The "Chosen Race" feeling is deeper than it was in Cromwell's day, the conviction that men alien in religion and blood are necessarily inferior; but there is not felt as there was in Cromwell's day the *right* to despoil such inferiors, to kill them wholesale, to torture them, to betray them and to drive them from their homes.

Even had not the Catholic menace been what it was throughout Europe, and what it was in England, to that large part of Englishmen whereof Cromwell was representative and which was already Puritan, the Papist idolator had no rights. The Irish, in the nature of things, must be subjected to alien rule, ousted, and if they resisted, destroyed. Whether we approve these morals or not, has no connection with the historical fact of their existence: such was the moral conviction of the very large Puritan faction; it was a conviction held with an intensity proportionate to the convictions of the individual—and held perhaps with more intensity by Cromwell than anyone upon his side of the quarrel not actually insane.

We may sum up, therefore, and say that this great news of late 1641, the tremendous shock received by the general pride of England and the particular Puritan conviction when the noise of the Irish massacres was heard, had the effect on Cromwell of persuading him that myth was truth—he did believe that the event had been enormously larger than it had really been and especially the atrocity of it vastly greater than it really was—though it was bad enough in sober truth. He knew what there was to excuse it, but the excuse was to him of no moral value whatsoever. It was like trying to excuse Hell and a diabolical deed proceeding from Hell—it was excusing men already utterly condemned by his own enormous and justly angered God.

All this must be remembered in our general estimate of the man, when we judge him for the things that were done later on the other side of the sea.

The massacres in Ireland had been directly due to the withdrawal by the King of the English troops and the intention to withdraw them in still greater numbers, for his own defence in what was now certainly going to be an armed struggle in England. And it is in the heat of the excitement upon the Irish massacres that Cromwell's next important appearance takes place upon the public stage.

It is on the 6th of November, 1641, that he moved to appoint Essex to the command of the Trained Bands south of the Trent. That was an act preparatory to war, and it is significant that Cromwell's name, though he was still no more than prominent and not as yet a leader, should come in so conspicuously. A few weeks later, on the 14th of January, 1642, he proposes the Parliamentary committee for "defence"—that is, for the preparation of arms.

Immediately afterwards he again appears as one of the first speculators in the proposed reconquest of Ireland, which was destined to be so long postponed but which, when it was undertaken, proceeded from beginning to end a joint-stock affair in which those who had bought shares should reap their reward out of further lands to be seized from the already despoiled Irish people. Cromwell, though he had a good income proportionate to his rank, some thousands a year as we should put it, was not as yet a man with much free cash at any one time. He put down as a first instalment rather less than £2,000 of our money. But the speculators were to be adjudged, should they succeed, lands of very much more value than their original share. They were coming in on the ground floor.

Not quite two months later, in the last days of March, he was able to raise in cash a larger instalment. He put down another £500, which we may call, say, £3,000 today at least. He was engaged therefore altogether for some £5,000 or more; but that was to give him a right (if the experiment succeeded, and the speculators believed its achievement to be much nearer than it was) to many times the value in Irish land.

Meanwhile he begins to act for direct armament. He spent some six to seven hundred pounds (a hundred pounds in the money of that day) on arms for the men to be levied in his own district in the county of Cambridgeshire; it was to be regarded as a loan repayable out of taxes, and was in fact repaid in the course of the summer. He moved for the sending of ships to the Tyne, for controlling the Armourers' Guild in London, for the search of foreign ships which might be importing arms for the King across the North Sea. He again raised a matter of some three thousand or more for the army which was now rapidly forming. He secured the magazine at Cambridge, and supported his two brothers-in-law, Walton and Desborough, in seizing for the Revolution the College plate which the University had designed to send in aid of the King.

OLIVER CROMWELL

FROM A COPY IN THE NATIONAL PORTRAIT GALLERY, LONDON, OF A
WATER-COLOUR BY SAMUEL COOPER, ABOUT 1657, THE PROPERTY OF
THE DUKE OF BUCCLEUCH

At last he appears with a Commission, a Captain at the head of a troop which he has raised and is training, the number of his troop being the 67th: and side by side with his relatives in similar positions he marches to join the army which Essex that summer was to lead against the army being raised by the King.

At this point that phase in his life which I have called "The Soldier Out of Place" is over, and the soldier in action appears. Henceforward we are to see developing very rapidly all that Oliver Cromwell was to be in that function for which nature had intended him and on which he thus so tardily entered. He was already in his forty-fourth year.

WE now approach the problems connected with Cromwell in active warfare. Those problems present the task of judging what element of good fortune was present side by side with Cromwell's genius and aiding it; how much he owed to the incompetence of opponents, to their insufficient strength in numbers, to their lack of armament; what part was played by other commanders and their troops on his own side. These sometimes increased his chance of success, sometimes diminished it. We have further to satisfy ourselves on the nature of the tactic he employed, and why apparently he alone was able to employ it with uniform success. We have to examine his opportunities in siege work, the nature of his general success and his occasional failure in this; and we have to ask ourselves to what degree he possessed or carried out the art of strategy.

All these questions must be answered in some elementary fashion at least if we are to understand Cromwell, and we must deal with these particular points of his soldiering as we have dealt with the more general points of his character; remembering that there has been a religious and political tendency of the strongest kind—now established for more than two generations—which reads into all he did the maximum of talent; just as in the general matter of character there has been a corresponding tendency to read into all he did the maximum of virtue and strength. Against that tendency to myth we must guard ourselves if we are to see the thing as it was. But there remains the overshadowing fact that in nothing did Cromwell ever *ultimately* fail where soldiering was concerned. He decided most actions in which he was involved, he reduced most strongholds which he besieged; he obtained a decision under circumstances most unfavourable and even, as at Dunbar, in face of apparently hopeless difficulties, impossible to overcome; while the upshot of those many years during which he was continually in the saddle was a complete domination of his instrument, of his enemies and of the country as a whole.

He was, one may say, as a soldier fully successful. He did not indeed as have some few (Marlborough is the chief example in English history) win every battle he engaged in and reduce every fortress he besieged; but he had at the end complete civil mastery, achieved as a soldier, over all men in these islands, a power such as Marlborough neither desired nor obtained.

In order to judge the quality of the man in such a brief survey as this I have chosen four actions in especial with their surroundings: Winceby, Marston Moor, Newbury (the second battle) and Naseby; selecting each of these as tests. The campaigns against the Scotch present a different type of problem, for three reasons: in the first place because there was not the complication of civil war; in the second because they involved long isolated marches, each concluding in one decisive action (Preston, Dunbar, Worcester); and thirdly because in these alone do we see Cromwell acting in complete independence with no interference by political superiors or military colleagues as to his actions and his plans.

I have hesitated whether to make one continuous study of all the military affair, or to take it in historical order, interrupting it with the critical political tests of Oliver's character which intervened between the battles and campaigns. In the end I have decided to compromise: I have put the all-important test of Cromwell, his negotiations with Charles Stuart, his manœuvres for the putting of that King to death, in the midst of the military survey, where it properly belongs in order of time, coming as it does between the Civil War and the Irish and Scottish conquests which followed it. But I have made an exception in the campaign of Preston, which properly belongs to the story of the political manœuvring against the King, and treated it as one of the three campaigns against a Scottish army.

. . . . . .

All these tests by which we may judge Cromwell, these marches, checks and victories, demand for their comprehension a general view of the military circumstances in these islands at that time and on these the first remark we make is that the war began as a chance untried thing on both sides. It had throughout the defects and good qualities of the amateur until the actual fighting was over.

Oddly enough it is not till the fighting stops that full professionalism appears. At the end of the war—but not before—Cromwell had in hand a true and finally formed professional army, which was that sword in his hand whereby he governed England absolutely, first in reality and practice and then officially as well, for seven years. From the battle of Worcester (3rd September, 1651) till his death on the same day seven years later (3rd September, 1658) the great force upon which he relied was an army in the modern sense of the word and in the sense of Roman antiquity. It was indeed more of such an army than most modern ones are. It was perfectly disciplined, it was kept up to strength, and it consisted of mature men, including a large proportion of veterans. But throughout the fighting, up to the very end, it was only gradually acquiring these characters, though it had almost wholly acquired them by the last year.

At the very outset in 1642 the forces on either side of the struggle were inchoate to a degree which is nearly always under-estimated. Men deserted wholesale; they had a confused idea (which in actual life worked out not confusedly at all but most definitely) that no one had a right to make them serve far from home or even for lengthy periods, and this disability was especially marked upon the Parliamentary side.

The discipline was bad, the command divided, the breakdowns rapid. If anyone will be at the pains of comparing the

Civil Wars in England as a whole with the contemporary and earlier work upon the Continent the contrast is striking. Actions, whether decisive or indecisive, are usually settled in a very brief space of time. Compare the two hours at most of Marston Moor, the hour and a half at most of Naseby, or even the work on that late autumn afternoon (3.30 to 7 p.m.) at Worcester, with the work in the Thirty Years' War and the Franco-Spanish Wars.

At Breitenfeld (1631) the first big battle of Gustavus Adolphus, the Imperial foot under Tilly held out for hours against the combined attacks of the three arms. Again at Lutzen in 1632 neither side could break the infantry of the other. At Rocroi (1643) the Spanish infantry beat off Condé's cavalry with big loss, resisted many combined attacks, and only surrendered at nightfall. There is no parallel to these in the English Civil Wars. The infantry of the English Civil Wars were but slowly trained to manœuvre. The nature of the recruitment largely accounts for this, and it must be remembered that the New Model had only a few weeks to work in before Naseby.

Discipline improved as time went on, but it improved slowly, especially on the Parliamentary side.

Even as late as 1649 and the beginning of 1650 Oliver Cromwell in Ireland was under the anxiety of threatened mutiny. It is true that he was dealing with troops far from their homes, engaged in country much of which was wild and ill-suited to the sustenance of the army and the winter was bound to be a trying one under such conditions. But with his forces such as they became a year or two later Cromwell would not have been thus hampered.

This amateurish quality was naturally more apparent in the early stages. You get a vivid example at the very beginning in the first action at Edgehill. There is no scouting, the Parliamentary army goes forward with its guns and a great portion of its men a day's march away behind the main advanced body. The Royalist horse on the left wing, with all the advantage of charging downhill, actually *misses its opponent!* The Parliamentary horse opposite to it is able to act freely in the gap thus left open and to take the Royalist infantry in flank. In that same action the Parliamentary right wing attacks in the old deep formation, not having learnt the Swedish lesson. Edgehill, which might have been a decision on the one side or the other with even moderate instruction, was a series of blunders and a draw.

Now all this aspect of the English Civil Wars is of special value to a study of Cromwell in this: that it was Cromwell, more than any other man, who gradually changed the quality of troops and action. The original defects were remedied largely by the skill, energy and ubiquity of Cromwell himself. The steps towards the final result are the forming of Cromwell's own unit of cavalry until at last it spreads throughout all the Eastern Association (1643); the formation of the New Model (the first approach to a professional army, 1644-45) and thirdly the welding, by the mere practice of arms, and the prestige of victory, of the army which marched to Preston and did what it did at the end of such a march; the still better force which was victorious at Dunbar, and the finally homogeneous body which advanced with such regularity and rapidity from the Firth of Forth to Worcester.

Next we remark the sporadic character of the fighting. It is nearly always so in civil wars to some degree, but the English Civil Wars showed it at its fullest. There was not a district in England where the two sides were not engaged one against the other. There was spread throughout the territory a mass of smaller and larger garrisons holding more or less "strong" posts of every kind, from walled towns to isolated country houses, and it was this feature of the Civil Wars which maintained, until quite near the end, a character of confusion. There could be no training in strategy, and therefore very little exhibition of it. The modern mind has read into more than one series of marches and combinations a thought-out plan which was not there at all. We shall see several examples of this, of which perhaps the most striking in the way of wrong judgment is the modern effort at seeing grand strategy in the earlier part of the campaign of Worcester.

Next let us consider the material basis of the Civil War and how the opposing forces stood in this, apart from instruction and *morale*.

There are here three elements closely connected: money, the recruiting field, and command of the sea. In all these three things the Revolutionaries had a very marked advantage, in some aspects an overwhelming one.

To begin with, they had the money power of the City of London. It was this money power which ultimately defeated the monarchy, not only in this first phase of the Civil War and the killing of the monarch himself, but on through another lifetime until the climax was reached with the foundation of the Bank of England and its preponderance over Government throughout the succeeding centuries. The King had to rely as best he could upon the generosity of loyal supporters—witness the magnificent examples of Lord Winchester, Lord Newcastle and Lord Worcester, the three wealthiest of the peers who rallied to the support of the Crown. He had more and more to quarter his soldiers upon the inhabitants, he had to levy supplies by force, and as the struggle proceeds this lack of financial resources became acute and at length disastrous. The great mass of the people, naturally monarchist in feeling, detested the disturbance of their homes and the seizure of their horses and cattle and corn, and were more turned against the Royalist forces in the west towards the end of the fighting by these desperate necessities under which they suffered than by any other thing.

The financial supremacy of London—three-quarters of the Customs Revenue of the kingdom, and only a somewhat less proportion of the accumulated liquid wealth—showed itself by the continual hold the Revolutionaries maintained over the south and east. Draw a line from near the Wash to Southampton Water, make a big bulge in the middle of it towards the west along the main western roads to near Basingstoke, and you have the field in which the revolution could act securely for the levying of men and means. The war taken on its economic side may be regarded as an advance northwards and westwards from this secure base. The Parliament obtained Lincolnshire—largely Cromwell's own doing—in 1643; in the next year, after Marston Moor, it gets at one blow all the richest parts of the north, that to the east of the Pennines. It holds the greater part of the sea ports, with the exception of Bristol, lost earlier in the war, and with every new victory it reduces the area from which the King can draw men and supplies.

Further, it is the revolutionary side which has command of the sea. It is not an absolute command; the Queen was able early in the struggle to bring munitionment by water from the Low Countries; but this control of sea communication had continual and increasing effect. Without it Cromwell could never have conducted the campaign against Scotland or the conquest of Ireland.

The war in one of its many aspects may be regarded as a war of attrition, during which the Royalist forces are being steadily worn down and their opponents gradually established. All this had its effect on the moral as well as the material side; and it had its effect especially upon discipline. For soldiers who plunder tend to lose their cohesion, apart from the animosity they provoke in the mass of neutrals.

The astonishing thing is that in spite of such handicaps Charles's cause should have been maintained as gallantly as it was and for so long. There were moments when it might, in spite of the heavy odds against it, have triumphed. Thus the one clear strategical conception of the whole affair was the

Royalist idea of a triple convergence upon London in 1643. It broke down, as very wide efforts at convergence usually do; but the particular cause was the inability of Newcastle to make his men march south. That, coupled with Cromwell's energy in the east (about to be described under the general title of "Winceby") was the first step towards the final Parliamentary victory.

The second opportunity which the Royalists had was that of Marston Moor itself. Outnumbered (because the Scottish alliance with the Rebellion, so admirably achieved by Pym, was now fully at work) the King's forces none the less all but destroyed the army in the field against them. And here again it was Cromwell (in the main) who reversed the battle, and from what looked like a lost action retrieved a complete and crushing victory.

After Marston Moor Charles had no chance; but even so you get his striking success in the west against Essex, and the blunders and failure of the Parliamentary forces in the second battle of Newbury. They had the advantage of two to one, and missed it.

In general, and looking on the large picture of the whole of the fighting from 1642 to 1645, it is the recurrent partial failure of the Parliamentary side which had the trumps in their hands against their opponents and who ought, by all the rules of warfare, to have felt themselves to be dominant. The upshot was a final victory gained by the greatly superior money power and recruiting field of the Parliament, coupled with their command of the sea.

Yet not even these considerable advantages would have effected what they did but for the particular talents of Cromwell. It was he who formed from the beginning those special units in the mounted arm whose spirit gradually spread; he who won the two critical actions at the head of his own mounted troops, and did this by his own commands, his own tactic, his own rapidity, promptitude and eye for the moment and the place.

Throughout, for reasons that will appear when we consider Cromwell in action, cavalry was, under the conditions of the England at that time the decisive arm and in Cromwell the Revolutionaries possessed a man unequalled in the use of it.

CROMWELL, taking up soldiering, discovered himself to be what he was. He entered fully into his own nature for the first time. The rapidity of the transition was as remarkable as its thoroughness. It is a great error that men after a certain age take on no new faculties; the seed must have been there, of course, but the plant may pierce very late. It has been seen even in the faculty of verse; it has been seen in commerce, in the management of a great business or in any great organisation; men who had hitherto led one kind of life and exercised one set of activities, performed well enough but without remark one set of tasks, suddenly show supreme ability in another, and aptitudes which no one had suspected.

It is true that Cromwell had had in him certain talents apparent and in exercise during his civilian days which were of just the sort most necessary to the soldier; he had lucidity, he was tenacious, his energy was abundant, but what no one could know and what he did not know himself was the answer to this question—Could he manage men?

He certainly in the event proved that he could not manage men in the political sense of management; but the qualities required for the management of men as soldiers are very different from those required for civil government: they are the qualities of command. Command contains an element of persuasion, but its strength lies much more in limitation than in approach—by which I mean that the faculty of command lies much more in commanding thoroughly and knowing the limits beyond which you must not go, than it does in the gradualness of your advance to control over that which it is your business to order.

But command has in it something much more than this. The

faculty of command is a mysterious gift which you may perceive such and such men to be endowed with in various degrees. At first sight one observing Oliver Cromwell in his civilian days would have said that this, the highest of military qualities, had been denied him. He was harsh, he was quarrelsome and even explosive, he would suddenly blurt out his thoughts at inconvenient times and even in moments when he weakened himself by so doing.

What would seem still worse for the faculty of command, he was ready to change. For instance, he had evidently taken up some position and then retired from it in the mysterious Steward negotiations, when there was that discussion about the controlling of his uncle's fortune and the doubts upon that uncle's sanity. Again, he had conspicuously shown his proneness to change in the business of the Fens, though there the underlying motive was ultimately clear—he had no objection to the freeholders being sacrificed to the Russells because the Russells were the head of his party, but he protested vehemently against their being sacrificed to the King because the King was the object of his opposition. Later this same readiness to change is seen in his withdrawal of the accusations against Manchester, but there again we must remember that there underlay a permanent motive, and though he withdrew for the moment he got rid of Manchester in the end. Anyhow, he did suffer from his changeability, and as all the world knows, nothing is more fatal to command.

Now the interesting point about this is, that the man was so destined by nature to be a soldier, that in his military command such fluctuation did not appear. Politically he was unstable, as when he manœuvred back and forth in his attitude towards the discontents of the Army during the quarrel with Parliament, but in the actual military function of command he never wavered. No one under his orders had to complain of contradiction, or vacillation. He acted always at once with authority, and his violence did not here detract from the plenitude of his effect, as it does when one is concerned with equals and debaters. When Cromwell was in the face of lawyers, that violence appeared futile and certainly lessened him in their eyes, as we have seen it did in those of Hyde before the outbreak of war. But it went well enough with sudden decisions shouted from the saddle, with immediate judgments directing, checking, converting a charge.

Note further that Cromwell increased prodigiously in his capacity to "form and to inform," that is, to mould by order from without, and to quicken by the spirit from within, the men whom he was to bind into an instrument of war.

There is no truer word than the old Greek, "You become a carpenter by doing carpenter's work." Cromwell's genius grew in the active exercise of it, and this was the more plainly seen because it grew by successive steps, from a smaller to a greater model. He begins with the training of a troop, the teaching of that small body while he himself was learning at the same time: he was a good horsemaster, he could judge their control of their mounts, he could advise as well as dictate, and he immediately discovered that out of the material afforded him (and at first largely chosen by him; the sons of yeomen for the most part it would seem), he could make with his own hands a first-rate unit in but a few weeks.

It was in a way an advantage (though paradoxical) that the period between the beginning of their training and their first active service was so short. For the particular ordeal with which he and they were to be faced a long period of peace training or of service different from that in which they were about to engage would have been a disadvantage.

What was the cavalry in which he was now forming a fierce zeal? We have seen that cavalry was at that place and time a decisive arm. Whether it can be called the decisive arm in the early seventeenth century everywhere and especially upon the Continent of Europe, where wars had been continual and where professional soldiers, veteran and of high quality, were familiar with it, is debatable. Cavalry was indeed regarded as of such importance that the proportion of one mounted man to two on foot was everywhere advanced, and if possible everywhere maintained; but it did not always win battles as it did in England. Perhaps the decisive arm of Gustavus Adolphus from ten to a dozen years before was rather artillery than horse. With the Spaniards and notably with Spinola it was rather the infantry—that matchless infantry the reputation of which still ran throughout Europe; the glory of Spain even as her sun was setting. But in England the supremacy of cavalry in the coming struggle was bound to be supreme.

There were two reasons for this, not to be found elsewhere. In the first place the war was essentially a struggle between the greater tax-payers, that is the big landowners, and their following of the smaller freeholders, the yeomen. These men could all ride and most of them could ride well. It is true that perhaps the backbone of and certainly the most effective factor in the revolution was the body of great merchants and money-lenders in the City of London, and they were not remarkable in the saddle; but the squires were riders, and so were the young farmers who came into these first troops, often providing their own mounts and all knowing the ABC of what was to be their trade. Each could manage a horse, and therefore the training of a troop was founded before it was begun. Opposed to them were men of the same type, the great landowners and the small.

In the second place the infantry of the Civil Wars was, as we said, especially at their origin, ill requited and ill disciplined.

The infantry were on a lower scale, socially and of course in pay, but also in all that makes for military quality. In the first year of the war they had too much freedom, and soon many of them were pressed men, unwilling. All through the struggle up to the appearance of the New Model the infantry were unreliable, and particularly on the Parliamentary side. They were, if I may so express myself, "meat for the horse."

They were largely picked up from the riff-raff. We have seen that they deserted freely and almost as matter of course when they were asked to act at any great distance from home. The London Trained Bands were something of an exception, but not very much of one; they were better drilled and had something of a common spirit, but they were not of the first quality, and it must always be remembered that, though London was controlled by the Puritan faction and though its money power was the very basis of the revolution, yet the populace was divided: Pym had been able to provide organised mobs of Londoners to bully the King and the Royalist members of Parliament and Lords, but London had also provided spontaneous mobs upon the other side.

Artillery, until it became siege artillery at the very end of the war, was almost negligible. It played a certain part at Dunbar and here and there one hears of a local effect, but no one was specially skilled in the handling of it, it was not of sufficient interest to leave a record.

Further let it be remarked that in the nature of things competent cavalry was at a greater advantage than ever over competent infantry, on account of the weakness of the infantry flank and the difficulty of rapid conversion, especially with the poor manœuvring capacity of the foot in that England as compared with the contemporary Swedes or Spaniards.

Cavalry fronting good infantry armed with the musket and pike would indeed find them formidable opponents, but if ever cavalry got to work against the flank of an infantry line it could reach its very vitals with hardly anything to check it. Infantry was drawn up in the centre of the line of battle, cavalry stood in two bodies on either wing, and when, say, the cavalry of the right wing was dispersed by the shock of the enemy's left, then the flank of the infantry in the centre was exposed. This in especial, the swinging round after a successful charge, the piercing of the infantry flank by the attacking cavalry was to form Cromwell's prime tactics. It decided

[ 135 ]

Naseby and it decided Marston Moor. But it could only be done by troops exceptionally well held and cohesive, and that is why Cromwell alone was uniformly successful in it.

A troop of cavalry in that day, such as Cromwell was forming and informing during the July and August of 1642, consisted in its full complement of sixty sabres, officered by one Captain with a Lieutenant and a Cornet and a Quartermaster. An average of seven such troops, that is at full strength 420 sabres, formed a regiment under a Colonel. The pay at the beginning (but only at the very beginning) was regular, and it was what we should call today nearer four than three pounds a week for the man and his horse. It was not less than 2s. and later 2s. 6d. a day—but we must multiply by six at least to get the social value of the money today. The multiple would be more than six were it not that, in this case, grain plays so large a part; the price of oats and wheat fluctuated enormously during the wars and was always, in comparison with other things, far higher than it is today.

The officers were very much better paid in proportion, a thing only to be expected from the nature of the revolution, which was essentially that of rich men against the Crown. A Captain got from six to eight times what a private soldier got; a Lieutenant rather more than three times, a Cornet and a Quartermaster somewhat less. As for the Colonels, they had the equivalent of a great deal more than what £2,000 a year would buy today, and allowance for horses as well. It was important to make sure of one's cadres, and there was a very large proportion (it is impossible to say quite how much, but at least one-third), in the class from which the officers were drawn, who, even at the beginning of the war, hesitated between one side and the other. Apart from political passions, which were full of cross-currents, there was the knowledge that a man who took the wrong side—if he were a landowning squire—might end by losing all he had.

Such was cavalry. As for its armament, it is probable that

many of the men carried short carbines, though there are some accounts in which it looks as though only the officers had these, at any rate in certain units. But by way of fire-arms every private had two pistols, and he had, of course, his sword.

The formation was a close one, in three ranks for the most part, after the fashion which Gustavus Adolphus had taught. The older formation had been in six ranks, for the sake of weight in the shock of the charge; but the development of firing in the charge and the advantage of outflanking with a longer line had produced the change. It was not completed in these first months of the war; at Edgehill some of the Parliamentary cavalry seem to have been drawn up in six lines. The horsemen rode knee to knee, in very close formation. They would discharge their pistols just on contact and after discharge hurl them at the opponent, and then immediately set on with the sword, whereupon, however close the original formation, a mêlée began.

Apart from the general type of mounted soldier there were the "dragons"—dragoons as they are now called. Their function was that of mounted infantry and they were, of course, but a small number compared with the cavalry; they would line hedges on the flank of an action especially to interfere with an enemy's charge, several men dismounted to fire, one holding the horses of those dismounted.

This 67th troop which Cromwell was so excellently forming was part of the Eastern Counties Association, later to be very famous and largely to be famous through the example which Cromwell himself had set. The idea of County Associations had arisen on the Royalist side, and in Yorkshire; it was quickly adopted on the other. All Cromwell's own neighbourhood, Cambridgeshire (for the capital of which he was a member and in which he drilled these first men), Essex and Hertfordshire, and beyond them Norfolk and Suffolk, were the first five counties of the Association, later to be joined by two others, Huntingdon and Lincolnshire, making seven. This sort of training of men by the local gentry (and especially by the members of Parliament as chief officers) was going on everywhere on the Parliamentary side. Cromwell's very famous cousin Hampden was at it, with the rank of Colonel (natural to his great wealth) and working in Buckinghamshire as Oliver was in Cambridge. Under him was Oliver's son, as Cornet.

We know very little of Oliver's action in all that first year, 1642, save that he had formed a remarkable troop of his own, perhaps two.

On a Sunday in August (almost certainly the 7th of the month) two young men (the sons of a Judge whom Charles had summoned and who had hesitated to go to the King) were arrested near Huntingdon on suspicion of being Royalist agents as they came back from the north, and were told that they must be examined by Cromwell, who was apparently then in the town. But they got off by giving the troopers a bribe of a few shillings.

How Cromwell had already seized the plate of the Colleges and the rest has already been mentioned. His troop joined the army which Essex was leading against the King, the cavalry of which was under Bedford as Lieutenant-General; it seems certain that he was at Edgehill on the right wing of the Parliamentary army. Holles denies his presence there, but Baxter, who had better opportunities, affirms it.

It is also about this time that he made, if he did make it (it is probable that he did so, but it is not related till a long time after) his famous comment on the quality of the troops recruited for the Parliament. He is said to have told his cousin that they could not win unless they pitted men of "religion" against the men of "honour." It is likely enough that he said something of the sort. There has been based upon it, of course, a super-structure of exaggeration, as though all those who rode in the Parliamentary ranks were Puritans and enthusiasts of Oliver's own type; but there was already an element of this and in some degree (in what degree we cannot tell) Puritan zeal had impressed itself upon these first levies of the Parliament.

There is a characteristic letter of Cromwell's written in the January of the next year, during the lull in the fighting, to the same Mr. Robert Barnard who had been his opponent years before in the troubles of the new Town Charter of Huntingdon. It is interesting as showing again in Oliver just that same tenacious anger which we found in the larger matter of the Montagus. It is also characteristic of the spirit shown in so many other letters of his during the course of the wars, when he summons a house or a town or wrangles with an opponent. It is a bullying letter, apparently in reply to a protest on the part of Barnard, whose house had been invaded and himself treated as a suspect: he tells his old enemy that if he is not opposed to the revolution, well and good; but that if he is, he must expect what is coming to him. It is exactly the tone you get years later in message after message sent to those into whom he would strike fear.

Cromwell had extended his drilling to a double regiment and had been given the rank of Colonel some time in the early part of this year. He is already mentioned as Colonel on the 2nd of March. On the 13th of March of this same opening second year of the war, 1643, there was a fray in St. Albans, hardly a skirmish, between mounted men. The Sheriff, and round him a multitude who were on the King's side, was trying to recruit, when Cromwell's Dragoons slashed in among them to arrest him. The populace being Royalist, the Dragoons had to barricade themselves in the inn, but they carried off their Sheriff and the Commons imprisoned him for years.

It was a day or two later that Cromwell again appeared in the Eastern Counties to meet an attempted Royalist movement from Lowestoft. He put guards on the gates of Norwich to prevent any going out in aid of the effort, attacked

Lowestoft himself, took two cannon and eighteen of the gentry of his own class who were forming the nucleus of the Royalist effort. There was no fighting, for the townsmen, though on the King's side, did not even hold to their guns.

The last notice we have of Cromwell in this early time is a skirmish on a considerable scale near Grantham in the middle of May, where he was in action with twelve troops, say six to seven hundred sabres. Its chief interest is another characteristic letter written in that other tone which we shall find appearing more than once. His troopers, whom he knew to be excellent, appear in it as "poor broken men, helped by God." He was always at it. The most extravagant example we have already seen in the letter concerning Naseby. But we must remember that however ridiculous such falsehood appears to the detached reader, it was not unsoldierly at the time. It was propaganda; bunkum, of course, but useful bunkum. If those soldiers of his whom he had formed upon so good a model could be got to believe that they were thus mysteriously supported by the Creator of the World, that He had them in His special favour, there need not be too much fear that they would behave in action as "poor broken men"—however necessary the phrase might be for enhancing the value of their success.

To sum up these first fragments of the very little remaining from those first moments of the war: Cromwell from the outset has become something new: he has been a soldier more than the others. He was already a soldier altogether, and soldiering will be his trade from now to the end. We must always think of him in that fashion: most of the rest of him was striking and plays its part, but this military spirit is the soul in him which quickens all the rest. He was doing his own work; he was at home; in his own skin. I say again, had all Cromwell's other qualities, not connected with soldiering, been other than what they were, had he been profoundly Catholic or cynically indifferent to any creed, had he been as sensual as he was controlled, ambitious, greedy for gain—or any other thing which he was not—yet still he would have been a soldier, a mounted soldier and supreme in that capacity: "forming and informing."

## I

### WINCEBY

THE first considerable movement in which Cromwell's name appears in any prominence may be called the Campaign of Winceby, and occurs in 1643 when the first year of the war is ending. It consisted in a defence upon the northern front of that "London Area" which was the soul and essential of the revolutionary cause. The great population of London furnished a recruiting field of its own; the size of the City was such that it could not be besieged by the armies of those days, and rushing of it by storm was not conceivable. There was of course in London (as everywhere) a large part of the population upon the side of the King; but the financial organisation of the City was in all the earlier part of the war directly opposed to the interests of the Crown. It was their business to maintain the money power. It was the size of London and the presence of her half-trained militia bands in great numbers, and the great ring of her fortifications put up by enforced and voluntary labour, which had presumably convinced the King and his advisers that it would be hopeless to attack the city with one army on one approach.

The London area included what we call the Home Counties: Bucks, Surrey, Sussex, Kent, Essex, and most of Hertfordshire; but it also included the people who had been formed into "The Eastern Association," of which Cromwell was the most energetic organiser: Huntingdon, Cambridge, etc.

Now to reduce the London area and to destroy the effect of London upon the war there had been drawn up this plan of Royalist convergence. The capital was to be marched upon

SITES OF THE CIVIL WARS

from the south and west; the City, if possible, was to be isolated by cannon upon the Thames well below bridges, and of course the keystone of such convergence would be a simultaneous successful march from the north. The north was still held for Charles, and there was a wealthy man of some lineage to whom masses of tenants were devoted and who would bring, it was thought, sufficient force down south.

The man through whom this menace was coming upon the northern front of the London area, the man whose effect "The Eastern Association" had to meet, was Newcastle.

Newcastle was typical of those among the enriched landed class who had come down on the King's side when it had come to an open quarrel. He forms a sort of bridge between those who were quite whole-hearted, who understood what popular monarchy meant and were determined to save it, and those who, though willing to support the King, had a class feeling in sympathy with the revolt of the rich; a sympathy sufficient to weaken their loyalty to the King under severe trials.

For the first sort—those who would save the monarchy in its fullness with enthusiasm—we have such men as Winchester; pouring out the whole of their wealth and giving all their reputation and their very selves as well. Of the other sort, those who would just barely join the King but felt at heart upon the other side, those among the very richest of the squires, we have Southampton. Newcastle, I say, stands in between. He poured out his wealth unstintedly; in *that* he sacrificed himself wholly for the cause; but he would not carry on his sacrifice to the highest point and endure the moral suffering of failure. Therefore after Marston Moor he gave up the struggle.

But at the moment, in this first twelve months when the war was going well for Charles through the incompetence of the revolutionary leaders, Newcastle was, after Rupert, the most serious factor on the Royalist side. He was a Cavendish, the head of a legal family who were already gentlemen well before the Reformation, but whose first rise to great fortune was based on Abbey lands. His grandfather had been that Sir William Cavendish who as a young man had been Commissioner for the visiting of the monasteries, Auditor for the Court of Augmentations when their estates were seized, getting Sheen for part of his loot and much monastic land in Hertfordshire. It was he who began to build Chatsworth, six years after the death of his master and maker, Henry VIII. But of Newcastle's own vast wealth the greater part came from his mother, who brought in the estates of the Ogles. Newcastle had been the first to form those county associations which later the revolutionaries copied, and of which the most famous became the group of the Eastern Counties, "The Eastern Association," with which we are now dealing.

Newcastle's own county, the one from which he recruited nearly all his troops, was Yorkshire. These County Associations on both sides had the defects and the advantages of local patriotism: such units had cohesion so far as local feeling went, but they had also the grave weakness of losing their willingness to fight outside their own borders, and of subordinating a general plan to their own particular interests. Thus the reason Newcastle delayed in front of Hull, as we shall see him doing in a moment, was that the Yorkshiremen of the surrounding district complained of the way in which the Parliamentary garrison in Hull ravaged their flocks and levied tribute upon them. Much graver was the refusal (for it amounted to that) of the Yorkshiremen to go far south: it was this reluctance of theirs to do more than defend their local interests which destroyed Charles's strategical plan of converging upon London in the summer of 1643.

Newcastle had already attempted to hold Hull for the King at the very beginning of the Civil War. The revolutionaries had been too quick for him, and he now found himself in front of Hull under the following conditions:

He had already raised long before, what was, for the haphazard conditions of the early Civil War, a fairly reliable force; he had made himself master of nearly all Yorkshire and particularly the West Riding; after the fall of Bradford the two Fairfaxes rode eastward across to Hull and were there received.

In this month of August, 1643, Newcastle received direct orders from the King to take part in the general plan, and march south against the London area, that is, immediately against the Eastern Association. We have seen why he had thus entangled himself in the siege of Hull; it would have been better for him and for the cause if he could have marshalled his whole strength for the march southward, but there was that second and grave source of weakness, the reluctance of the northerners to fight out of their own district—and this must be remembered in all that follows.

Anyhow, he had so far carried out the beginning of the plan as to besiege Gainsborough, and here we must take a general view of the situation, at this moment in the summer of 1643, when those operations in Lincolnshire began which are the first important occasion of Cromwell's action as a soldier.

The situation which now brought Cromwell into prominence is comparatively simple, and yet it is not always clearly understood, because the Civil War was of its nature such a confusion of petty incidents.

Further it must be appreciated that though we can now see the general lines clearly enough, they were necessarily more obscure to the men of the time; and it is an interesting question how far in this first emergence of Cromwell, the first military action in which his own initiative begins to count (as distinguished from the preparatory phase, when he was acting as an obscure troop captain) he himself saw the situation, and how far his action was instinctive.

The position was this:

When the fighting began ready cash was needed in great quantities by both sides. Now this could only be obtained by levies from the areas controlled by either party. Therefore, apart from political advantage, to extend its area of control was vital to each.

The area covered by the influence of London was, as we have seen, the south-east; the all-important capital itself, by far the greatest port of entry; the lesser ports up to the Wash on the east and to Portsmouth along the south coast, with a certain wide sweep to the west of London along the Thames valley. Now the elongated shape of the island is such that the hold possessed by London, its numbers, wealth and material, under conditions where twenty miles was a long day's effort in the transport of goods or men, lessened as one went northwards along the east coast, and left everything north of the Wash, at least, outside the influence of the capital.

Lincolnshire, the great area of Yorkshire, Durham and Northumberland along the east coast were not affected by that capital factor in favour of the Parliament—the preponderance of London. But here the Parliament held, as we saw, the very important isolated point of Hull, a seaport of entry of the first value and a great store of munitionment, for, as we know, from the beginning of the year it had held the Royal magazines. The country around Hull, however, was open to the influence of the legitimate Government against the revolution, and the Royalists further held the nodal point of Newark. Yorkshire and the northern part of the coast were subject to the influence of an army which was commanded by Newcastle; and this army was preparing to take Hull if it could. Should it succeed in doing so, the mass of north-eastern England would be secured for the King. The importance of the nodal point of Newark lay in this: not only was it the crossing point of the Great North Road over a main river, so that anyone who held it could interrupt the facility of communications from the North to the South, but in a highly sporadic form of warfare where isolated posts were held one against

[ 147 ]

the other all over the place and comparatively small bodies marched to and fro, it was a central rallying point.

Newark, also counted high, prevented free communication between East Anglia, Essex and Cambridgeshire and Huntingdonshire, Suffolk and most of Norfolk—all Parliamentarian—and the Parliamentary garrisons in the Midlands, and conversely it was a strong place for which Royalist reinforcement could aim. The attempt to take Newark was a leading feature right through the war till the very end, for it was being held by the Royalists when the complete collapse of their cause came in '46, after the King surrendered.

Only secondary in importance at this moment to Newark was Gainsborough. Gainsborough was held by the Parliament. It cut that important line of communication, the water-way of the Trent, and lay so far to the north as to be a sort of outpost of revolutionary influence. Therefore the Royalist forces were besieging it. If, or when, Gainsborough fell, Lincolnshire might all be overrun by the strength of the Royalists, while masking Hull they could be pressing southwards upon the very frontiers of the area held by the Parliament in the south-east.

To prevent the fall of Gainsborough, to free Lincolnshire from the menace under which it lay, and if possible to raise the siege of Hull—these were the three main objects which, whether consciously perceived or instinctively felt, formed the main task of the Revolutionary leaders on the east side of England.

Of these Cromwell was the most clear-sighted and the most energetic. He attempts all three points: he misses at the first, failing to relieve Gainsborough; but after that by an extreme use of energy and rapidity he saves Lincolnshire, and it is probably he—at any rate he in combination with others—who manages at last to disengage Hull. This is the effort we are about to follow.

On the 25th of July, 1643, Gainsborough had been seized

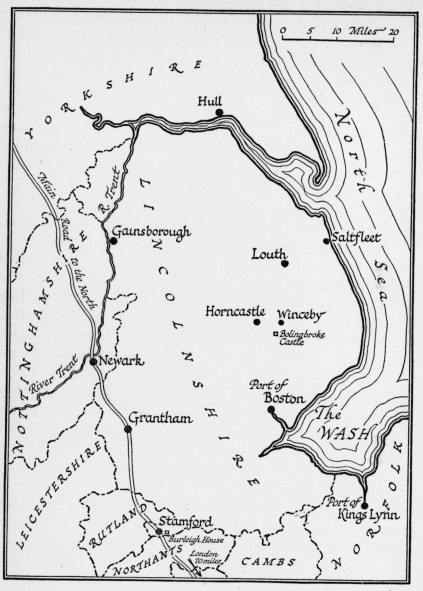

THE CAMPAIGN OF WINCEBY

for the Parliament by their General, Willoughby. It was the time when the revolutionary movement was approaching its most critical moment, and it is part of Cromwell's good fortune that he first came into prominent notice precisely at this juncture. For the day after Gainsborough had been seized that much more important thing, the fall of Bristol, took place. It was on the 26th of July that the revolution lost this second port of the United Kingdom, with all it meant as an opportunity for support from the sea, and still more as a centre of wealth and support for the Crown. It was further the moment in which the popular movement in favour of peace among the lesser Londoners—in spite of their being dominated by the wealthy merchants—was coming to a head. It was the moment when Charles made his solemn declaration in support of Protestantism on taking the Communion at Oxford.

On the same day, Tuesday the 25th of July, that Willoughby had seized Gainsborough, Cromwell had stormed Burghley House. This fortified mansion outside Stamford commanded the great road to the North, and the taking of it by Cromwell was part of the effort to get more and more elbow-room for the South-Eastern revolutionary forces—that is, to extend "The London Area."

The revolutionary hold on Gainsborough was short-lived. Cromwell began going north with the greatest rapidity on the morning of Wednesday the 26th, taking with him 600 horse, units of that excellent sort which he had already informed and trained. The rapidity of his march must be noted, because though there was nothing abnormal about it for unhampered cavalry he was taking with him a mass of provisions and munitionment, especially powder, for the reinforcement of Gainsborough. On that day he reached Grantham after a march of twenty-one miles, to be joined by 300 more horse from Nottingham; on the day after, Thursday the 27th, he was to get yet further reinforcement from Lincoln, troops which were to meet him at North Scarle. That was another march of twenty-five miles. It is an example of his use of time that he led his cavalry out of North Scarle at 2 a.m. on the Friday morning, the 28th, along the Gainsborough road. They had about a dozen miles before them, and so bad was the scouting, or so defective the intelligence, that Cromwell evidently thought the dozen miles held nothing to stop him. The blunder might have cost him very dear, for what happened was this:

He found on the sky-line of a ridge about one and a half miles south of his objective a patrol of Newcastle's army. When he had driven this in he discovered behind it an advance body of horse which the northern General had sent forward preparatory to establishing the siege of Gainsborough. This advance body of horse he and his cousin Whalley, who acted as Cromwell's lieutenant in this operation, drove back—the whole thing was no more than a skirmish. It permitted Cromwell's entry into Gainsborough, so that he effected the first object of his march, the provisionment of the town; but his information was still so bad that he had in effect only given a present to his opponents, who were in a few hours to become masters of all that food and powder. For on marching out again northward, upon the news of some further advance body upon that side of the town, he was all but surprised by Newcastle's main body. He came unexpectedly upon it on reaching the summit of a rise, finding the enemy in force spread out before him— a far superior mounted body and three regiments of foot.

What followed was a retreat, successful enough, well conducted, but necessarily extremely rapid. He had just escaped disaster. In his advance on Gainsborough he had covered between fifty and fifty-five miles in forty-eight hours; in getting back again he covered eighty in less. Exactly how much less we cannot tell, for we do not know at what hour he left Gainsborough on the Friday, but he was in Huntingdon writing his account of the whole affair by Monday.

Cromwell rode with but a small body as far as Huntingdon itself: but there is ample proof that the retreat was precipitate.

[ 151 ]

However, he brought off his cavalry without loss in spite of suffering surprise in front of Gainsborough, and actual disaster had been avoided. But of course Gainsborough was lost; Newcastle was master of it, while Cromwell was still flying down the road south, for the town was occupied by Sunday, the 30th of July.

The loss of Gainsborough was not the only burning anxiety of those perilous days: Gloucester might follow at any moment the fate of Bristol, the siege against it was soon to open; and a mob of women crying for peace had raged round the House of Commons and only been dispersed with bloodshed: while Willoughby sent news that after Gainsborough, Lincoln also had gone, and the reason of its going was more serious than the news alone. Lincoln had been abandoned because Willoughby's troops would not hold, his command had gone to pieces.

It was in the midst of this strain that those famous words were written which, hackneyed as they are, I will repeat here because they do so vividly illustrate the mind of Cromwell working at high pressure, the keenness of his view, the intensity of his aim, and his grasp of the factor of time:

"It is no longer disputing, but act instantly all you can! Raise all your bands; send them to Huntingdon; get up what volunteers you can; hasten your horses. Send these letters to Norfolk, Suffolk and Essex without delay. I beseech you spare not, but be expeditious and industrious. Almost all our foot have quitted Stamford: there is nothing to interrupt an enemy but our horse, which is considerable. You must act lively! Do it without distraction! Neglect no means!"

All this excitement turned upon the threatened pressure of Newcastle, coupled of course with the danger of the fall of Gloucester. If or when Gloucester fell the convergence upon London would begin, and meanwhile if or when Newcastle took Hull, or even marched southward masking Hull, "The

London Area" would be threatened. Lincolnshire was still mainly dominated by the Royalists as to its northern part. If they should advance into the country south of Boston, taking Boston itself, their plan would be half accomplished.

On the 10th of August the Royalists summoned Gloucester, and on the same day Manchester was appointed by the Parliament to take over the command of the Eastern Counties Association. The revolutionaries had acted with vigour, as is the fashion of revolutionaries with their backs to the wall: they had shot down and trampled down with cavalry the great crowd of women who had stormed round the House of Commons shrieking for the blood of the "dog Pym" and demanding peace. But Pym was more active than ever. His emissaries had already been in Scotland begging for the army of the alliance—at least 11,000 men—and a forced loan had been levied upon London, which must have regretted the happy days when all the wealthy would have foamed at the mouth at the idea of five subsidies, for this time the wealthy of London had to send fifty subsidies; the grinding taxation of the revolutionaries which in the long run was to ruin their cause and to bring back Charles II was begun. Before the end of that month of August, Essex had been sent off with 15,000 men (of whom the nucleus were Londoners) and Manchester was at work in the eastern counties.

But all this would have availed nothing if Newcastle had marched; and the reason he could not march was a moral one—the condition of his northerners and their reluctance to act in the south, just as his entanglement in front of Hull was due to a similar moral cause.

Manchester's first business in his command was to raise recruits and get them trained. Of the four Colonels he had under him, Cromwell, the most energetic, threw himself into this task and saw the numbers swell until the Parliament had in this district, between the Lincolnshire Wolds and Norfolk, anything between ten and fourteen thousand men, mobile and available. The port of King's Lynn, opposite Boston, on the other side of the Wash had gone back to the King and had to be taken by force: Manchester's forces got hold of it on the 16th of September, shortly after the news had come in that Essex had relieved Gloucester. And still Newcastle delayed! Still the threatened blow did not fall!

Meanwhile it became clear even to those who were compelling the reluctant Newcastle to pursue the siege of Hull, that Hull would never be taken, because the Parliament commanded the sea. Fairfax and his horse were withdrawn from the town by water (Newcastle could do nothing to prevent it); they came up the narrow ditch of a stream which leads from the North Sea to the shore at Saltfleet, through the immense flat of Hile Sands; and whether at Saltfleet or at Louth, Fairfax met Cromwell. This additional body, this additional commander, joined up with Willoughby and Cromwell in South Lincolnshire.

The three held a conference together on the 2nd of October; three days later reinforcement was landed in Hull, and it became clearer than ever that Newcastle was wasting his time in front of the place. But then, if he was wasting his time in front of the place, might he not abandon it and move southward to overrun the Boston district? No: for his unwilling army would not have stood the strain. Yet the Parliamentarians were nervous enough and thought it necessary to establish themselves in South Lincolnshire before the expected blow should fall. Manchester summoned his subordinates to meet him for the siege of Bolingbroke Castle, which had a Royalist garrison: this reduced, he would march westward against Horncastle at the foot of the Wolds. A resolution was taken upon Monday, the 9th of October, there being present as an active and mobile force some 5,000 men: Winnington thought it possible, though his total available strength was insufficient to frustrate the Parliamentary attack. He could move with a force equal or nearly equal to the force actually in the field near Bolingbroke, for the rest of Manchester's command was scattered in various posts within a radius of from ten to fifteen miles round Boston, the safety of which port was ever in his mind. The Parliamentary force moved westward * to occupy Horncastle on the morning of Wednesday, the 11th of October. The distance between their place of concentration and Horncastle town was by road a little over six miles. But the Royalist force starting before them from Horncastle, the two bodies came in contact rather less than half-way between the two places; on the rising ground near the Church of Winceby hamlet, not quite four miles as the crow flies east by a quarter south from Horncastle.

The skirmish opened with fire from dismounted dragoon troops on the Royalist side, who had lined the hedge in front of the Royalist body. Against these the Parliamentarians charged, and just as they came within close range Cromwell, leading his troop, had his horse shot under him. At the same moment the Royalists counter-charged; even as Cromwell rose, bruised and shaken, he was knocked over again by the rush of enemy horse, extricated in the mêlée, mounted again on a much worse beast, and plunged himself into the turmoil.

The struggle was confused, violent and brief; and the military interest of it lies in this, that it gave evidence of how much work by way of formation had been done among the cavalry of the Eastern Counties Association. For there is no doubt that the issue of this little action proved the superiority of the Parliamentary horse in this particular field, and under this particular command, over its opponents. The forces were nearly equal, the result was complete. The Royalist body broke, fled westward and was pursued with heavy loss right through

---

* I have not cared to interrupt the text with too many allusions to Carlyle's errors; but there is one in this connection so bad that it would be a sin to leave it unnoticed. He makes out the whole business to have taken place on *the other side* of Horncastle, and Winceby to be on the west of that town instead of the east. This is not the kind of error due to the misunderstanding of technical terms or to confused accounts of a battle: it simply means that Carlyle did not take the trouble to look at the map, or if he did, could not understand it.

Horncastle itself in a running fight, thundering along the high road through Thanker Hollow and High Toynton for mile after mile. They had covered over four miles in the pursuit before they drew rein and saw the scattered disorganised rout disappear over the edge of Langton Hill; at least one-fifth, or it may have been one-quarter of Winnington's command was killed and an equal number taken prisoners. Of the colours more than a third fell to Manchester's men and 1,500 sets of arms. Such was the work of that Wednesday.

Its importance has been exaggerated, of course, because Cromwell, who played so great a part in it, was to have so vast a fame: this first success in which he had taken a personal part (and a large one) could not but be made out more significant by posterity than it really was. The legend is still further swelled by the fact that the siege of Hull was raised on the very next day—though that had nothing to do with the affair at Winceby. Obviously the success at Winceby would have been of no avail against the mass of Newcastle's army had it been possible to move that army southward.

But what Winceby did prove was this:

That the Eastern Association had formed a trained cavalry of permanent value. The report of the defeated Royalist commander is clear upon the impression that cavalry had made, and he dwells especially upon the superiority of his opponents' armament. Now in this result the personality and energy of Cromwell had played a very great part—perhaps the chief part —and Winceby may therefore be taken as the starting point of that great career in action.

## II

### MARSTON MOOR

Marston Moor was the action which established Cromwell, and of described actions in which great captains have taken part, Marston Moor is one of those which best illustrates the mixture of talent and good fortune which makes up a complete reputation. That reputation, once established, of itself strengthens a man, he does better for being suspected of invincibility. There is thus nearly always in the career of any great captain a moment after which all changes with him. Before that moment he was known to have such and such capacity, which might be disputed or criticised: after that moment his fame— sure to be exaggerated—is fixed, he is indispensable and the army begins, in spirit if not by definite appointment, to regard him as the one leader.

So it was with Cromwell at Marston Moor. It was so because he retrieved what had become in a very short interval of fighting more than a desperate—rather a wholly ruined— situation; something approaching a rout. The situation was not only retrieved but completely reversed; an action which had already become as to more than three-quarters of it a breakdown of the Parliamentary forces, was turned in something over half an hour into a total defeat of the Royalists. And that turning was due to, and coincident with, a victorious movement which Cromwell led on his own extreme end of the field. Had he been one of other successful leaders in a general victory such as the superiority of the numbers of his side would have warranted, Marston Moor would never have had this effect upon his career: it was the vivid contrast between what he did and the failure of all the rest that served him. We shall see how much in this was due to the advantage of numbers and to the aid of others: but the decisive act was his own.

The battle of Marston Moor was in itself so confused that no one present there could have told you properly what happened. In the accounts which have come down to us the confusion has, of course, got a great deal worse. One eye-witness gives us the right for the left, sometimes writing in terms of the Parliamentary and sometimes of the Royalist line of battle. The various Parliamentary commanders gave, as was common form, their various accounts, which, seeing the very poor part most of them played, are naturally full of lies. Nor (as we have seen) does Cromwell himself escape from this frailty.

But the action has been elucidated by patient research, and we may fairly say that, since Mr. Firth's study was published,* a number of quite certain points have been established. Notably, there is a contemporary plan of the action, which makes what is common to the various accounts reasonable, and with this the historian just quoted has dealt very fully.

Among the things which are certain are those which permit us to establish the personal effect of Cromwell upon the decision. It may fairly be said that he won the battle, and why this is true we shall see. On the other hand, among the things that are not quite so certain lies, unfortunately, the proportion between the part he played and the part played by his Scottish allies, whom he so disliked and his ultimate triumph over whom was one of his chief satisfactions.

The action was of the oddest kind. In the very short time it lasted (from about seven p.m. till nearly dark, on July 2nd, 1644), in the haphazard way in which it began, in the lack of all calculation of time and place, it thoroughly conforms to the nondescript character of the Civil War as a whole.

The great plan achieved by Pym had been accomplished this six months past, the Scottish army—ill-mounted as to its cavalry, but of excellent quality in men and with plenty of experienced officers—had been across the Border for more than six months. Newcastle could not face the combination between them and the Parliamentary army; he was being besieged by the two in York. King Charles, who now as always had a good general view of the war, perceived that the fall of York would be fatal. It would mean the loss of the north, and the loss of the north might mean the loss of the war, for the north to the east of the Pennines was a recruiting field and a source of wealth such as the north to the west of the Pennines was not. Therefore the King urged his nephew Prince Rupert to

* "English Historical Review," New Series, Vol. 14.

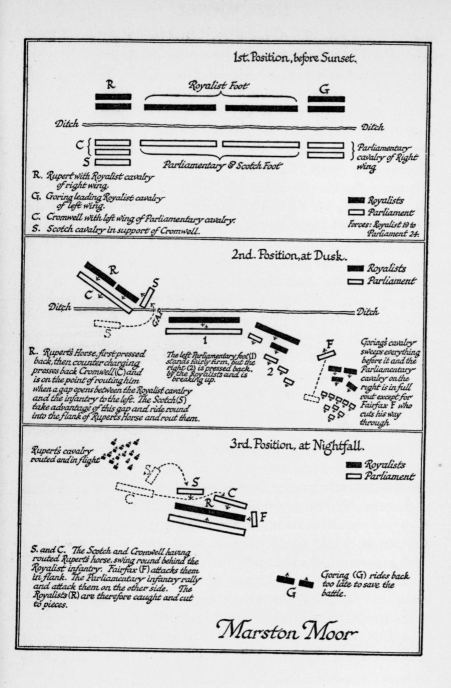

1st. Position, before Sunset.

R    Royalist Foot    G

Ditch — Ditch

C { Parliamentary & Scotch Foot } Parliamentary cavalry of Right wing

R. Rupert with Royalist cavalry of right wing.
G. Goring leading Royalist cavalry of left wing.
C. Cromwell with left wing of Parliamentary cavalry.
S. Scotch cavalry in support of Cromwell.

Royalists
Parliament
Forces: Royalist 19 to Parliament 24.

2nd. Position, at Dusk.

Royalists
Parliament

R
S
C
Ditch — GAP — Ditch
S
1
2
F

R. Rupert's Horse, first pressed back, then counter charging presses back Cromwell (C) and is on the point of routing him when a gap opens between the Royalist cavalry and the infantry to the left. The Scotch (S) take advantage of this gap and ride round into the flank of Rupert's Horse and rout them.

The left Parliamentary foot (1) stands fairly firm, but the right (2) is pressed back by the Royalists and is breaking up.

Goring's cavalry sweeps everything before it and the Parliamentary cavalry on the right is in full rout except for Fairfax F who cuts his way through

3rd. Position, at Nightfall.

Royalists
Parliament

Rupert's cavalry routed and in flight

S
S
C
R    C
F

S. and C. The Scotch and Cromwell having routed Rupert's horse, swing round behind the Royalist infantry. Fairfax (F) attacks them in flank. The Parliamentary infantry rally and attack them on the other side. The Royalists (R) are therefore caught and cut to pieces.

G    Goring (G) rides back too late to save the battle.

Marston Moor

relieve the town. Rupert did so, effected his junction with Newcastle, and the siege was raised.

The commanders of the Parliamentary and Scotch armies proposed to retire southward and stand between the newly joined Royalist forces and all that area controlled from London which was vital to them. They were still in superior numbers to Rupert and Newcastle combined. There was some discussion between the latter as to whether the enemy should be attacked as he retired, and made to stand, or be allowed to go. Rupert's advice prevailed, and the whole Royalist command, save a fraction left for garrison in York, filed out westward to the open space of Marston Moor, the centre of which was five miles from the town. The allied Revolutionary armies, Scotch and English, were marching away southwards towards Tadcaster when the news came that the Royalists were close upon them and harrying the baggage and the rear. Cromwell himself was with the rearguard.

It was necessary, therefore, for the Parliamentary leaders to accept battle, lest they should be caught by the enemy in column of route. They retraced their steps, and formed in line of battle on the slopes which look northward towards Marston Moor, over the lane between Long Marston and Tockwith. Opposite them, seeing the battle was challenged, Rupert and Newcastle drew up their troops on the moor to the north of that lane. The opposing forces were in number probably about 19,000 on the Royalist, 24,000 on the Parliamentary side. On both sides the usual formation was adopted, the infantry in the centre, the cavalry on either wing. On the Royalist side, facing southward and drawn up upon the Moor itself, Rupert at the head of the Royalist cavalry and with him Byron at the head of the Irish troops, were upon the extreme right or west. On the Parliamentary side the cavalry of the corresponding wing, that is, the left of the Parliamentarians, was under the command of Cromwell. As the retirement of one force and the acceptation of battle by the other had taken a considerable time, it was afternoon before the lines were being ordered, and late afternoon before the formation was complete. The Parliamentary forces and their Scotch allies stood in fields of rye on a slope facing northward and overlooking the Royalists.

Cromwell there upon the left opposite Rupert had a superiority over his immediate opponents in face of him which should be noted: that superiority was due to the presence of a considerable Scottish contingent, nearly one-third of the total mounted force at that point. The actual number of sabres present, English and Scottish, under Cromwell's command as head of the mounted forces on this left wing of the Parliamentarians, over against Rupert, can of course only be a matter of conjecture, because we do not know the difference between the "paper strength" and the actual strength. There were seventy troops, of which twenty-two were Scottish. With full complement this would mean 4,200 sabres, of whom just over 1,300 would be Scottish—very nearly one-third. But we are certain, of course, that the full complement was not present with either force; for it is always so in war, after long trials such as are involved in a siege and lengthy marches. The Scottish contingent has even been put as low as 600 sabres; it was probably something between that and a thousand. It was commanded by David Leslie. They were excellent soldiers, but ill-mounted on small and insufficient horses. Cromwell's men, five-sevenths of the total, were heavily armed, still carrying the cuirass, which was gradually eliminated in the course of the war—it was Cromwell's clinging to this form of defensive armour which had caused Rupert to give him the nickname of "Ironsides," after the old Anglo-Saxon Prince of history, and, as we know, the title spread gradually until it was attached to the Parliamentary cavalry in general; it has been changed by modern writers into a sort of laudatory epithet.

The cavalry thus under Cromwell's command upon the left Parliamentary wing was certainly greatly superior to the cavalry of the Royalist command. How much superior we do not know; the total superiority of the Parliamentary forces and the Scottish combined was to their opponents roughly as twenty-five to nineteen, possibly as twenty-five to eighteen. The numerical preponderance of the revolutionary cavalry over the constitutional Royalist cavalry was not so high; but here on the western side of the battle where Rupert stood on the right of the Royalist line and Cromwell on the left of his, facing Rupert, there was a considerable preponderance, because this wing had been specially strengthened.

Between the two forces lay a ditch. It was not so difficult an obstacle as at the other, eastern, end, but it did have this effect—it would interrupt the movement of cavalry and make either side hesitate to take the first step. For there could be no properly ordered charge over such an obstruction.

Although the two forces were thus drawn up for battle it seemed unlikely that the struggle would begin so late in the day, and more probable that it would be joined at the first dawn of the next morning. It was after four o'clock before the two lines were fully formed, and five before a desultory cannonade of no effect was over. There was still some daylight left, as the date was Tuesday, the 2nd of July, but still it was very late to begin an action. Neither side would risk the disadvantage of attempting an advance across the ditch.

The afternoon wore on till nearly seven without motion along these two opposing columns of men, a mile in length. It would seem, though we are not absolutely certain of it, that the determination to attack came first from the Parliamentary side. It is possible that the initiative lay with Cromwell, but unlikely, for his position was still subordinate; the left, of which he formed a part, was under Manchester, and we may be certain that if his had been the deciding voice or act it would later, after the victory, have been plentifully advertised. At any rate, the whole Parliamentary line did attack at that very late hour. And what happened in the succeeding thirty minutes was roughly this:

I say "roughly," because the accounts are so confused and the result so extraordinary that it is impossible to present a clear plan. The Royalist left had a complete success against the Parliamentary right, their horse here under Goring scattered and pursued their opponents, turned on the flank of the abandoned infantry, and the mass of the Parliamentary body broke and fled. The Royalist infantry in this part of the field and the centre, the kernel of which was the very fine body of Newcastle's own tenants and followers, conspicuous in their rough white coats of undyed wool, pressed forward triumphantly. On the right and the right centre of the Parliamentary line the battle was lost for the revolution. Just about sunset there was a disorganised mass of men flying down the Tadcaster road with one part of Goring's cavalry sabring in pursuit, and the rest wheeling round to attack such units as had tried to stand. Among these certain isolated Scottish were conspicuous; but the Parliamentary foot went to pieces.

The battle seemed so obviously lost even while the sun was setting that the three commanders, the elder Fairfax, Manchester and Lord Leven, fled (as the classical phrase goes) "in all directions." Each had determined that the defeat was final. The younger Fairfax—a strange episode in this mere turmoil—cut his way through to the back of the advancing Royalists, with what results we shall see.

Meanwhile, in that very brief last hour of the sinking sun and the advancing night, what happened on the Parliamentary left and the Royalist right—that is on the west of the line—was strange, and at variance with the fortunes of the rest. Cromwell's cuirassed mounted men had crossed the ditch and attacked the first line of Rupert's command—the Irish cavalry under Byron. In the first shock against this first line Cromwell's men had the best of it, but Rupert, who, like Newcastle, had little expected an attack at such an hour, was immediately in the saddle and on the spot, and the counter-attack by his second line was successful. It threw Cromwell and his cuirassiers in spite of their superiority of numbers back towards the ditch. In the mêlée Oliver himself was slightly wounded, in the neck it would seem, and the pressure of Rupert's energy and his men, though in slightly inferior numbers, bid fair to do here upon the west of the battle (the Royalist right) what was being done upon the Royalist left. Had he succeeded, Marston Moor would have been a complete decision for the King. It would have been the beginning of the end of the war—in his favour.

The account of such a hurly-burly, even were it possible to get one from an unbiased witness suffering neither from vanity nor excitement, would be confused enough—we can only see it as the success of the Royalist counter-charge, with the leader of the Parliamentary cavalry, Cromwell himself, out of action for the moment.

Now note carefully what certainly followed. In this successful counter-attack of Rupert's and the pushing back by force of Cromwell's cuirassiers, a gap had opened between the Royalist horse and the Royalist foot to the east (or left) of them. It was not the wounded and occupied Cromwell who saw the opportunity, it was David Leslie. His some hundred sabres were directed at once from the reserve and rear of Cromwell's body where they had stood, right into this gap, and appeared upon the flank of Rupert's so far victorious cavalry. And it was this which decided the issue.

The Scottish mounts were bad, as I have said, and the Scottish force was acting alone, for their English allies were already very nearly in rout; but they had the advantage of coming suddenly upon a flank, and the fierceness of their onslaught did the trick. The pressure upon Cromwell's immediate command was relieved, Rupert's began to lose order, the English Parliamentary horse rallied and pressed forward, the Royalist horse—now attacked in front as well as in flank—began to break. With the dusk still gathering they broke altogether and were driven in disordered masses towards Wilstrop Wood, some six furlongs to the north, half a mile behind their original line.

Reading of how that gap was pierced by Leslie, of how through such advantage the whole line was turned and a decision attained, the mind reverts, not without sadness, to the Battle of the Marne.

It is comparing small things with great, but the mournful parallel is there. During the Marne also, in a front of not one mile but over a hundred, a gap opened; and on the Marne also it opened between the extreme right wing of the enemy and the mass of his troops. Through that gap also the line might have been turned, and the security of our civilisation saved. But there were none present to take advantage: those who should have done at that place what Leslie did were from ten to twenty miles away.

There remained with the Scottish and with Leslie the feeling that they had done the whole thing—that naturally became their tradition. Cromwell himself must have been detained, if only to have his wound dressed, but he was now once again at the head of the pursuit and ordering his men before the light should fail altogether.

Then it was, with Rupert's men in flight, with the Parliamentary infantry which had stood just beyond the Scottish horse to the east still in good formation and standing up well to the Royalist infantry in front of them—though with all the rest of the Parliamentary line gone to pieces—that Cromwell executed his manœuvre.

It was, so far as we know, the first time he used it; like all great commanders who have discovered a method of their own, he was to repeat it. He reined up his men, left a detachment to follow the flying and defeated Royalist horse, and with those whom he had checked and kept with him he wheeled round to the right. Part of his men were thus on the flank of the Royalist foot in their immediate neighbourhood, and the rest were extended eastwards behind the whole Royalist line as they rapidly advanced in the gathering darkness.

The successful Royalist centre, Newcastle's men, hitherto pressing forward victoriously against the revolutionary foot in front of them, hitherto cheered by seeing the complete breakdown of the revolutionary horse to the east, with Goring thundering in pursuit of them, suddenly found themselves attacked from the rear. Their comrades of the foot upon the right flank, to the west of them, were already in confusion through the repeated Parliamentary charge of Cromwell's men —and still the rapidly advancing line of his horse drew eastward, until all the Royalist centre, but a few minutes ago certain of victory, found themselves surrounded. Those whom they were driving back in defeat would rally; the rear ranks of the Royalist centre had to turn to receive the shock of this new unexpected assault from the north—the whole shape of the battle had changed. Cromwell riding eastward with his bandaged neck found in the gloaming the younger Fairfax, his face open with a wound—the man who had cut his way through from the rout of the rest of the Parliamentary cavalry. Such horse as he had with him joined with Cromwell's own forces. The enclosed and now doomed—so recently confident and victorious—Royalist foot, centre and left, were trapped and at the mercy of the foot and horse from the south, from the east, from the north and the outflanking movement now begun from the west as well.

Then was seen one of the few sublime passages of these wars, the death and sacrifice of Newcastle's men. The white coats would not surrender to the rebels nor ask for quarter: their fate certain, they preferred to meet it. At the end of the slaughter forty were left alive to find their way off through the darkness: no more.

Men hardly knew what had happened. It was full dark under the showery clouds: there was no moon: the battle—and for that matter though men could not tell it yet, the war also—was won.

How many were killed we cannot certainly tell: the account on the Parliamentary side that they lost only 300 is ridiculous and need not be entertained. The Royalists can hardly have lost less than 4,000; 1,500 officers and men were prisoners; 10,000 stands of arms were piled, 130 barrels of powder and all the twenty-five guns of the King; and of the colours sheaves upon sheaves.

It was not till the next day, the Wednesday, that the fugitive Parliamentary Generals returned; and by that time the dead had been stripped and plundered by the Puritan soldiery. On the day after, the 4th of July, Cromwell set off on a pursuit of Rupert and his remaining 6,000 men, whom he had kept sufficiently in hand to save them from their pursuers: the pursuit therefore failed. The little garrison in York stood out for another eleven days under Glenham; it got good terms, capitulating with the right to march out with the whole garrison intact for the King. Manchester's soldiers who were to escort the retirement of these men plundered them. It is to be remembered that by the time they had reached Cromwell to the west, in his futile pursuit of Rupert, they were better treated.

Oliver Cromwell through this day of Marston Moor became fully famous. His name was now first among the soldiers. Had he been but one in a general victory, as he might well have been, seeing the superiority of the forces upon the revolutionary side, he would not have attained so rapidly and so immediately the reputation due to his high talent. Fortune had favoured him greatly, in that he was thus conspicuous in succeeding where the rest had failed and marked him out in contrast, the hero of the day. Fortune had favoured him also most conspicuously in lending him the Scotch (whom he despised and disliked) just at the moment when his fate lay in the balance. But it would be a great error to belittle Cromwell by too much emphasis upon these advantages. But for him—his

eye, his will, his clarity of perception, his flash of decision—
the dreadful harvest of that day would never have been reached.

Remember once again the famous epigram of Foch, which
cannot be too often repeated: "It was not a Carthaginian Army
which crossed the Alps, it was Hannibal." So one may say
of Marston Moor: "It was not the well-disciplined English
horse, saved by the Scottish charge, which won the battle,
nor was it propitious fortune: it was Oliver Cromwell."

## III

### THE SECOND BATTLE OF NEWBURY

This great Parliamentary and Scottish victory of Marston
Moor, which we can now clearly see to have been the turning-
point of the war, had not, then, at the time and for contemporaries the importance that it should have had.

Although the north was lost to the King, its loss might not
(it was hoped) be permanent, and everyone had been struck
by the weakness displayed during the action on the Parliamentary side. The Parliamentary foot had for the most part
broken down absurdly within the first few minutes of the
strain; the horse on the right had been swept away by Goring
at the first attack; the two revolutionary nobles at the head
of the Parliamentary army, Manchester and the elder Fairfax,
had fled for their lives. They only returned on the morrow,
upon hearing the unexpected news that someone else had won
the field for them in their absence.

With the opinion of London in this condition—and London
was what counted—there came the news of a serious disaster.
Charles, with his usual sense of country, and his military direction, had marched against the incompetent Essex in the west.
That anodyne commander had got his army into a cleft stick,
north of Fowey on the last waters of the harbour at Lostwithiel. He himself had escaped by boat, his cavalry had cut
its way out, but the whole of his infantry had ignominiously

surrendered. It was in appearance a worse blow to Parliamentary prestige than Marston Moor just before had been to the Royalist. The Londoners especially had been humiliated and their own guns taken.

To try and retrieve the situation it was necessary to raise yet

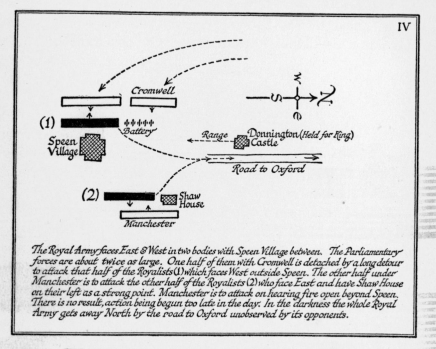

The Royal Army faces East & West in two bodies with Speen Village between. The Parliamentary forces are about twice as large. One half of them with Cromwell is detached by a long detour to attack that half of the Royalists (1) which faces West outside Speen. The other half under Manchester is to attack the other half of the Royalists (2) who face East and have Shaw House on their left as a strong point. Manchester is to attack on hearing fire open beyond Speen. There is no result, action being begun too late in the day. In the darkness the whole Royal Army gets away North by the road to Oxford unobserved by its opponents.

THE ELEMENTS OF THE 2ND BATTLE OF NEWBURY

another army, and deal with Charles as he returned eastward from his triumph.

The part played by Cromwell in the second battle of Newbury, fought on Saturday, the 27th of October, 1644, O.S., is of this special interest in the study of his career; that we can note, and estimate the reasons for, a military failure; and can see how failure acted on his soldier's mind. He did not do what he had expected to do nor perhaps what had been expected of him. He was bitter about the check; he used it as an opportunity for making his chief attack on Manchester;

Manchester's reply was judged sufficient by many contemporaries. It is our business to extricate the truth from the entanglement as well as we can. But it is also our business to see Cromwell as he was under a humiliation; the quality of his resentment; the way in which his energy turned it to profit.

The position was this: The King having had his great success in the west, enforcing the surrender of most of Essex's army in Cornwall and the flight of that unfortunate commander almost alone by sea to Plymouth, was coming back east with the captured guns. The City of London (or rather its rich merchants) had made a somewhat belated effort, but one more than sufficient when the shock should come to achieve a decisive victory. They sent 20,000 men down the road westward under Manchester's command—if that command can be called Manchester's, which was by the specific orders of the Parliament shared with his Council of Officers. It was his task to destroy the King's force—only half his own—before Rupert, who was coming up to join Charles, should arrive.

Charles entered the town of Newbury on Friday, October the 25th, just at the moment when the head of the Parliamentary army advancing against him had reached Bucklebury Common, four and a half miles away. On the next day the Parliamentary command decided upon a manœuvre which is common when a greatly superior force is acting against an inferior, and which we shall see securing a complete victory at the battle of Worcester, seven years later. They proposed to divide their forces into two, hold the enemy with one half upon one side and, marching round him, attack on the other side with the other half. It is a manœuvre obviously tempting to forces which have the advantage of two to one over their opponents, for if the plan is well conducted and succeeds the enemy cannot escape, he is enclosed and destroyed. It has also an obvious danger about it, which is that the division of forces necessitates very accurate co-ordination if it is to have the desired result, and accurate co-ordination between wholly separated bodies is difficult to achieve. Charles was aware of the manœuvre and acted as follows:

He drew up the mass of his men and nearly all his cavalry north of Newbury in the open land between the Lambourne brook and the Kennet river, where his position was defended by a stream connecting the two water-courses. He thus faced eastward towards the main Parliamentary body, with Manchester at its head, lying very much along the line of where the railway from Newbury to Didcot runs now, and standing as Charles did between the two rivers. Behind the town of Newbury to the west is a rising tongue of land on which is the village of Speen; immediately to the west of this village on the ridge Charles had placed Prince Maurice, his nephew and Rupert's brother, with a battery of guns which that commander defended with earth-works. Thus Maurice's command, with its guns faced westward along the top of the hill of Speen, and the mass of Charles's command faced eastward, about a mile away to the east along the flat between the two rivers. It is to be noted that beyond the Lambourne opposite Speen on the far side of the valley and standing on a height there which dominated the stream was Donnington Castle, a stronghold long to remain untaken and in Royalist hands. Its guns were far out of range from Speen, the distance of the Castle from Prince Maurice's battery being very nearly a mile. But they would prevent any force from acting with ease close to the Lambourne itself. It is further to be noted that in front of Charles's position just south of the Lambourne stream was a fortified house known as Shaw House, or, from the name of its owner, Dolman's. While Manchester remained on the east side facing Charles the other half of the Parliamentary army was sent round well to the north of Donnington Castle during the night of Friday. They camped at North Heath and were due to attack the next day, the Saturday, along Speen Hill against Prince Maurice's battery of five guns. The force thus sent round included Cromwell's regiment of horse. They had to cross the Lambourne stream rather high up; they were not in a position to attack the battery in front of Speen until the afternoon.

The foot was drawn up on the right, that is to the south of the line which was advancing a-straddle of the road to Speen, and the horse under Lieutenant-General Cromwell on the left, that is to the north of the line. In this order the attack was delivered. But one important point must first be noticed. The work against the battery was done by the foot. In all the confusion of detail and the contradictory accounts of what happened there runs throughout a general impression that Cromwell's horse hardly came into play. It may be that this was because they had no opportunity for doing so, the infantry having rushed the battery and poured into the streets of Speen, so that the horse could only have acted outside to the north of the houses. It may have been that they did not even do much work there after the battery was taken for fear of getting too near to the guns of Donnington Castle on the north side of the narrow vale. At any rate it is clear that Cromwell for one reason or another did very little on that day. And it was permanently reproached against him, as though in the opinion of some he had been deliberately inactive (which is unlikely) through his hatred of Montagu, Lord Manchester, now come to a head.

This point being mentioned, we must turn to another doubt, which is the exact hour at which the attack on Maurice's guns was launched. Now at this point there is a dispute—such an uncertainty of hour as is perpetually cropping up in every story of an action. But we can be fairly certain that it was not earlier than 2.30 p.m. and almost certainly not earlier than 2.45 p.m., but not so late as 3.30 p.m. The attacking force was ultimately successful and had carried the battery by somewhere about 4 p.m.

Here again there enters some little doubt: certain witnesses would have it that there was still "one hour to sunset," and the sun does not set on the 27th of October (O.S.) before 4.23 p.m.* Our judgment of the Cromwell-Manchester quarrel largely depends upon the precise moment when the thing was done; and it seems probable on the whole that the later rather than the earlier estimate is correct, for these things do not go to a time-table, and all that anyone would realize at the moment was that it was still full day.

There was a good deal of fighting in the streets of the village of Speen after the guns had been carried, and in all this some time must have been consumed. It was therefore perhaps about sunset or a little before that Cromwell's horse had an opportunity of moving eastward. If indeed they had an opportunity at all, for it may be that they were checked by the fire from the hedges in the dusk, for there was plenty of cover and a vigorous defence was kept up; they certainly could not have extended their left any distance for fear of the guns of Donnington Castle.

Now at this moment, not long before dusk began to gather, an attack was vigorously proceeding on the other side from the men with Manchester against the forces of the King, where these faced eastward in Newbury field between the two watercourses. That attack had been launched at four o'clock. Cromwell himself, in his bitter intrigue against Manchester during the next month, said that Manchester had not attacked until it was dark, and therefore too late, but he is unsupported by any other account, Royalist or Parliamentarian—all agree that it was daylight. So much seems to be certain. It was necessary, if Manchester was to strike with force against Charles that he should first carry Shaw House. He was still engaged in that operation when night fell.

There was a certain amount of desultory fighting carried on in the first hours after it was fully night, but the moon-

* October the 27th (O.S.), 1644, is by the true calendar November the 6th, and the date of sunset on that date in the latitude of Newbury is just after 4.20 p.m.

light was short and insufficient, the moon being only in her first quarter, setting at midnight.* She was to set behind high land upon a misty evening. Astronomically she was above the horizon until nearly midnight, but it is certain that the firing ceased long before that and all chance of active operations, while it is possible that it ceased not more than an hour or an hour and a half after the full fall of darkness. According to one account, Cromwell was actually drawing off his horse through the town about eight o'clock.

What followed is more surprising than the failure of the attack, including in particular, the failure of Cromwell to charge home on his front south of the Lambourne. For Charles, after the moon had set and complete darkness covered everything, withdrew the whole of his force past Donnington Castle, where he left his baggage and guns, and thence made directly northward for Oxford. He got the whole of his army away intact, and he got it away from the very front of two large bodies which ought to have had him under observation! The very noise of the march would, one might have thought, have betrayed it—yet all night long nothing was noticed, whether by the force that had come down from Speen or by the force that had been attacking Shaw House. In all the tale of military insufficiency during this sporadic warfare the escape of a whole army under such conditions is perhaps the most astonishing.

The first question attaching to the action, after the question, "How could the Parliamentary Commanders have allowed Charles to make off unnoticed?" is the question, "Why did Manchester attack so late?" It had been arranged that he was to move when he heard the sound of the guns of the attack on the far westward side of the field. That he certainly did

* Gardiner got information which he sets down in his history making out the moon to be five days old. He refers the reader to a Mr. Hind; but in point of fact the new moon was at five o'clock in the afternoon of October the 20th. October (O.S.) that year (1644), and was therefore exactly at the quarter on the day of the fight at Speen.

not do. There was at least half an hour's interval, perhaps three-quarters, and just possibly an hour between the first of that firing and Manchester's attack at four o'clock on Shaw House.

Why was there this interval? I suggest that it was due to no deliberate intention: it certainly cannot have been due (as Manchester's enemies hinted) to a desire to spare the King. But any man who has seen a slow commander at work and heard him angrily criticised by quick-thinking subordinates will I think be able to visualize the business of that late afternoon. I take it that Manchester waited for the sound of the guns before making *any* dispositions, instead of having them all ready to fall on and attack Shaw House the moment the first gun-fire was heard from Speen. If this was so, a preliminary delay in giving orders, and then possible blunders and readjustment would account amply for at least half an hour; there would be some interval between the first advance party's cautious feeling of the ground and the main attack, which main attack was perhaps the first of Manchester's fire to be heard by those on Speen Hill.

That there was some undue delay on Manchester's part is certain. It is equally certain that Cromwell, whether from bad faith or mere impetuosity and anger exaggerated that delay. He puts the hour of the attack on Speen much earlier than anybody else, and he puts the hour of Manchester's attack on Shaw House much later. I take it that if we were to have the full story impartially told it would run somewhat as follows:

The marching wing which had been sent round behind the position of Donnington had been fatigued and got delayed. Its attack on Maurice and his battery therefore was not of any weight until the latter part of that short autumn afternoon, not being fully developed perhaps until well after three o'clock or even nearly three-thirty. The struggle for the guns was heavy and after the battery had been taken the continued resistance was stubborn even in the streets of Speen itself, as

Maurice's command fell back on the King's main body. Manchester to the west being a slow man and overcautious, had not established positions preparatory to move at a moment's notice. He waited for the first sound of a gun from Speen Hill before doing so. It was from half to three-quarters of an hour before the fully developed attack on Shaw House was taking place, at about four o'clock, and by that time it was too late to obtain a decision. Cromwell's horse had not a fair chance of coming into play, they could not act in the streets of Speen, and the space to the north of the houses was nowhere quite free from the fire of Donnington, save over a belt too narrow for the mounted force to manœuvre in properly. Darkness fell while both operations were proceeding, that on the west and that on the east. The moon, only at her first quarter and low in the heavens, gave very little light wherewith to continue the action, and none worth having after about nine o'clock; by which time Cromwell had already withdrawn his men into the streets of Newbury, and the attack on Shaw House could not be continued in the darkness.

.    .    .    .    .    .    .

As to the escape of the King, that was sheer bad soldiering on the part of the Parliamentary leaders, all of whom were equally to blame. It was one of those amateur blunders of which the Civil Wars are full. There could have been no proper outpost work, or the King certainly would not have got away. It is even possible that the Parliamentary commanders imagined (as later Leslie was to imagine at Dunbar) that Charles would hardly make the attempt in the night. There had been a full day's fighting, and it was judged improbable or impossible that he could impose upon his men another long march before they had had time to sleep. Perhaps it was calculated that being hampered with his train and artillery he could not have undertaken it. They forgot that Donnington was hard at hand to receive the custody of all that, so that the Royal forces could go off northward marching light.

It is from this second battle of Newbury that we should date the advance of Cromwell to political power. Marston Moor had given him a new, though disputed, reputation, it had made him securely the favourite leader of the soldiers, but it had not launched him on the road which was to lead to the Protectorate. Nor did he follow that road consciously so early. He certainly had no plan in this regard. He goes forward not knowing where he is going, and each step that profits him is a step taken for some reason disconnected with his own advancement.

One such step is taken because he feels that he is the one man required for this or that operation; another step is taken because his colleagues, and notably Fairfax, his nominal superior, feel the same thing. Another step is taken because he feels himself to be personally in danger for the moment; another step is taken from impulse, and as the result of a private quarrel.

But the result of all these things is a continuous advance. We have seen how badly the Newbury affair was bungled. The war might have been ended; instead of that the King had got away with his army intact in face of forces double his own. Cromwell had mishandled his own part of it, Manchester had probably been too cautious in his part of it—anyhow Newbury was a very disturbing event, and it had all the more depressing effect upon the supporters of the Rebellion because it came after the dramatic collapse of Essex in the west, and the surrender of his army. To the men of the time, as we have said, that blow more than counterbalanced the advantages of Marston Moor. They were wrong (for the capitulation of Lostwithiel gave the King no more men and no more money, no more recruiting area and no more taxation area, whereas Marston Moor had given all these in a sudden and very great accession to the cause of the Revolution), but contemporaries did not understand this, and therefore the fiasco at Newbury, coming after the disaster at Lostwithiel, had bred a general sense of failure.

Cromwell took advantage of this feeling to push what was at once a personal and a public grievance. It is unjust to say that the action he took on the morrow of Newbury was only due to personal pique and to a long-standing general quarrel. He was also moved by his smouldering instinct demanding greater efficiency; but to leave out the element of personal feeling, to forget the standing quarrel between himself and the house of Montagu is silly hagiolatry. Both motives were present, and to judge him by the general standards applicable to human affairs, the personal motive was presumably the stronger.

Cromwell considered long. It was on November the 25th, that is, four weeks after the battle, that he took advantage of his dual position as Parliamentarian and General to lay before the House of Commons his complaints against Manchester. The burden of his attack was that his superior officer did not at heart desire a definite victory over the King. The errors of Manchester at Newbury and elsewhere, his delays, his imperfect action, were not to be thought mere incompetence— rather were they treason to the Revolutionary cause. How far Cromwell believed this no one can say without getting inside the man's mind; there was a certain amount of truth in it, for Manchester certainly did not think that the war could be brought to the complete destruction of the Royal cause, and hardly wished that it should be; but that this feeling—in which he certainly was not alone, it was naturally widespread among his colleagues, for the extremists of a revolution must always be a minority—accounted for his particular actions in the field may be doubted. If he had attacked a little too late at Shaw House (and it is by no means certain that he did) that was not because he did not desire to win a victory. Nor do any of his actions from the Lincolnshire campaign onwards, betray a character of this kind.

No, the fact rather is that Cromwell found the acute anxiety following on the disaster of Lostwithiel and the breakdown at Newbury an opportunity for a decisive attack against Manchester.

It failed. But it is most interesting to see how out of that very failure Cromwell accidentally drew further strength. To his attack Manchester replied by publishing a whole list of things which he had heard Cromwell say, and they certainly ring true, they are just the kind of things he would have said in his excitements, which were frequent enough, and they certainly conform to what was passing in his mind. He could not bear the idea of the Scotch imposing their strict religious organisation upon himself or his country; he was quite willing to fight the King personally; he had certainly become thorough in his revolutionary temper since the war had inspired him, and all these scandalous things to which Manchester testified give one today a better, not a worse, opinion of the man. For instance, he told Manchester once that it would be a good deal better if there were no Lords: an unpleasant thing for Manchester to hear, but a great relief for Oliver to say; for this rich family which had ousted his own family had got hold of two peerages, while the Williams-Cromwells had none.

Anyhow, Manchester's revelations gave that commander the victory. Cromwell backed out. The Scotch were annoyed at what he had said about them, in private; so were the Lords; so was the Presbyterian majority in the Commons. In the face of that coalition, Oliver gave way. And it is amusing to see how he eats his words. The whole point of his accusation had been that Manchester at heart was betraying the cause: now, only a fortnight after his original onslaught, Cromwell becomes as gentle as he had been blustering. He is sure that he never meant anything against Manchester personally; not a bit of it—besides which the House of Commons must not be disturbed with personalities. Let them rather consider the remedies which are urgently needed to prevent the Revolution from collapse.

And thenceforward he canalises his energies into what was to be the making of the New Model and the Self-Denying Ordinance.

With the New Model, Cromwell was to bring the war to its end. And as for the Self-Denying Ordinance, it was to do exactly the opposite of what it had been designed to do, it was to turn every other politician out of the Army except Cromwell himself—but to leave *him*. He alone was to have the special position of standing in the Army and the House of Commons at the same time, a unique advantage from which all his further advancement was secured.

"I hope," he had said, "that no members will scruple to deny themselves." Nor did any so scruple. They all gave up their military commands—except Cromwell himself. So ended the first great crisis through which he had to pass at the beginning of what may be called his civilian advance, his advance towards command over the State as distinguished from the Army.

It is to be remarked that Cromwell was not the creator of the New Model. The first idea of it is to be found in a letter of Waller's. But indeed it was already apparent to all who looked around them that the construction of a professional and regular force was necessary. Once the idea was started, however, Cromwell's lucid mind and uninterrupted energy were exactly suited to the support and development of the idea.

The idea of the New Model was to produce on the Parliamentary side something like a professional force, which hitherto they had not had. The Royalist levies were better trained and of longer service. There was less desertion from them, they were more efficiently kept together, although one could hardly talk even among these of a professional body.

The Revolutionaries had started with everything in their favour, all the elements we have already enumerated—the command of the sea, a greater recruiting area and vastly superior money power; yet upon the whole they had had the worst of the fighting until they had been able, through the political talent of Pym, to bring in the Scotch to their succour. Their commanders had complained bitterly of the quality of the men they had under them, of whom by this time more than half were being unwillingly pressed for service. The regimental officers noted that the best material they got were the prisoners from the Royalist side, re-enlisted on their own. The New Model was an effort to set all that right, and upon the whole it succeeded.

The other factor at work was the Self-Denying Ordinance.

It was not an easy thing to carry this proposal through the House of which Cromwell was a member, as well as being the all-important officer he had now become. Command in the army meant patronage; it meant also what must always be remembered in any affair whatsoever where politicians are concerned—money. Not only their direct pay, though that was large enough in all conscience, but gifts of land and all manner of opportunities for perquisites.

It took a long time to get the measure through. The little handful of Lords remaining on the Parliamentary side were most reluctant, because the old state of affairs was all in their favour. It was not till the spring of 1645 that the New Model was established in law.

This professional nucleus of the whole Parliamentary fighting body was to consist of 21,000 men: 6,000 horse organised in ten regiments; 1,000 dragoons, and 14,000 foot, the whole to be complete with its baggage train and every detail of equipment. It was to cost £45,000 a month—say, not quite a third of a million of our money—and that had to be raised from the area which the revolution controlled. Sir Thomas Fairfax, the younger Fairfax, that is, was to be the Commander-in-Chief of the special force, with Skippon as Major-General.

But note this significant point: no man was put forward to command the horse, the decisive arm of the time—and Cromwell was the leading mind on the committee. Fairfax and Skippon were not members of either House.

After the first false start, the second Self-Denying Ordinance was finally adopted as late as the 3rd of April, 1645. Cromwell had been specially eloquent in the House upon the necessity for members foregoing the glory and advantages of command. He kept his own.

Modern apologists (and nearly all modern writers have been apologists for Cromwell) have pretended that there was nothing remarkable in this. The new Ordinance did indeed demand (they say) the resignation of officers who were also politicians, but it did not in so many words forbid their reappointment. Arguments of this sort remind one of the worst kind of equally modern theology. That Cromwell should be allowed not only to keep a commission but to be at the head of the horse in the New Model was clearly a flagrant contradiction of all that he had himself urged; but it would be a great error to say that he acted in this from ambition.

He acted thus because the army could not do without him. It would have been suicide for the revolutionaries to try to do without Cromwell at the head of their cavalry. His nominal commander, Fairfax, was determined to have him. Therefore a special privilege was voted for him, whereby he might retain what was the most important military command without giving up his seat in the House. "Both Houses ordered that Lieutenant-General Cromwell should be dispensed with for his personal attendance in the House and continue his service and command in the Army for 40 days longer, notwithstanding the Self-Denying Ordinance."

This was on the 10th of May, at the end of the first forty days' grace after the passing of the original Ordinance. Later one or two other exceptions were made, but they are of no importance except as masking this special contradiction of the original principle, made for the advantage of Cromwell, still more for the necessity of using his abilities.

It is not true that the New Model decided the issue of the war. The Royalist cause was already weakening through the loss of the northern recruiting field, through the triple strain of its finance, and the presence of the Scottish allies upon the Parliamentary side. It must weaken still further, its end was by now certain. But the New Model did put backbone into the revolutionary army after a fashion it had hitherto lacked. It was to spread its influence throughout that army, its effect was very soon felt, and it hastened the inevitable end.

The Parliament was again nervous about the London area. They were afraid lest the weakened King, even so late in the day as this, might attack it. Fairfax had been ordered to besiege Oxford, the King's headquarters. But the advance of the Royalist forces eastwards towards Leicester made the nervousness of the politicians acute. They might come down further eastward and to the south, and they bade Fairfax follow them and engage. There were to be rallied to the Commander-in-Chief such forces as could be summoned for the business of a final duel with the King.

Cromwell at that moment was himself in the Eastern Association, at Ely, where he had his family. He set out to join Fairfax, and sundry of the militia were to effect that junction also.

Fairfax's force was seeking the King's; the King's force was scouting to find whether it might be in the neighbourhood. The Royalists had just stormed Leicester—but weakened themselves by the garrison they had to leave in that captured town. There followed the battle of Naseby, which was the conclusive victory of the war.

## IV

### NASEBY

The work done by Cromwell at Naseby needs careful estimation. For there are elements in the action which make for severe misjudgments on both sides—an overestimate of his effect and an underestimate of it.

[ 183 ]

On the other hand you could so arrange the facts if you liked as to make it yet another tactical marvel to his credit, worthy of being put side by side with the later feat of Dunbar. He can be represented as "snatching victory out of the jaws of defeat." That commonplace phrase has been written of Cromwell at Naseby, I suppose, a hundred times. But for Oliver's power over his command, the rapidity of his decision, etc., a Royalist triumph was certain—and indeed had already been achieved. Oliver almost miraculously changes all this— etc., etc.

On the other hand you could emphasise the gross disparity of numbers and in particular the overwhelming superiority of Oliver's own command against the Royalist cavalry to which he was immediately opposed. The Royal army as a whole was barely half the revolutionary army, and Cromwell in his own part of the battle commanded 3,600 sabres, with the opportunity of charging downhill against Langdale, his opponent, leading only 2,000 at the most and these compelled to open the action uphill.

If these last are the features of Naseby which you choose to put forward as a piece of advocacy and make specially significant, then Oliver's function at Naseby would seem negligible—one might make it out that anyone with such advantages could have done as he did and that the result was a foregone conclusion, almost, as later, Worcester was to be.

Now the truth does not lie between these two conceptions, but to one side of them. It is perfectly true that things were going against his side when Cromwell restored the fortunes of the day. It is also true that the disparity of numbers both on the whole field and in the particular place and time of Cromwell's charge was overwhelming. Yet by a mere comparison of these two sets of truths we cannot see the essence of Cromwell's effect in that really decisive and final action of the war.

In spite of its great superiority of numbers the Parliamentary army was on the way to defeat when Cromwell charged, and it was his charge which turned the tide. Further, although it is true that Cromwell had this great numerical superiority (nine to five) in the cavalry work which was his special task and that superiority of ground which I have mentioned, yet the decision was achieved not by the mere throwing back of his opponents—which would have been no decision—but by these now tried tactics of the "interrupted charge." But for Cromwell's successful use of these tactics Naseby might have been a drawn battle even though his success against Langdale had been as complete as that of Rupert against Ireton. It is therefore true to say that, making every allowance for his obvious advantages in number and position, Cromwell was the true author of the complete victory which virtually ended the war.

To appreciate this it is sufficient to follow the story of the battle which, unlike that of Marston Moor, is simple in its elements and in their combination. Prince Rupert and the King had come down south with an army of some 7,000 to 7,500 men, and lay a dozen miles south of Leicester. It had been known by contact that the Parliamentary army lay on Friday, June the 13th, in the country to the south of them; its strength was as a matter of fact nearly double their own. Cromwell had joined it the day before with 600 sabres, to whom another 3,000 were added; and Fairfax, the Commander-in-Chief, was thus at the head of a total force of some 14,000. Rupert, going south on the morning of Saturday the 14th to find the enemy, saw them a long way off falling back from a low ridge to the plateau which stands just in front of Naseby village.* The field is situated right on the watershed of England, from five

* The ridge at the point where Rupert moved for his first charge is some 50 feet above the depression below it, and the rise from this to the plateau something more, 70 or perhaps 80 feet above the depression. But such a difference of level spread over half a mile is not considerable.

It should be noted that the obelisk on the Clipstone road just to the northeast of Naseby village which was set up to mark the site of the battle is to the east and south of all the fighting; the furthest extension of Cromwell's cavalry on this side cannot have got to within a quarter of a mile of it, and was also well to the north in front of it.

to six hundred feet above the sea at the beginning of the Avon on the west of it and of the Ise on the east. The ridge from which the Parliamentarians were falling back bears the general name of Dust Hill; it falls by a very gentle slope southward to a shallow valley called the Broad Moor, to the south of which again the ground rises equally gently to the plateau. The whole system, from the highest part of the ridge to the high edge of the plateau, is about a mile across from north to south, and the differences of level everywhere less than a hundred feet.

This falling back of the Parliamentarians on the plateau from the ridge of Dust Hill was taken by Rupert for the beginning of a retreat. He was in error. The first position on the ridge had been taken up by Fairfax when Cromwell gave him the good advice of falling back on to the plateau, because there would be more room there for deployment and if necessary manœuvre. Further, the position had this advantage, that much of the Parliamentarian army would be just behind the highest point of the plateau and its superior numbers would thus not be guessed by the Royalists watching from the opposite ridge. Bounding the field on the left and running across the shallow valley from north to south was and still is a hedge of high growth, while right across the field from north to south, cutting the positions of the two armies, runs the road from Silbertoft to Naseby village. Lastly, we should remark rough ground on the east side of the field, full of rabbit-holes. This rough ground prevented the cavalry of either side from deploying to the east in as long a line as it might otherwise have done, but the point was not to prove of much importance.

The elements of the battle therefore are quite simple: on the ridge where the Royalist army deployed, Rupert was on the right with some 1,500 horse, perhaps rather more; Langdale with the remainder of the horse (some 2,000 or possibly rather less) on the left; in the centre immediately to the west of the road the Royalist infantry under Astley, and of these there

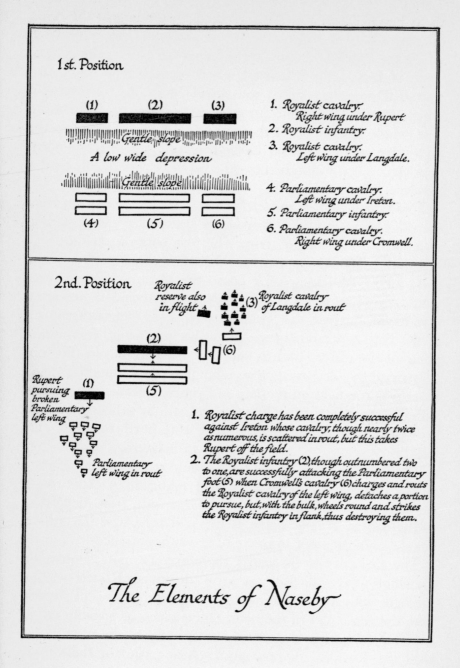

**1st. Position**

(1)    (2)    (3)

Gentle slope

A low wide depression

Gentle slope

(4)    (5)    (6)

1. Royalist cavalry.
    Right wing under Rupert
2. Royalist infantry.
3. Royalist cavalry.
    Left wing under Langdale.

4. Parliamentary cavalry.
    Left wing under Ireton.
5. Parliamentary infantry.
6. Parliamentary cavalry.
    Right wing under Cromwell.

**2nd. Position**

Royalist reserve also in flight

(3) Royalist cavalry of Langdale in rout

(2)

(6)

(5)

Rupert pursuing broken Parliamentary left wing

(1)

Parliamentary left wing in rout

1. Royalist charge has been completely successful against Ireton whose cavalry, though nearly twice as numerous, is scattered in rout, but this takes Rupert off the field.
2. The Royalist infantry (2), though outnumbered two to one, are successfully attacking the Parliamentary foot (5) when Cromwell's cavalry (6) charges and routs the Royalist cavalry of the left wing, detaches a portion to pursue, but, with the bulk, wheels round and strikes the Royalist infantry in flank, thus destroying them.

## The Elements of Naseby

were less than 4,000. It is to be remembered that this infantry was largely composed of Welshmen, and that Langdale's horse were northerners who looked to return to their own part of the country as soon as possible. On the plateau the Parliamentary disposition was the cavalry of Ireton, some 3,400 men, facing Rupert across the valley; from these a small detachment of men dismounted and acting as dragoons lined the hedge; in the centre just west of the road was the Parliamentary infantry, 7,000 strong, and to the east of the road the mass of Cromwell's horse, 3,600 in strength and facing Langdale on the opposite ridge.

The action opened with a charge of Rupert's which completely overthrew Ireton's greatly superior body of horse in spite of the fire which the dragoons in the hedge delivered in flank upon the Royalists as they charged up the slope of the plateau after crossing the depression. The Welshmen of the infantry came upward and began a struggle with the infantry of Fairfax in the centre, while to the west of them Rupert's horse were driving Ireton's off the field. Langdale's horse advanced in turn across the depression and began to come up the hill against Cromwell's wing: Cromwell counter-charged, threw Langdale back, and soon turned the Royalist cavalry of that commander to flight.

As Cromwell's superior numbers of mounted men poured up the slope of the ridge with Langdale's horsemen making off before them, while to the left of both these bodies the Welsh infantry were struggling with Fairfax's superior numbers of Parliamentary foot, Cromwell executed the manœuvre which determined the action. He continued the pursuit of Langdale's men with a portion of his own, retained the other portion in his own hand and swung them round at right angles to the general advance, to the left, across the road, and against the flank of the Royalist infantry. There was still left unbroken on the Royalist side a small reserve of horse, among whom was the King, and with this the King desired to attempt a counter-charge. But a wrong order was given in the confusion, the reserve joined in the flight, the Welsh infantry thus abandoned to Cromwell's cavalry upon their exposed flank were ridden down and cut to pieces. Rupert, riding back again from the pursuit, which he had carried a mile beyond the top of the plateau, found nothing on the field but a completely disintegrated force, its cavalry and the King in flight, the infantry of its centre destroyed, and the Parliamentary forces—which had at one moment seemed so near dissolution—restored and triumphant even upon their broken left. Their infantry could do what it willed, and Cromwell's cavalry was right round and behind the whole line.

The thing was so complete that nothing of the Royalist army remained but the mounted fugitives making for Leicester with the King, and joined by such of Rupert's command as were still rallied. Perhaps 1,500 men got away all together; 5,000 prisoners, all the guns, the King's baggage (including his most important and secret documents), 8,000 stand of arms—these were the immediate trophies on the field. Some 700 of the Royalists had been killed in the battle, perhaps 300 in the pursuit.

The Royalist army had ceased to exist as an organised body, and it was the last force of consequence in the field on the legitimist side. There were still of course a large number of Royalist garrisons scattered up and down the country, and there was still the possibility—though it was a desperate one— of further recruitment. But the blow was mortal, and more especially for this reason, that of the Royalist prisoners at Naseby a very large proportion were officers—the cadres of the Royalist army—and these could not be replaced.

. . . . . . . .

After Naseby, although to contemporaries things looked still confused, though certain advisers of the King still hoped that there might be a chance of recovery, the situation was really quite clear and of chances of recovery there were none.

The sole military task left to the successful revolutionary cause was the isolation of the Devon-Cornwall peninsula, with its Royalist forces and considerable Royalist recruiting field, the defeat of the King's remaining small bodies in the field there and, most important of all, the reduction of the Royalist garrisons.

The isolation of the Devon-Cornwall peninsula was effected by the occupation of three key points, making a chain from the Severn sea to the Channel. Lyme Regis, on the southern sea-coast, they already held, and it was their business to occupy Taunton in the centre and Bridgewater on the northern coast-line, or rather river-line, forming a barrier as far as the northern coast.

The forcing of Langport against Goring has remained famous, though the thing was on a small scale.

I do not deal with Langport because it was hardly a general action and gives us little that is new to illustrate Cromwell himself, though it had a value as illustrating the efficiency in cavalry of the New Model. It is true that they were opposed to very demoralised cavalry on the other side. Plenty has been written about the inefficiency of Goring, and, by writers who prefer the Puritan morals to those of the ordinary man, such writing is accompanied by denunciations of his undoubted looseness—which is little to the point. But the interesting thing about the lack of discipline in Goring's cavalry at Langport, which was the cause of the defeat, is that it was due to that one of the main causes which lay behind the King's failure— lack of money. The Royalist cavalry and especially Goring's horse had been demoralised; they were billeted out on the inhabitants to live as they could on the countryside and take provisions by force. That meant not only a breakdown in *morale* but also a breakdown in physical cohesion, for the soldiers scattered to plunder. It also meant, of course, the disaffection of the countryside.

Neither will I go into detail on the taking of Bridgewater,

the completion of the chain of posts. The siege is interesting as having been conducted against what was rare in the civil war, tolerable earthworks; and especially from the character of the ditches, which were filled with a rush of water at flood-tide and thus difficult to negotiate. But the town was not properly held; if it had been, being divided by its river and the defence being therefore able to concentrate at will all its efforts against the besiegers, it might surely have been preserved longer for the King. The interest of the episode really lies in the proof it gives of the disheartening of the Royalist forces; they felt that the end had already come.

The fall of Bristol followed; Rupert surrendered it of necessity. He surrendered it on good terms, but the King's strength was now so depleted that there was no real question of the issue. On the 11th of September, 1645, he marched out under good escort, and the second port in the kingdom was gone.

It is a good example of how things fall out of proportion in the excitement of war that this inevitable loss—part of the general collapse at the very fag-end of the struggle—struck the imagination of Charles with the violence it did.

Cromwell had now appeared in the conduct of siege work, for which his campaign in Ireland was to be conspicuous. I will select three consecutive examples of this, following immediately upon the fall of Bristol: those of Devizes, Winchester and Basing House. The last of these has a double value. It illustrates the power of the new siege train under Cromwell's hand; it illustrates still better the point in Cromwell's character which will, in the long run, make his most permanent impress upon history, and chiefly establish his reputation. I mean the effect upon him of the Catholic Menace.

Basing House was the first occasion in which this frenzied emotion of his appears: his subsequent slaughterings and rapine in Ireland complete the impression of this passion, which, being the most profound in himself and the most vivid in its results, will be the longest remembered.

BEHIND the army lay a certain number of isolated hostile garrisons, between it and London along the western roads.

Off the main road of retirement between Bristol and London was the garrison of Devizes, which blocked communications along the main road south-west to Exeter and would interfere with anything less than a considerable armed force going along the Bristol road, from which it was distant less than a day's march. Further east, menacing the main part of the London-Bristol road, standing just north of Newbury, was the garrison of Donnington Castle. The road from London to the south-west, that is, the main road from London to Exeter, passing through Salisbury, was interfered with by a private house which had been fortified and continuously held for the King, Basing House, owned by Lord Winchester. It stood only four marches from London (indeed only three forced marches), and directly commanded the main western road, standing but a mile and a half to the north of it. Intermediately, the town of Winchester was held and its castle garrisoned by Royalist forces. They cut the alternative road to the south-west, with its direct approach to Southampton and Poole, the garrison being available for interference with anything short of a very considerable convoy.

These three, then, concern our study: Devizes, the nearest to Bristol and the first to be taken; Basing House, outside Basingstoke, the nearest to London; and Winchester, with its castle, to the south of the line and in between.

The fate of each was certain, for Cromwell now had a powerful siege train, and his opponents insufficient knowledge of the growing art of supplementary fortification with earth as it was developing on the Continent of Europe. They understood all about the making of lines, and those who had served abroad had seen the use of earth for packing stone walls; but they had not thoroughly woken up to the fact that no stone wall could stand against the more accurate heavy artillery which had developed before the mid-seventeenth century. It it is strange that a dozen years after the birth of Vauban and half a century after the publication of Errard's book you still see scores of places attempting to stand up to heavy and fairly accurate cannon—twenty- and forty-pounders—with nothing better than medieval defences. The Italians had been developing the use of earthworks to cover stone for nearly a century before the English Civil Wars. Cromwell himself was as little practised in such defence as his opponents, but that did not matter so much, for there was now no peril of the fall of Parliamentary garrisons through Royalist sieges.

These three places, therefore, fell as a matter of course, and Devizes was the first to be taken. Cromwell summoned it; Lloyd, who held it for the King, asked for time to communicate with his master and finding he could not have it he stood out. His determination to do so was apparently better justified than were the other cases of resistance. The walls were especially thick and solid, and Cromwell's heavies, though he seems to have had at least one forty-pounder among them, might either have failed to effect a breach or been so delayed doing it as to hamper the campaign.

What decided the fall of the castle at Devizes was a very good example of the amateur way in which the Civil Wars were conducted. The defence was of course no more than a curtain, that is, the interior court of the castle was open to the sky. In this interior court Lloyd had left his stores and powder exposed. He forgot the peril from high-angle fire. Cromwell had only to use shells from the big bombards he had with him and drop those shells into the exposed courtyard behind the wall to make certain of his result. Lloyd, suffering at once from explosions of his powder which killed several of his men, determined that against such methods the castle was untenable, and surrendered.

The taking of Winchester in the following week and the contrast between that success and the butchery at Basing House is an especial episode which stands out in high relief. For that contrast vividly illustrates the character of the General who commanded the twin operations. So far as Cromwell as a soldier is concerned each tells exactly the same story—the facile success of a siege train against insufficient and essentially antiquated defences. But whereas Devizes gives us no illustration of Cromwell's self, Winchester and Basing amply do so. For a comparison between Cromwell's behaviour in the two places is the most vivid illustration we have of the condition of his spirit in the chief matter of his time, the duel between the old and the new religions.

It was exactly a week after the first summoning of Devizes that Cromwell's force appeared (on the 28th of September, Sunday) and summoned the town of Winchester, after a march of over fifty miles; somewhat circuitous, for a direct road was lacking. The city was in no condition for defence and was occupied at once; but when Cromwell summoned the castle it would not yield—though it was far less strong than Devizes, the fate of which it had heard.

Here, almost at the beginning of the story of the siege work that followed the army operations in the field, we must appreciate a point in seventeenth-century warfare which affected England as much as the rest of Christendom. It was a point of honour in any place that could put up something of a resistance not to yield at a first summons; it was even a point of honour to fight it out as best might be when it was clear that the besieging force was certain to win. In pure military science such points of honour are absurd. As war grew more and more intense with modern times they were abandoned; but in this earlier half of the seventeenth century they still played a great part. Winchester Castle knew it was doomed

—or rather knew that the odds were very heavy against it—as shortly Basing House was to know; but that was no reason, according to the ideas of the time, for yielding at the first demand.

It is very important to appreciate this if we are to understand the peculiar character of what did happen later at Basing House, compared with what happened at Winchester. When the defence had put up as good a fight as honour demanded, they might by the conventions of the time demand a parley, and bargain upon terms. They would be prepared to capitulate (the very meaning of the word "capitulation" is a bargain or compromise arranged under "capitula," i.e., heads of clauses). On offering to capitulate after parley, storm and massacre were spared.

That is what happened at Winchester. The siege train required repair, as the heavies often did after a march along those roads, and these repairs were not completed until the Friday following, the 2nd of October, but when they had been made the battery could be mounted, and fire was opened upon the Saturday, the 3rd of October, against the walls of the castle. There were six guns, and the mere battering down of the wall was only a question of time—and not a long time either. The garrison made a sally through the breach, actually reached the battery and were for a moment in possession of the guns, but they were driven back, asked for a parley, and were graciously admitted to the peace of the victor.

All this episode at Winchester is filled with the spirit which marked the Civil Wars in England. Everything was done strictly to a military purpose only, there is no indiscriminate killing and no mere orgy of plunder. The Bishop, Dr. Quarle, had been offered a safe conduct by Cromwell when he was in the town, and chose of his own free will to go into the Castle. When it surrendered Cromwell gave him an armed escort to save him and his accompanying clergy (who were in their clerical dress) from insult by the scum of his army.

[ 195 ]

Moreover Cromwell did more than this; in his desire to impress the people with his justice and to affirm the discipline of his troops he condemned six men for pillage and actually hanged one of them. That was how things went at Winchester.

Now mark how they went at Basing. At Basing he had to deal, not with a Protestant Bishop of the Protestant English Church, but with a great noble, the Marquis of Winchester, a Catholic and surrounded by Catholics. It was as a stronghold of that large Catholic minority, which minority was the nucleus of the so much larger surviving general Catholic sympathy in England, that Basing House stood in Oliver's mind. The Marquis of Winchester (a Paulet), a man now not far off his fiftieth year and immensely wealthy, had put all his fortune at the disposal of the King. He was utterly devoted to the ancient constitution of his country. He was untouched by that ambition to supplant the monarchy, so prevalent in his own class, which had produced the Civil War—making so very many of the Royalist leaders sympathise in part with the revolutionary demands. To him the whole revolutionary movement was an abomination.

But it was not as the typical Royalist that Cromwell regarded him, as he pondered on that objective during his march from Winchester, it was as an abettor of the Mass, a protector of priests, a servitor of Babylon—or the Fiend. Cromwell marched against Lord Winchester and his little garrison as against the intolerable enemies of his God; for Basing House had been announced for years as "a nest of Papistry." Its garrison was some 400 in number, and largely made up of Catholic gentlemen who had gathered round its master.

Here then was Basing House, two things in one, the stronghold nearest to London, commanding the main road, which had repeatedly maintained itself against attack; and a plague spot of Catholicism. Now that the mopping up was on, Basing House was a place to be reduced as a matter of course. But it was also much more than a stronghold, for it was a last but typical Catholic focus of resistance.

It was on Wednesday, the 8th of October (for Cromwell had come up from Winchester in one day) that he appeared before the walls and joined his considerable force of six or seven thousand men to the body under Dalbier which had been maintaining the blockade of Basing. Cromwell's rival Manchester, before he had been driven out of command, had earlier made every effort to take the place and had failed; Cromwell had refused to help him—one of his last ill turns to the detested Montagu—and thereby had put yet another spoke in the Montagu's wheel. That had taken place before the New Model was in the field. Manchester's men had mutinied and deserted, marching on their own account disorderly to Reading to seize food. *Now* it was to be a very different matter; Cromwell's 7,000 in this October of 1645 were members of a force consciously united, well disciplined, and above all well gunned for the purpose they had in hand. Nor could any doubt the issue.

Dalbier, an elderly German officer, knowing much of war, once serving under Buckingham and ready to serve anyone for pay, was now serving the revolutionary Government of London. Cromwell had in his siege train six heavy pieces as well as the lighter ones. It is possible, however, that he could only mount five. At any rate his heaviest piece was again his "cannon," that is his forty-pounder, and with it his two "demi-cannon," the twenty-pounders which flanked their bigger brother. It was upon the accurate delivery of these heavies that he mainly relied.

There was something like a mile of trench and low earthwork round Basing House, that is, four quarter-mile fronts; but there could be no hope of holding these now with so small a garrison. The house itself was in two parts. One of these was like so much that had been disputed in the Civil War, a medieval castle; the other was a new Elizabethan house, a very splendid thing, built by that Paulet who had been Elizabeth's Treasurer and the first with the title of Winchester.

It took as usual some little time to set up the battery; the work was completed by Saturday, October the 11th; on that day the place was summoned and the summons was, of course, refused. The chances of the defence were indefinitely less than they had been elsewhere, but Winchester and his little body of gentlemen could not think of surrender before saving the point of honour.

Sunday passed, and we must believe that the priests within the doomed place said then their last Masses before the men in arms attendant. Were not Vespers also sung that afternoon? For them the Psalm, "In Fexitu," with its solemn mode in Latin Chaunt, intoned something that was to be in the minds of others than the besieged. For it is the Vesper psalm in which you have the verse in denunciation of idols:

*"Aures habent et non audient: manus habent et non palpabunt."*

and around them as they sang were the images of Catholic usage: The Abomination.

It was on Monday, the 13th of October, that the roar began, the crash of the great iron balls against the brick and masonry, and before the end of the light two wide breaches had been made; all was ready for storming on the morrow. In the hours of darkness the plan of the storm was drawn up, and Cromwell's thousands disposed for it in their places, nearly twenty men to each of the defenders, and all the guns as well. There was nothing on the side of the besieged which could silence or even meet the fire which had destroyed their walls save small guns, muskets and swords, and only 400 hands to use them.

The Revolutionary soldiers slept at their posts with orders to attack at six in the morning; the first grey light.

Cromwell, when he had ranged about somewhat, seen to all, tested and questioned, withdrew to commune with God; and to him also, but in a medium most sacred to him, the new rhythms of that new English Bible which had so possessed him from his boyhood, came these words of that same Psalm for a text:

*"Their idols are silver and gold. They have ears but they hear not . . . They that make them are like unto them."*

He sat or knelt there alone in the dark, preparing himself for that offering up of victims that was to come with the first dawn; the slaughter of the idolaters.

The rush of such numbers, nearly twenty to one, was, and could not but be, overwhelming as a great wave. It poured through the breaches, the first walls were taken, the grateful holocaust had begun. Pickering's men had taken the new house and forced the gate of the old one, when, as at Winchester, the trumpets of the defenders sounded for a parley. But Basing was not Winchester; nor did these Papists count as human. "Our men would not hear," wrote Cromwell after. No, neither would Cromwell.

No parley was granted, and therefore no quarter. A second detached body attacking the place from the other side had met the main body of the assaulters within, and all combined flooded through the glorious rooms, where the killing continued and the looting had begun. The soldiers gorged themselves with every sort of plunder and with the frenzy of destruction, where all that great and ancient wealth lay to their hands. And in the midst of clamour and explosions great flames arose, how started none now know, and the men with their loot were forced out as from a furnace.

Old Winchester himself (for men of fifty were counted old in that age) was brought forth, proud to have maintained his loyalty to the end. He had to suffer the insults of Peters, the fanatical Chaplain, but to a man of his temper the ruins of that great palace and the flames that consumed it and the end of all his substance was a glory. He had written long before on every pane of glass the word *"Loyauté,"* he had called it

"Loyalty House," and it was fitting that if it were to fall into the hands of such beasts as these, only its charred shell should so fall. From the building others were brought out, women whose clothes were stripped off them for the value of the loot they afforded, and old Inigo Jones—really old he was, seventy-two years old—having been stripped stark for the value of his linen and his very boots, so that they had to wrap him up in a blanket, was carried forth.

It was the "blessed Word of God" fulfilled. "They that make them are like unto them, and so is every one that trusteth in them." And among the heaps of corpses was the body of a woman, the daughter of Griffith, a clergyman of the Church of England dispossessed from his living; she had replied proudly to the invaders and been knocked on the head for her pains. The priests were massacred as a matter of course—all but four of them, who were kept back for the more formal business of mutilation, the boiling pot, the torn heart, the fire and the knife, strangling and the gallows—whatever had been now used for seventy years on end against their kind in England.

The work was accomplished. It was Tuesday, the 14th of October, 1645, and Cromwell, in the calm leisure following on such an evening, somewhat apart, wrote his account to the Parliament. It was succinct and exact enough, and is summarised in his conclusion:

"God exceedingly abounds in his goodness to us." But not to the idolaters.

Bᴇᴛᴡᴇᴇɴ the end of the Civil War proper on the 6th of May, 1646, when the unfortunate Charles rode to the headquarters of the Scottish from Southwell, which he had left the day before, up to the fatal 30th of January, 1649, is a period within which we have to solve the most important of all questions remaining open today upon the character of Cromwell.

This question is the following: "At what date did Cromwell determine to kill the King?"

Upon the answer to it depends the nature and gravity of Oliver's action in that one act of his life by which he will be most strictly judged. The earlier his decision was taken the greater his duplicity becomes, the more tenacious his purpose: the later we place it the more excusable we make it, by a plea of acute necessity or by pressure from others than Cromwell himself.

At one point therefore between these two dates, the 6th of May, 1646, and the January morning thirty-two months later we must be able to place Cromwell's decision.

We must of course from the outset postulate the plain truth that Cromwell was the man who killed Charles Stuart. There were a great many other factors as there always are in any event whatsoever, and particularly in a public event where thousands of disputing men are concerned. But the one man mainly responsible before history for the death of the King is Oliver Cromwell. He did it.

There runs through the whole story a connected chain of happenings all leading to one end, each suited in its exact time and place to produce the final thing. Either this chain is a succession of miraculous coincidences or it is evidence of one plan. If of one plan, then of one brain, for the process is carefully concealed, duly retarded at the right moments when haste would ruin it; similarly, at exactly the right moments, especially towards the end, given impetus and hurried forward. Such co-ordination is the fruit of one mind, and the only mind to which it can be laid is Cromwell's.

Yes: he did it. We must postulate that.

Next we must postulate what I think is equally undoubted —that a determination to put the King to death must have been considerably later than May, 1646. He remained long after that a bargaining asset of high value though whether he would have permanently so remained is another matter. We must also take a somewhat earlier limiting date than the actual death of Charles for the end of the period under examination: we may say for instance that as there is no reasonable doubt upon Cromwell's intention to kill the King after the sending of him to Hurst Castle on December 1st, 1648. *That* date is the last term of the discussion. The final question is, then, where can we put the decision between well after May, 1646, and December, 1648.

First we must note the sequence of events—the principal facts in their order: and then consider those facts in relation to Cromwell's personal character, necessary motives and sur-rounding circumstances. All these three things can be judged and known as well as the patent facts.

The factors are clear and their order simple. The King's flight from Oxford having ended on that 5th of May, 1646, after which he was in the hands of the Scotch, from whom he thought he would get better terms than from the Army or from Parliament.

Nine months after, at the end of January, 1647, he was handed over to the Commissioners of the Parliament as against a payment of half the arrears due to the Scotch on the sums they were to have received for helping the Rebellion. The date of this transaction is the 26th of January, 1647, and the King left Newcastle for the south on the third of the following month.

He was kept by the Parliament at Holmby House for four months, under custody of the Parliamentarians.*

In the first days of June, 1647, a Cornet of the name of Joyce commanding a body of cavalry appeared and took him away by force on the 4th of the month, whenceforward he was the prisoner of the Army. The thing had been secretly planned in Cromwell's own house in London. It is after this act of brute force that the active problem begins, for whatever was passing in Cromwell's head before the Army had physical possession of the King can only be matter for conjecture.

The sequence of events after Cromwell, by use of the Army, had thus captured the King is as follows:

There arose conflict, complicated by four elements. There was the captured King on the one side, intent upon saving the monarchy for himself and his descendants and, as the peril increased, intent upon saving his life. He had to deal with three separate opponents, each of which was at once a possible enemy and a possible ally against or with either of the other two. These three opponents of Charles were, the Parliament, the Scotch and the Army. It was the business of Charles Stuart to play off one against the other with such skill as he could summon, so that, by the mutual neutralisation of these hostile forces, he should regain his rights and liberty.

* There is a tragic irony in the choice of Holmby (Holdenby by its full title). It was the most magnificent private house in England, a palace rather, and had been built by the dancing man, Hatton, whom Elizabeth had so singularly favoured. It arose out of the huge profits of the promotion she so astonishingly gave him to the Chancellorship; and also out of the plunder of the Crown, in which such men as he indulged at large under the decaying monarchial power of Elizabeth's reign. James I had bought it back for use as a summer residence and for his Queen and her children: later the Parliament sold it in their straits for money, and today nothing remains of it but the gate houses. A man may be pardoned a certain superstitious awe when he considers Charles held a prisoner in this place which his childhood had known, and the magnificence of which was a testimony in stone to those evil forces which had ruined the Crown of England, especially under Elizabeth.

What were the qualities of these very different potential allies, all openly hostile to the King and each secretly hostile to the two others?

The Parliament was, in the speech of men, in legal terms, and even in their own opinion for some time to come, the *de facto* ruler governing the country. We call it "The Parliament" for the sake of brevity, but it was of course not the Parliament at all; there were only a handful of the Lords, say one-tenth, and only the rebel part—towards the end only a remnant—of the Commons; somewhat over a half on a full roll at first; before the death of the King a tenth which never became a fifth of the total membership.

The Scotch had this to say for themselves, that they still possessed a large striking force, or at any rate one that could be renewed at short notice; a delegation of them and their power was already planted in the English capital as allies of the Parliament, and as allies who could and would act independently. They were still owed an enormous sum of money, arrears of wages due to them; and they had bound the English politicians to them by an open pact. True, pacts can be broken, but the moral effect of that pact was strong, and at the beginning of the business the majority of the so-called Commons called themselves Presbyterian. With all this it must be remembered that this body of men calling themselves the House of Commons knew that they were in peril. Their power was an abstraction; it was there so long as it was obeyed, but they had no instrument for enforcing it. Real power lay obviously with the Army, which stood within striking distance of their meeting place—and could at any moment make itself actually their master as it had for so long been potentially their master.

This third opponent of Charles, the Army, was of a texture which needs close appreciation.

It had now nearly become something to be found nowhere else in the world at that time (save in patches under the Spanish monarchy), a true professional force. It was gorged with victory; it was fairly well disciplined. To say that it had any common opinion except pride in its achievements and the general soldierly feeling which so rapidly inspires men in the course of campaigns would not be true. The great majority were riff-raff, hired or compelled to serve during the fighting, though since the fighting had ceased recruitment was much more free, the same pay remaining without risk and without an expectation of toil. It was owed enormous sums by the Parliament, which had been unable to pay its way. It was naturally sore at seeing all that gold given to the Scotch which might have gone to meet its own arrears. It had developed what is very rare in the history of the mass of the English populace during all the centuries, a power of corporate egalitarian action, the opposite of the national instinct for following leaders. Hence it was capable of mutiny and of a revolutionary movement of its own against its officers. But it developed this new and short-lived quality insufficiently. The attempt at self-assertion by the rank and file, when it came to a head, was at once suppressed; and one may say that the Army meant, in practice, the chief officers and, above all, Cromwell. For the soldiers regarded him as victory personified, and worshipped in him a special excellence in all that soldiers admire.

But though Cromwell was their virtual chief (nominally Second-in-Command under Fairfax), and though one may say, "Cromwell was the Army," such a phrase is but shorthand. His power could only be exercised indirectly. He had to join in the Council of Officers with the rest; he had, in some degree, as had the other chiefs, to humour the men; he could not turn back openly from the cause for which they had all fought in common; nor did he wish to do so; it was sincerely his own cause also. In general, when one says "the action of the Army" or "the proposals of the Army," there is meant "the actions of Cromwell" or "the proposals of Cromwell," and the phrase, "Cromwell was the Army," though too short and crude, is an epitome of the truth even as early as May, 1647. But the actions and the proposals of the Army were only Cromwell's in the sense that he was their chief man, and he could neither propose nor act save by carefully watching and shepherding others.

These things being so, let us see how the problem works out. The initiative is obviously with the soldiers. They not only have force on their side but the King in their hands, and as the tradition of monarchy was that of the overwhelming mass of the English people he was the trump card of whoever held him. The Army treated the King with far more respect than ever his Parliamentary jailers at Holmby had done, or his earlier Scottish jailers either. He was fairly free to move about, he was allowed to pay visits, to see his children and to hunt; he was surrounded by servants. The idea in the mind of Cromwell and of those who worked with him, notably his son-in-law Ireton, was that the King, being treated thus freely, would become their puppet-ally in their own struggle with the remnant of the Parliament, and lend the authority of his name to their side.

There are therefore put before the King, just after the middle of July, 1647, certain "Heads of Proposals," that is, the sketch of a constitutional scheme for his acceptance. He is asked to agree to the dissolution of the existing Parliament (nothing could please him better), the date of such dissolution to be determined by the Parliament itself: after that to Parliaments every two years which should be indissoluble during the first third of the year on which they were called; with a better redistribution of seats, a high property qualification for voters, and so on. It is all moonshine, because it is only a paper fabric; but the underlying spirit is that the King shall cease to be King and the Church of England shall cease to be that well-endowed and national establishment to which Charles had all his life been more devoted than to anything else on earth.

In the first draft of these "Proposals" there was probably a provision for the destruction of the Church's revenues. In their final form there was also great power given to a "Council of State." Voting for these projected Parliaments was not to be allowed to the King's party, and the right to deal with at first seven, later five, of his friends as criminals was reserved.

I say the whole thing was paper and could not have held. It was intended only to get the King definitely on the side of the Army in their rising movement against the Parliament. Nor did it much matter, for the King necessarily refused the proposals. His grounds of refusal were that he would not sacrifice his friends, and that, as none of his supporters might sit, the proposed Parliament was not free, also that there was no scheme of guarantees for the Church of England. There would be of course no enforcement of the Church of England ritual or doctrine.

But we need not delay upon this affair, which has been a great deal over-emphasised. Charles could not have accepted complete alliance with one of the three which he was playing off one against the other without tying his own hands: when the Parliament approaches him in its turn with a set of proposals leaving even less of his power to him, even less chance of seeing the Church of England restored, he tells them that he so much dislikes *their* scheme that he would even prefer the Army's; but he will not have either. The Scotch he can fall back upon later.

He keeps the three in play somewhat clumsily—for he was most unskilful in falsehood—ready, then as later, to promise to each in turn incompatible terms; and so until the autumn the thing hangs undecided.

We may affirm with fair certitude that during those late summer weeks of 1647 and on until October there had presumably been no fatal decision taken in Cromwell's mind. What would have happened if the King had been so foolish as to surrender morally to Cromwell and his Army we cannot tell. Some imagine that he might have remained as a sort of puppet with Cromwell the real ruler—but the whole thing is guesswork, for Charles had no intention of yielding but only of continuing to manœuvre the separate hostile forces until he could arrive at some tangible result worth his while.

It is in October, 1647, that things begin to change. And it is by the end of that month, or perhaps at the latest in the first days of November, that Cromwell determines on ultimately getting rid of the King.

Whether such an idea had occurred to him earlier or no we cannot certainly tell. There is evidence for it, but it is not very good evidence; it is based on the evidence given by Young at the trial of Peters in 1660. Young then testified that Peters had told him (Young) that he, Peters, and Cromwell had both resolved early in 1647, when they were fearing arrest at the hands of the Parliament to "Try him" (Charles) "for his life and cut off his head." There is no reason why Young should be lying; but Peters, our only informant, was always an irresponsible fanatic, nearly mad. The period of decision during which Cromwell turns to consider the elimination of Charles, must fall after the moment in which he is certain that he can never get the King into his power by mere negotiation, nor use him as a puppet. He was already certain of that by September, when Charles, though rejecting alliance with the Parliament, had left the door open for further negotiation with them and the Army combined. It was quite evident that the King would never henceforward voluntarily yield to the Army alone, nor be taken in by any flattery or good treatment on their part.

Meanwhile in this month of October a thing of capital importance was being decided; and from what we know of Cromwell's excellent intelligence department (yet another proof of his value as a soldier) we may be certain that he knew more or less what was going on—indeed, he complains to Ashburnham at that time of the King's duplicity. This thing of capital importance was a growing understanding between the King and the Scotch.

After all this, the breakdown of the attempt to cajole Charles into a puppet position under the Army and the discovery of the Scottish plan, there was nothing left for Cromwell but to pursue the King's destruction. Once more had arisen that parting of the ways which you meet over and over again in history—"It is your life or mine." That is what the group led by the genius of Cecil had felt with regard to Charles's grandmother, Mary Queen of Scots; that is what Charles's son was to say in so many words when he permitted the due execution of William Russell, who had plotted to destroy him. "It is his life or mine," was Charles II to say in that crisis, and here, now, today Cromwell could see defined in vivid contrast the double issue between Charles I and himself, "It is his life or mine."

There is no need to credit the romantic story that Cromwell had intercepted a letter from Charles to his Queen, saying that if ever he was in power again Cromwell should be hanged. Whether such a letter were written or not, it is not required in further confirmation of a situation so evident. Those two qualities which had served Oliver so conspicuously in battle, clarity and decision, had shown him what the clean issue now was, and permitted him to do what a man less endowed would have hesitated to do, and to carry it through with hidden tenacity to the end. Many of the Army leaders must have known that they had gone too far to retreat and that the King, if ever he should be restored to power, would (he himself or those supporting him) take vengeance; but Cromwell saw this better than any of them. Had he been able to lure Charles into a sort of alliance in which the King should be his servant he might or might not have chosen to eliminate him later; but there was no longer a choice. The only question was how the elimination of Charles was to be carried out. And the way in which it was carried out, the careful steering to avoid this danger and that, the manipulation of all the forces to his hand, adverse and favourable, is the best example we have of Cromwell's talent in the carrying out of a scheme.

To begin with, there was a formidable peril of premature action. This peril arose from the ferment rising in the Army, the faction among the soldiers which was soon to be called that of the Levellers.

All wars have an egalitarian effect. They produce that spirit which is sometimes, today, loosely and inaccurately called "democratic." Men submitted to great hardship in common may retain respect for officers, but they will hardly maintain the illusions of civil life—especially the prime illusion that money in some way makes the rich of a different clay from the poor. The long strain had bred among the soldiers a desire for human equality which they desired to see transplanted into the new constitution of the state, and which prepared them also for mutiny.

On the top of that the soldiers had seen their pay refused them by perpetual procrastination until it was weeks and months in arrear, and they had suffered this injustice while the Scotch had gone off with a wagon-train full of gold. This ferment among the soldiers was for Cromwell an advantage in that it could be used as a driving power to make familiar the demand for the King's trial—which would mean, of course, for his death. But it had the disadvantage of being a grave threat to the existence of this very weapon on which he depended: the Army, and the fuller disadvantage of rousing resistance in favour of the King from all who dreaded social disorder. Disorganisation is the end of an army, indeed that is all "a rout" means. An army is destroyed by its enemy when its organisation is shattered under that enemy's blows; it is destroyed by its own self, when its organisation dissolves from within. Now, but for the Army there would be no Cromwell —moreover, as the Levellers clamouring for the King's trial were also clamouring for the poor against the rich, property and rank and all ordered forces would be mobilised to save

[ 210 ]

the King. Both issues would be fatal to Cromwell's object.

It was therefore the very first task before him to master and to canalise in favour of his own more deliberate scheme this dangerous spirit abroad among the soldiery. And it was imperative that no mere chaotic enthusiasm on their part should propose too early to destroy the King. Were that to happen the threatened murder at *this* stage could not but rouse the whole mass of the English people, cowed though they were under the power of the sword. Such a blunder would have been as much the end of Cromwell and all he sincerely desired to achieve as would have been the restoration of Charles to his full power. Cromwell had become what he was through the Army; he had in a sense made that Army, he was the leader and deservedly the idol of that Army; but he had to manage it, and an army victorious is not of its nature docile, especially if it be made to suffer; the leaders of an armed revolution stand themselves in peril of what they lead. Who rides a tiger must never let go its ears.

Even were Cromwell successful in mastering military rebellion and disorder, there would lie before him the second obstacle, implying a second task; he would have to meet what was certainly coming in the next year, a Scottish invasion and presumably a Royalist rising also and a renewal of the civil war.

Were he successful in surmounting this second obstacle, in suppressing the revolt from within and defeating the invasion from beyond the Border, there would yet remain a third obstacle—the remaining authority of the Parliament. The majority of its members would refuse to be mere dependents of the Army and its virtual chief. They would still, almost certainly and in spite of earlier disappointment, play once more the card of alliance with the King against the soldiers. They would not consent to Charles's trial and death. Therefore, somehow or other, that Parliamentary majority must be got rid of.

Only when Cromwell should have managed to get the better of these three successive obstacles could he attain his end. He did attain it; and to watch the skill and perseverance with which he carried out his plan has something fascinating about it.

On the 9th of October appeared the first public demand for equality. It was called "The Case of the Army Truly Stated." In the new Constitution that was ready for discussion this document demanded manhood suffrage, Parliaments every two years, and all the rest of it. It was the rank and file ominously dictating to the Council of Officers, although so far the thing was only political.

Two days later the fanatical Chaplin Peters published his "Word for the Army and Two Words to the Kingdom." It aimed at the King; it complained that men were "more afraid of a dead dog than of a living lion." This was an incitement to attack Charles himself.

A week later, five of the Regiments, acting through their now permanent committees (what we should call today "Soviets") presented the Commander-in-Chief with their demands. All this Cromwell in public opposed, he spoke for hours in Parliament in defence of the Monarchy, swearing he had nothing to do with the new revolutionary movement; in private also, within the Council of Officers, he and his son-in-law, Ireton, met those Colonels who leant towards the Levellers. Nor was Cromwell insincere in this; for Monarchy in the abstract did appeal to him, he thought it the only rational form of Government, and subversive unco-ordinated action from below was most certainly odious to him; and still more certainly the soldiery getting out of hand and attacking the King at this early stage of the affair he could see to be disastrous.

The Levellers began talking more and more wildly against the King, the true author, they said, of all the bloodshed; the true culprit and the one who should therefore be the expiatory victim. And meanwhile there was danger not only of Charles's assassination, but of his rescue. What was Cromwell to do?

What he did was a master stroke. He secured the King in a place where neither Levellers nor rescuers could get at him, and yet he did it without the open use of force and under the appearance of the thing being done by Charles himself. He got the King into the Isle of Wight, there to be in the hands of the Military Governor, with whom Cromwell was closely connected.

This Military Governor was a well-born, well-to-do, pampered, not very pleasant young gentleman called Robert Hammond. By paternal descent he came from the learned professions, his grandfather having been a famous physician; it was through the women that he had both his noble blood and his fortune. He was at this moment only twenty-six years of age, and he owed his unusual and disgracefully rapid promotion to connection with the incompetent Essex. But he was still more closely connected with the present chiefs of the Parliamentary Army. One of his uncles was Master of Ordnance; his father-in-law was that millionaire Hampden, who was the leading figure during the early Rebellion and the debates preceding it, and who had fallen in the first year of the war. Hammond was therefore by this marriage a cousin-in-law to Cromwell himself, but he was also a familiar; to Cromwell, Hammond was always "dear Robin," the recipient of long, affectionate hortatory letters, almost like a favourite son.

Hammond had played the young blood, killed his man in a duel, fought through the war, and got rather sick of it; he had been taken prisoner at Basing House and was given £1,000 of public money to compensate him for that momentary inconvenience—for the garrison had spared his life. He had made all sorts of difficulties about further service in Ireland; he wanted a soft job, and suggested the Governorship of the Island, which he duly received on the 6th of February, 1647. Let it be remembered, however, that this young Robert Hammond had thus been appointed Governor of the Isle of Wight by special Ordinance of Parliament; at the demand of the Army and of Cromwell, no doubt, but still on special Parliamentary authority. Armed with this knowledge of the young man, we can proceed to follow the part he played.

Charles was, therefore, to be got into the custody of this young man, of whom, though Cromwell could not be certain (it was his chief anxiety), he could at least say that the odds were in favour of his proving dependable during the anxious months that were to come. Charles once lured on to the Island, where there was a well-defended stronghold and no chance of a force coming against it, could be kept there in what may be called by a modern metaphor "cold storage," until the other obstacles in Cromwell's way should be overcome. When the extravagant picture of Cromwell was universal, one of his most detailed worshippers and biographers * wrote, fifty years ago, this sentence with regard to the statement and conviction of Cromwell's contemporaries that he was the true author of the King's being caught in the trap of the Island. "It is now felt to be too absurd for discussion."

A little discussion will soon show whether so obvious a truth is absurd or no. I will first state the facts in their order, and then recapitulate their effect.

On Thursday, the 11th of November, 1647, just when the outcry of the Levellers for the King's blood was rising to its height, Colonel Whalley, Cromwell's first cousin, who had the command at Hampton Court and whose business it was to prevent the King from escaping, showed Charles a certain letter which he had received from Cromwell himself. In this letter Oliver insisted upon the grave danger of the King's assassination. That same day an anonymous letter reached Charles, signed only with the letters "E. R."; it professed to be from a well-wisher and loyal subject, praying for His Majesty's safety, which can never be secure "while you are in those

* J. A. Picton.

hands"—the hands of Whalley and his master Cromwell—and wishing with all his soul that His Majesty were with the writer under his safe and private roof. Whalley's own Chaplain, Baxter, assures us that when the letter was first heard of most thought it was contrived by Cromwell.

That same day the various guards at the issues from Hampton Court were doubled; but there was one issue to the river across the garden from the King's lodgings which alone was kept unguarded; no sentries were put there.

Next let it be noted that on the other side of the river, at Ditton, the King's best friend and servant in those troubles, Ashburnham, was lodged, with horses; he was in position, if the King could get away over the river, to escort him, in company with another loyal gentleman, Berkeley, who had long been in negotiation between Cromwell and the King. Further let it be remembered that the whole district was in those days thinly inhabited, and the Governor of Hampton Court must have known perfectly well what was going on at Ditton, a few hundred yards away across the ferry. He cannot but have known that Ashburnham had sent his goods away some days before and had sent horses forward also, retaining only just so many as would be necessary for the enterprise that followed.

In the dark and stormy night of that Thursday, the 11th of November, the King went out of his lodgings through the garden, *there being no sentinel set there to stop him*, reached the river side and crossed; he at once rode off south with Ashburnham and Berkeley, towards Sutton in Hampshire, where remounts awaited them—and here let us remember Bulstrode's statement that the King expected to find a ship waiting at Southampton Water that would take him to Jersey.

There was no ship. The King went down the east side of that arm of the sea to Titchfield House, Lady Southampton's place; Berkeley and Ashburnham went down the west side and crossed over to the Island from Lymington and sought the

Governor of the Island, to sound him as to what his dispositions might be.

Hammond showed the most violent surprise, appeared to
be almost fainting, confessed to be terrified of the responsibility—torn between loyalty to the King and duty to the Army.
But he also broke out into quite contrary expressions. Both
Berkeley and Ashburnham have left accounts of what happened. Those accounts do not properly tally. But we know
the event. Robert Hammond, the Governor, said he would
go in person to see the King; he took Berkeley and Ashburnham with him and also the Commander of Cowes Castle.
Charles, on hearing that Hammond had come, cried out to
Ashburnham, "Oh, Jack! you have undone me!" Ashburnham
offered to kill Hammond, Charles would not allow him to do
so; and the upshot of it was that Charles was taken back by
Hammond to the Isle of Wight.

There are the facts as we know them. Charles must have
had a motive for going towards the sea; that motive was presumably to escape by sea, therefore presumably it had been
suggested to his companions and most probably to Ashburnham that a ship would be awaiting him—as we are also assured
upon other evidence.

Whence could such a suggestion have come, save from those
who had desired events to take this course, and to see Charles
safely shut up in the Island? Why, when such extraordinary
precautions were being taken to prevent Charles's leaving
Hampton Court, as also to preserve him from attack, was there
no sentry put at the one issue by which he could escape? Why
this feigned ignorance on Whalley's part of the movements
of Ashburnham at Thames Ditton, for half a week, close at
hand? Why the pretence of surprise at hearing that Ashburnham's horses and furniture had gone on, he having left his
house some days before? Above all, why this alarming letter
from Cromwell to Whalley and the still more alarming anonymous letter conveyed to the King? While Charles was under

such custody he could not have received it without Whalley knowing about it too, Whalley, Cromwell's own cousin and creature.

It is not possible for any man to read these facts in their order and still believe Cromwell ignorant of what was obviously a plan, carefully drawn up and thoroughly carried out. It begins with the departure of Charles from Hampton Court under circumstances which would have been impossible without Whalley's deliberately arranging them—a departure urged and almost forced by alarming letters, one of them anonymous, ascribed by those in the know to Cromwell, the other admittedly coming from Cromwell himself. It ends by the King being securely held in the only place within twenty-four hours of Hampton Court where he could be at the mercy of the Army, free at the same time from premature attack, and under an authority with whom Cromwell was in close and special relationship.*

* There is necessarily a considerable contradiction between the witnesses who have left accounts, and especially, as I have said, between Ashburnham and Berkeley, though the facts remain plainly enough in themselves. Thus Ashburnham, writing long afterwards, tells us that the King himself had desired to go to the Isle of Wight; but Berkeley contradicts this, and indeed the obvious facts are against this, especially Ashburnham's own testimony of Charles's despairing cry that he was undone when he heard that the Governor had come to take him. We must remember that later narratives were all written under the shadow of the tragedy that followed, and every loyal actor in that tragedy did what he could to shield himself from the accusation of having personally led the King into the trap.

Another point to be noted is that apologists for Cromwell talk of the King's having escaped "before the night guard was set." This is done in order to avoid the necessity of admitting Whalley's responsibility in laying the trap—and shows either bad faith on the part of the writers or their ignorance of conditions at Hampton Court. The sentries were doubled, and of course they were at their posts by day as well as by night. They would naturally be relieved at regular intervals; but when you relieve a sentry you do not leave his post unguarded, he remains there until he is replaced by his successor. The obvious issue by the back door over the garden to the Thames was left unguarded, and was deliberately left unguarded. Gardiner himself, who may be called our chief official apologist for Cromwell, suggests that he intended the King to escape in order that he might be free from the danger of assassination. He does not affirm as do less detailed writers, the impossible hypothesis that the King's escape came as a surprise to Whalley, and therefore to his cousin and master Cromwell. The only doubtful point is whether Ashburnham was a dupe or a knave, and from all

There is in the whole plan only one weak point, and that is the uncertainty of Hammond's temper, which, as we shall see, continued to give great anxiety to his close relation, patron and friend, Cromwell. But it was well worth risking Hammond's uncertainty as a servant, the danger of his obeying the Parliament rather than the Army, for the supreme advantage of having Charles firmly held and at the same time free from that immediate danger of assassination at the hands of fanatics which, had it taken place, would have ruined Cromwell himself and all his coming work.

We have now to deal with the three successive phases of that well-thought-out and admirably executed plan whereby the King was brought to the scaffold. Those three phases are as follows:

(1) The handling of the half-mutinous and increasingly radical Army which, if it had got out of hand, might have killed the King prematurely and, what was more, by mutiny wrecked everything and left the country in chaos.

(2) The overcoming of what Cromwell knew was already threatening and would later mature, a Royalist reaction in arms and a Scotch invasion to rescue the King.

(3) Supposing both (1) and (2) to be surmounted by Cromwell, the handling of the Parliament; either the obtaining from it a vote for the trial and execution of the King—or, failing this, the subjecting of it to the Army by force.

We shall see how Cromwell achieved all these three tasks triumphantly by careful manœuvre, by unceasing vigilance, by patience, by retreat when retreat was necessary, by the avoidance of exasperation, and, during the whole affair, by what was essential to success—the masking of his real intention; the playing of a moderate part.

we know of his character we can be morally certain that he was not a knave, but a dupe. He did not act as a decoy to lure the King to his doom, he was an unconscious agent of those who had caused it to be suggested that a flight towards Southampton Water would give the King his best chance of freedom.

That Cromwell played such a part caused him, we know, to be called a hypocrite by previous generations, who could not but believe that all his action during this critical period was designed for the obtaining of the power which ultimately fell into his hands. For the other later school, which, at the cost of all common sense desires to make Cromwell blameless, there is a much more difficult task to be performed. They have to reconcile what he said and wrote in public with what he *did*, with what he said and wrote in private and suggested to others. That task is an impossible one. The two sets of records are in glaring contradiction one to the other. All Cromwell wrote in private and *did* worked for the destruction of the King; what he said in public was, almost to the last moment, designed to prevent his appearing as the chief actor; for if he, the known master of the Army, had so appeared as the chief agent, the reaction against him would have been fatal.

The truth is that neither theory works, because Cromwell was neither on the one hand a saint, nor, on the other, a monster of ambitious cunning, sacrificing honour and morals to the one pursuit of power. He did dissimulate, of course, and continuously, in the course of those fourteen months. His outward aspect was the opposite of his inward intention. But his motive was not power. This contradiction between the outside and the inside was not the fruit of any native hypocrisy any more than is the concealment and false appearance practised by a commander in the conduct of a war; it was the necessary consequence of a plan which had to be carefully carried out amid successive dangers.

First then as to his dealings with the Army. The Army, I say, was half mutinous, and more and more permeated with that feeling for equality which used to be called in our politics "radicalism" or "republicanism." We have seen how this had been growing during the late summer and early autumn of 1647. When the news of the King's escape reached the Army there was an explosion. A general concentration and parade (or "rendezvous" as it was then called) was ordered by Fairfax to test the temper of the troops and to moderate that temper. The place of rendezvous was Corkbush Field near Ware, a couple of days' march north of London. Not all the regiments were summoned; two which were in a particularly excited state had been carefully omitted from the order. They came none the less, and their coming was in itself an act of mutiny. The date was the 15th of November, four days after Charles's flight and perhaps on the second day after that flight had become known to the whole Army. The mutinous regiments wore in their hat-bands papers of "The Agreement of the People"; one of them, Lilburne's Regiment, was in almost active mutiny, having driven out many of its officers.

This was the crisis of Cromwell's first peril in the business whereon he was now engaged. If the Army got out of hand, if mutiny spread, all was lost; the King might indeed be put to death, but put to death immediately and under conditions of such disorder that the cause for which the Civil War had been fought would collapse, and Cromwell himself would certainly go too.

He showed the most conspicuous courage. He rode up on his horse to the mutineers as they stood in rank. He had his drawn sword in his hand, and shouted to them to cast down the papers that they wore in their hats. One of the units, over-awed and cowed, obeyed; for there stood behind their General the Commander-in-Chief Fairfax and the mass of the troops whom he commanded. But Lilburne's regiment stood out.

It was then that Cromwell took personal action. By one account he laid hands on one of the mutineers himself; at any rate he saw to the arrest of the ringleaders; they were summarily convicted; three were condemned to death and forced to draw lots, and the one whom fortune served ill was summarily shot. The mutiny was quelled, and the moment of life or death for the Great Rebellion was passed.

Meanwhile the Parliament had drafted four Bills, embodying their demands upon the King. The first of these Bills laid it down that the command of the Militia (the only permanent armed force in the kingdom) should be vested in the Parliament for twenty years, and that its future after this limit should be determined by Parliament. By the second the King was asked to assent that all declarations he had made against the Parliament should be revoked; by the third all honours given by him since the outbreak of the Civil War should similarly be revoked; and by the fourth, Parliament was to be its own master, to adjourn when and where it chose.

When these four Bills should receive the Royal Assent and so become law the struggle would be at an end. The Bills were ready for presenting to the King in the Isle of Wight by the end of December.

But Charles was under no immediate compulsion, by giving his assent, to destroy the powers of the Monarchy and surrender the rights of his posterity, for he still had ready to his hand those allies whose presence had determined Cromwell to destroy the King—the Scotch. They prepared another document, or set of proposals, which came to be called "The Engagement." By this it was proposed that an experiment in Presbyterianism should be established in England for three years, after which the ordering of the Church should be arranged by the Assembly of Divines and twenty members nominated by the King himself. A certain proportion of Scottish notables were to be received into the King's Council, all Armies were to be suppressed, and equality of trade and the rest between the two nations established. These proposals were to be put before the English Parliament and Army. Should the Army refuse, the Scotch would pledge themselves to bring their forces into England and re-establish the Royal power, at the same time publishing a declaration demanding the aid of all loyal Englishmen.

Charles signed "The Engagement" on the 26th of December, and two days later rejected the four Bills of Parliament.

There followed a very sharp change in his position. From being treated with respect and as a free man he found himself subjected to rigorous restraint in Carisbrooke Castle. Ashburnham and Berkeley were dismissed; and on the 3rd of December, the remnant of the Commons, by a vote of 141 to 91,* declared they would receive no more Addresses from the King.

As the news spread, both of the King's treatment and of the break with Parliament, ominous symptoms of rebellion in favour of the prisoner began to appear. All England was shocked at seeing the King treated as though he were a criminal. He had indeed been the captive first of the Scotch and then of the Parliament and then of the Army, but the outward respect paid to him had at least been sufficient and the mass of Englishmen believed that he would in the long run be restored to power. These new indignities and all they meant roused a new spirit in his favour, and it was present everywhere. There had already been troubles in Kent against the Puritanical Government which forbade the observance of Christmas Day and public games. In the fear of further developments the first act of official violence was accomplished.

A loyal young gentleman of the name of Burley, shocked at the treatment of the King, had the drum beaten at Newport and proposed to rescue him. He was easily mastered, and for attempting to save his Sovereign was condemned and later butchered as a traitor. The incident is sometimes treated as a detail, for the rising was on a very small scale and futile; but it was very important as provoking the first act of terror— a declaration as it were, that the Revolution now regarded itself as the Government *de facto*, and any action taken against it to save the man whom the vast mass of Englishmen still called their King, as treason punishable by death.

It was during this passage to a new state of things, and on

* The full House of Commons would have been more than double these numbers; 493 had sat at the opening of the Long Parliament.

the same day that the House of Commons voted its refusal to continue negotiations with Charles, that Cromwell wrote to Hammond a letter of high significance. He warns his "dear Robin"—in that turgid style of which he was the victim—that he must stand by the Army; he must not vacillate. He urges him, implores him, half bullies him, for he knows how important is the issue. He talks of Hammond's hesitations in the matter of Charles as "temptations," he bids him remain "in the strength of the Lord." Indeed, Cromwell is very nervous about Hammond. After all, he had been appointed by the Parliament, and the Army hardly yet felt itself strong enough to do what it willed with the Governor of the Isle of Wight—that was to come. And if this jailer of the King should prove too kind or should previously insist upon the legal rights of Parliament as against the Army, Charles might be saved.

At any rate, by this opening of the year 1648 Cromwell could be fairly sure that, with the Army at least, his position was re-established. Mutiny had been suppressed; and though there was still this violent demand for immediate justice upon the King, and though therefore Cromwell's parade of continued negotiation still put him into some danger from the soldiers, the first obstacle may fairly be said to have been surmounted. There would be no immediate assassination of Charles, nor on the other hand any immediate release.

But now arose the second obstacle, and it was to prove a formidable one—Royalist reaction, rebellion upon every side, and invasion from Scotland to save the King.

The first significant date in this second phase, apart from grumblings and smouldering local riots, was the 22nd of February, 1648. On that day, Poyer, the Commander of Pembroke Castle, being ordered to hand over his charge to a successor, refused to do so—on the plea that the arrears of his pay had become too great and that a protest was needed. Ten days later the Duke of Hamilton at the first meeting of the Scottish Parliament obtained their support for a policy of invading England in the Royalist cause. All that month the effort increased to raise a large Army north of the Border; as the fighting season approached with the advent of spring the peril both in England and from beyond the frontier grew greater.

Just as it was about to break, Cromwell at some unknown date (but presumably towards the end of April) made a very able move. He summoned a meeting of officers at St. Albans where they should wrestle with God, examine their consciences, enjoy a feast of religious enthusiasm, and discover whether they had naught with which to reproach themselves. Especially he, Cromwell, would search his heart and make free confession if he had transgressed in any way. They met, they wrestled with God for three days—amid those transports of religious emotion which only the witnesses of a revival meeting can understand. They shed tears, they cried aloud—and Cromwell rehabilitated himself for good and all with the mass of the most sincere and even for the moment with the most republican, by his penitence if ever from carnal motives he had seemed to compromise in the matter of Charles Stuart. Even as they thus wept and writhed and suffered all the agonies of the Divine, news came that the storm had broken. There in South Wales where Poyer had defied their power the mass of the population had risen; not only Pembroke Castle but two key castles besides had been seized; the war of reaction, the war for the saving of the King, was well alight.

They did not separate without setting down in words that which was meant to bind Cromwell (though indeed had they known it, he needed no binding!) and they affirmed, none dissenting—least of all Cromwell—that, "Charles Stuart, that man of Blood, be called to an account for the blood he had shed."

Cromwell had taken the brakes off. With the Army now solidly behind him he prepared to master the new war.

The trial was to be severe. This novel idea of imprisoning the King, the evident and growing intention of sacrificing him, had moved all England. How large the fanatical faction might be which, outside the Army, would approve the dreadful end now vaguely surmised, we cannot tell; but it is certain that it can only have been a very small proportion of the English people. Resistance to unaccustomed taxation was natural enough and was one thing; to rise in armed rebellion was another; for the victorious rebels to usurp sovereign power was yet another, and far more violent, innovation, contrary to the traditions of the country. To imprison the sacred person of the King was a step much more extraordinary and therefore less tolerable than all that had preceded it: but the last extreme, the killing of the King, would be something almost inconceivable to the average Englishman outside the peculiar spirit of the Army itself and their more fanatical supporters.

Troubles broke out all over the place. The Scotch were arming during March, they were expected to join the northern Royalists in a few weeks; we have seen how South Wales had risen by the beginning of May. And—gravest symptom of all—the Fleet was disaffected. Revolutions often begin with sailors because it is more difficult to prevent their combining, living as they do at close quarters and in small units and their technical skill being indispensable to those who command them. The fine Navy which the King had so wisely built up during his days of power had, as we know, been betrayed to the Revolution and the crews had to do as they were told by their officers. But long arrears of pay moved the crews to revolt. No one knew when a naval mutiny might break out; and of all men Cromwell must have seen better than any other what the loss of the command of the sea would mean. It would mean the final loss of Ireland, the impossibility of conducting prolonged operations in Scotland, and almost certainly, sooner or later, invasion in the Royalist cause.

Had the general Royalist rising been properly timed and co-ordinated, with Hamilton able to march at once from the north, it would have succeeded. As it was the popular movement was not only premature but haphazard. In most places there was nothing more effective than riots, and the more serious movement in Kent was not organised to act until a fortnight after the first defeat of the Welsh rebels. It was defeated within ten days by Fairfax. What remained of the Royalist force crossed the Thames and, hoping to find recruitment in the Eastern Counties, occupied Colchester. The town was ill provisioned, and Fairfax sat down before it to reduce it by starvation.

Meanwhile Cromwell was away in South Wales with two regiments of horse and three of foot, attempting to reduce the one place which still held out there, Pembroke under Poyer. It was at the very moment of the Kentish rising that he prepared to storm Pembroke. He had with him that raving chaplain to his forces, Hugh Peters—who confidently prophesied that the walls of Pembroke would fall like those of Jericho— For why? For the obvious reason that they had against them the Living God.

The attempt failed ignominiously. Cromwell complained that it was the fault of the scaling ladders, which were too short, and estimated the loss of the Royalists as greater than his own. Cromwell had twenty-three dead on his side when he gave up the effort, but Poyer had lost only four men. The thing was to drag on for six weeks, and when Poyer did surrender on the 11th of July it was not the result of storming but of starvation.

Already Hamilton had crossed the Border, and there was soon to be in the North an army formidable, in size at least, against which Cromwell must gather what forces he could, and take his chance with certainly inferior numbers. I shall describe under another head (that of "The Scottish Campaigns") his advance to the Midlands, to Doncaster, his march across the Pennines and his decisive victory at Preston, which took place in the middle of August.

Colchester still held out; the threatened mutiny in the Fleet had materialised; six ships had dismissed their unwilling officers, declared for the King and put themselves under the Prince of Wales. They had sailed over to join him in Holland just as the siege of Pembroke began. The ships remaining at the disposal of the Parliament were not fitted out; Warwick, their Commander, was unable to act; if the Royalist ships, swollen to nine with others added under the young Prince's command, had boldly sailed for the Isle of Wight the King might yet have been saved. But unfortunately the trouble with all successful mutineers is that they have tasted power and may use it against their new masters. The sailors insisted on meeting and bringing over their fellows from the Parliamentary fleet, which during the month of August, lay in the Thames. They sailed therefore into the estuary of London River even as Colchester was at its last gasp (it surrendered on the 27th of August) and just after the news of Cromwell's great victory in the North had reached the capital. The Royalist ships were actually in contact with Warwick up the Thames, there was little doubt that the discontented Parliamentary crews would have gone over or have fought in confusion when—as happens so often in the history of England—the wind took charge. On the 30th of August it blew a furious gale from the north-west, there was no beating up against it, the Royalist craft had no choice but to run down river; they were at the end of their provisions, especially of water, and crossed the North Sea to replenish. Within a week the last stronghold in Kent, Sandown Castle, had surrendered—and the Second Civil War was over.

But it had been a near thing. And though so many accidents and so much individual talent had been at work to procure the result, though Lambert in the Pennines, Fairfax in the south-east had contributed, it was plain that the decisive blow had been delivered by Cromwell himself: at Preston he had crushed the Scotch invasion a fortnight before the ships had sailed away, and ten days before the surrender of Colchester.

[ 227 ]

He was greater than ever; more than ever the glory of the soldiery, and more than ever able to carry out his plan.

To that plan the third obstacle remained; the Commons, and also, in the background of the picture, that permanent cause of anxiety and annoyance, the doubts upon the attitude of Hammond. We have seen how Cromwell had appealed to him with vehemence, with insistence, with affection, with exhortation, to stand fast and hold the King tight. In the preceding December Cromwell had himself gone over to the Island to make as certain as he could by personal contact that "dear Robin" should not fail him. But "dear Robin" was an uncertain factor. He was peevish, selfish, lacking in decision—and, what was more, he knew his price.

As early as April, 1648, before the Royalist rebellion had grown serious, Cromwell had written him yet another letter which is very significant. He tells the young man that "his business is done"—that is, the House has been persuaded to give him money. His personal pay was doubled, he was given £6,000 as an immediate "refresher"; £3,000 a year was settled upon him and his heirs—really, even for a fine young officer still on the right side of thirty, this ought to have been enough to make him grateful, and even obediently so! True, the money was voted by the Parliament, but it was voted at a moment when the Parliament and the Army were standing together in their fear of an approaching Royalist rising and the Scottish invasion.

But in spite of all this Hammond remained what he had always been—a possible cause of failure. The time was not yet ripe to get rid of him, and yet so long as he was in command of the Isle of Wight he might let the King go—or at any rate refuse to hand him over when the time should arrive for the carrying out by Oliver and the Army of that dreadful purpose which was so steadily pursued.

Now that the fear of a Royalist success was over the Parliament showed a certain independence; what I have called the third obstacle in the way of Oliver's plan, an independent Commons at Westminster, grew more formidable with every week that passed. On the 24th of August, though Colchester had not surrendered yet, and though the Royalist ships still threatened the Thames, the resolution to receive no more Addresses from the King was repealed. On the 18th of September fifteen Commissioners were named, five Peers and ten from the Commons, to renew the negotiations with Charles; nor did the Army yet feel itself powerful enough to prevent so dangerous a renewal of that experiment. Hammond let Charles go to Newport on parole. For forty days the discussions dragged on, and even after that their prolongation was voted by the Commons. But though the spirit of the Commons rose—or their obstinacy—everything was making for the reality of the Army's power. In mid-October there was drawn up "The Army's Remonstrance," which was more or less a reassertion of the old terms of the "Agreement of the Nation" a year before. On the 6th of November there was written to Hammond, almost certainly by Cromwell, a curious and deeply interesting letter; it is very secret; odd fictitious names are used, but its involved repetitive style is almost unmistakably Cromwell's—and the burden of it is still the same. "Dear Robin" is implored to stick to it, not to give way, not to doubt where his true allegiance lies; he is told how much depends upon him. In his eagerness the writer says a little less about the Lord God than usual; he goes straight to the point.

In that moment of November things began to move more rapidly; the Remonstrance of the Army was presented to Parliament, or rather to the Commons, to whom alone it was addressed. Fairfax had had to yield.

This "Remonstrance" was an enormous document, but note its operative words: "The capital and grand author of all the troubles . . . should be speedily brought to justice for the treason, blood and mischief of which he has been guilty." And we have of course all the radical demands for new Parliaments with supreme power, the right to elect any future King—and so on.

A large majority in the Commons had the courage to throw it out (a majority of 34 in a House of 154 members; but in a second division a majority of 67 in a House of 183 members—let it again be remembered that these numbers mean less than half the full House of Commons).

Cromwell, while these things were toward, was in the north. He proceeded thither after his great victory at Preston, determined to be present in person among the Scots, to occupy their capital and to support with his troops the anti-Royalist faction, among whom Argyll was the principal figure. Leaving Lambert to garrison what one might call alternatively the conquered or the allied country north of the Border, he came south leisurely enough. He was determined to the very end not to appear in the front of the proceedings. It was from Knottingley, near Pontefract, on the 25th of November, that he wrote what all who desire to understand him should regard as the capital document in all his correspondence.

It was yet another last letter to "dear Robin," morally wrestling with him to make him stick to his allegiance and to make as sure as sure could be that the King would be kept in a tight grasp, ready to be handed over when the moment should come. It is in Cromwell's usual confused, redundant, difficult manner, but full of energy as well as of exhortation. He bids the all-important but uncertain Governor to comfort himself with St. James's Epistle, showing how, if he will but persevere to the end, Hammond shall be "made perfect." He "thanks God through Jesus Christ Our Lord," he "waits for redemption," he warns "dear Robin" that "our fleshly reasonings ensnare us"—so if Robin should reason that his allegiance was rather to the Parliament than to Cromwell and his soldiers, that would certainly be very carnal. He begs him to consider the manifest signs God has given to show which, between the two sides, Parliament or Cromwell, enjoys the favour of Jehovah.

If ever a man was dragged by the power of the spirit to do the right thing by a cousin and friend in a crisis, to hold the victim firmly down, and to have him ready for delivery when the order should come, that man was Robert Hammond.

It is probable that the letter was never delivered, for the plan necessitated alternative action. The letter might conceivably have got to the Isle of Wight in three days, but it is unlikely; and meanwhile what had happened in the Isle of Wight was this:

Fairfax and the Council of the Army had sent one "Eyre" or "Ewer" (the name is also spelt "Euer") with a Warrant to "seek the King's person" and "proceed with him according to Justice." That warrant Eyre showed to Hammond in the Island on the 27th of November, and there accompanied it an order direct to Hammond himself to come and discuss matters at headquarters. The poor dupe went off, possibly on the next day, possibly on the morning of the day after, making for Windsor, where he was due on Wednesday, the 29th of November. That day, at Farnham, he was put under arrest—and thus was the great problem of Hammond's vacillation settled. Sure hands now held the King.

Charles in those very days in Newport had been going through the last of the negotiations with the Parliament, saying sadly that they were certainly futile. On the 28th the Commissioners left. Rolph, by origin a cobbler, had taken Hammond's place. Charles had been hurried away, and on the 1st of December he was in Hurst Castle on the Hampshire shore, an isolated blockhouse of thick stone walls, with no approach save along a narrow spit of shingle hundreds of yards in length, and cut off from all human aid.

I will not here repeat the story of the King's *via dolorosa*, to Windsor, to London, to Westminster Hall; nor the details of the trial. But I will put as clearly as I can the succession of points in these two months, between the enforcement of the King in Hurst Castle and his death, which concern Oliver. Those points are few, but they are clear and all-important to our judgment of the man himself and his circumstance.

We left Cromwell still in the north, writing that confused, long, insistent, excited letter to Hammond, imploring him to hold the victim fast—until the time for cutting his throat should be come. That letter, as we have seen, Hammond probably never received. We have also seen that it is of little interest whether he did or no, because he no longer had power to obey or refuse—he had been arrested and was off the stage.

On the very day which saw the King shut up in Hurst Castle the Army moved towards London, and on the morrow, Saturday, the 2nd of December, it occupied Westminster. Hewson and his Regiment occupied the Palace of Whitehall. He was the man who was to be afterwards remembered for the massacre of Dunbar, and he was the man who spat in the King's face during his trial.

Though they were thus already in the hands of the Army, the politicians in the House plucked up a strange courage. It was the flare-up of the candle before its extinction. They boldly debated in the very teeth of the soldiers during all the Monday, whether they should accept the King's propositions or no. They debated all night. In the early morning of Tuesday, the 5th of December, by 140 to 104, they decided to accept the King's offer. It was as much as to say that, with the knife at their throats, they still refused to yield to the Army and to Cromwell. It was a very large House, nearly the full number of those who could have been present of all that revolutionary part of the Commons who continued to call themselves "The House." All this while Cromwell, from the conclusion of his northern campaign, had been advancing slowly towards the capital, and was now in touch with London. He could easily have been in Westminster while the debates were going on—he preferred to keep his distance.

On Wednesday, the 6th of December, came the exclusion from the House by force of all those who might conceivably have voted in favour of Charles. It is known to history as "Pride's Purge." Still Cromwell remains in the background, close at hand; but when the thing is done, on the morrow, Thursday, the 7th of December, he comes into London and is at the pains of writing to say that the thing was due to an inspiration from the Almighty. On Friday the Army seized the treasure at Goldsmith's Hall, upon which hitherto the Parliament had relied, paraded all day up and down the streets of the City to keep it in awe, and turned St. Paul's into a barracks for their common use. It so remained for more than eleven years, till the Restoration.

All this while Cromwell is still playing in the open the part of the moderate who wonders whether one ought to go to extremes. Things are still ticklish. To provoke reaction is still dangerous. All the great town lies there like a powder-barrel which may explode; and if once it were believed that he were the hand behind it all, he being known to be the true master-spirit of the Army, the powder-barrel *might* explode.

On the 19th poor Charles was taken off from Hurst Castle, spending a miserable dis-crowned Christmas at Windsor, and there received his fellow-victim, the Duke of Hamilton—the prisoner whose head also was marked to fall. Soon "they were parted and suffered to have no discourse."

Ten days earlier Cromwell himself had visited Hamilton, with the object of discovering further names of those who in England had abetted the effort of the Scottish Army to save the King. The Duke refused to betray, and thereby sacrificed his life; but probably it would have been lost in any case, for no pledge was now observed. He did well to keep his honour.

On Twelfth Day, the 6th of January, the unhappy last and pitiful group of forty-six commoners, sitting in their big empty room as puppets of the Army, debated with an absurd formality the arrangements for the King's doom. Even so, nearly half of them—twenty—hesitated. But the solemn rules of what had once been an Assembly and was now nothing still demanded a majority; and by a majority of six they passed an Act that the Lords (the fifteen remaining) who had already rejected the idea of a trial, did not count—and of course the King did not count. They set up a court of 135 persons, of which Bradshaw was to be the President.

Now three days after this, which one might think the very last decisive act, Cromwell was still playing his part. For it is on the 9th of January that we have report of a most significant thing that he said; the report has been challenged, but, after all, the words were noted within forty-eight hours, and they may fairly be accepted. "If any man whatsoever have carried out this design of deposing the King and disinheriting his posterity, or if any man still have such a design, he must be the greatest traitor and rebel in the world; but since the Providence of God has cast this upon us I cannot but submit to Providence, though I am not yet prepared to give you my advice."

And there you have the end of the comedy, or, let us say, of the strategy preliminary to action. Contact is established and the stroke is to be delivered. Indeed, how like a campaign has been all the procedure of this soldier in accomplishing his plan! The long approach, the overcoming of obstacles, the restraint, the convergence, the concealment of movements, the last rapid concentration—and then the blow.

There is no doubt at all how Cromwell acts from that moment on. We have the testimony of Algernon Sydney, telling us what words he used from man to man behind the public façade: "I tell you we will cut off the King's head with the Crown on it."

The Court meets, Cromwell is there among the first on the list of the roll, sitting conspicuous, almost next to Bradshaw—and all men know that his spirit informs the whole affair. The King refuses to acknowledge the authority of that Court; even of the nominated members only half have attended. But Cromwell is their master, and under his inspiration all goes forward; there is no more need for finesse, the battle is joined.

On the very last significant day, Saturday, the 27th of January, after the victim's protest, eloquent from circumstance and moving many among those who though already engaged hesitated to strike the final blow, one of those nominated as Judges, John Downe, could be heard protesting that he would not be party to the crime. He sat just behind Cromwell in the second row and next to Cromwell's brother-in-law, who should have kept him silent. That protest might have started a stampede, for not only did men dread in their consciences what they were doing—but they feared the future, and with good reason. But Cromwell knew well enough that a battle engaged must be won or lost, he turned round angrily to the interrupter and asked him if he were mad? Downe had this much success, that the Court adjourned; even one of its members protesting necessitated that.

When it came to deciding the Warrant for the coming death, Downe had not the strength to resist; yet it was a moment when many men abstained; only fifty-nine could be got to sign, and of these some have told us how they were constrained. When the thing was over the relief upon the strained nerves of Oliver was so great that he fell back upon one of those bits of horseplay which, time and again in his life, signalised such relaxation of tension. He played the fool with the disreputable Marten, one of the least responsible and most eager in the project—he daubed the fellow's face with ink from his pen.

Upon Tuesday, the 30th of January, all being prepared for the King's death, and the masked executioners ready, an order was still necessary for these to act. Cromwell was in the room of Ireton, his son-in-law; Colonel Harrison also was there, and Colonel Huncks. It was for this last man, or one of those present, to sign. Since all seemed reluctant, Cromwell turned to Huncks and told him to sign the Order. He refused. It lay there still unsigned upon a little table, with ink and paper and pen ready by. Then Cromwell himself stooped over and wrote, calling him who had refused "a froward peevish fellow." It was the last action. And thus, after all the delays for seeking an executioner and for getting the Order signed, things were ready for the headsman.

Meanwhile, lest Fairfax, who refused to judge the King and whose wife had made her famous protest, should, as the nominal head of the Army, attempt a rescue, Cromwell had put sentries at the door of his house in Queen Street, near Lincoln's Inn Fields.

There is a story the witness to which may be believed or disbelieved; it is of so dramatic a sort that many doubt it; but there is nothing impossible in it. It runs thus:

In the room where the King's body was lying at evening a figure entered which the watcher recognised as Cromwell's. He who so came in lifted the veil and looked upon the face, which was quiet even after such a death, and was heard to mutter, "Cruel necessity!"

## CROMWELL'S CAR

### SATIRICAL PRINT

Cromwell holds Liberty and Church at the point of the sword. The Kingdoms of England, Scotland and Ireland are asleep. The chariot, drawn by
dragons and driven by the devil, is running over Charles I whose head is
cut off.

# IRELAND

## I

### THE APPROACH

IT was upon the 10th of July, 1649, that Cromwell left London by the road for Bristol to take up the Irish command, accompanied out of the capital by crowds, as for a conquest. Four days later Bristol was reached; but it was a month (the 13th of August) before he could sail with the van of his force of thirty-two ships from Milford Haven; nor did the main body under his son-in-law Ireton take the sea till two days later, the 15th of August; while Hugh Peters, that Chaplain and prophet of the Puritans, came last with twenty sail. The force suffered from bad weather, many were prostrated, there was some confusion, and it was not till Friday, the 31st of August, that the muster was held outside Dublin and 17,000 men answered to the roll.

We must appreciate the conditions under which the abortive tragedy began: tragedy, for it was the profound wounding, mutilation and attempted murder of a nation; abortive, because that end was not fully reached. Neither the nationhood of Ireland nor the religion of which it is a chief custodian were destroyed.

The moral and material conditions under which the effort opened were these:

On the moral side the English Army and its Commander were beginning a Crusade. It was eight years since the great rising in the North of Ireland, the driving out of those who had usurped one-half of the native lands, despoiled their rightful native possessors and imposed a hated and alien religion. What the effect of that rising upon English opinion had been

[ 237 ]

we have already seen. The events of 1641 stood in the minds of Englishmen—and not of the Puritan faction alone—as an abomination, the letting loose of Hell on Earth. Whenever political or racial passions are violently excited, and especially when the religious feeling which commonly lies at the root of such excitements is working openly, the incredible is believed. We may argue as to the limits of this belief, we may discuss how far popular passion reaches the better-instructed ranks of society, how much of the error is due to wilful blindness—and so forth; but we all know from experience, and no one better than this generation, nearest to the Great War, that men under the influence of such emotions pass judgments hardly sane. In this case those emotions had been exasperated by an element of monstrosity; it seemed *monstrous*, out of nature, that the native Irish should even for a moment have obtained the upper hand over the plantation; nor did what remained of Catholic England sympathise with the rebels, still less the official Anglican England. As for the large Puritan minority now in power, and informing with its spirit the conscious and vocal part of the Army, its feeling upon such topsy-turvydom was of an intensity beyond description. To take vengeance upon so outrageous an inversion of all accepted order seemed to them a cosmic necessity. Further, this Catholic thing which they hated with a hatred intensified by national feeling and maddened by wounded pride, concentrated upon the Priests of the Irish.

But it is an error to see only a frenzied vengeance for 1641 in Cromwell's Irish massacres and robberies. There was another factor equally strong; the factor of fear. That Catholic menace, all-important to the Englishman in England, reposed not only upon the traditions of an English minority but, in a different fashion, upon Ireland. Ireland lying upon the flank of England was a standing monument of that menace, and this was felt so acutely that nothing short of the destruction of Ireland as a nation and therefore of the national religion therein, whereby tne nation lived, could allay the dread. It was this, combined with the memory of the rising, that inflamed such zeal.

The attackers therefore enjoyed upon the moral side that factor of absolute unity which is among the strongest factors in the conduct of a war; they acted with one motive and as one soul: that motive at its highest potential, that soul at its most vivid excitement.

In a less degree the remains of the Royal Army in Ireland under Ormonde's command attracted vengeance on itself. It was to be destroyed; not only because it was part of that general force against which Cromwell and his like had victoriously fought a great war of many years, but much more because it was now in alliance with the Irish nation—which it had been its main function in earlier years to garrison and keep down. Though so many of the officers were English, and among these a large proportion Protestant, like Ormonde himself, though even in the rank and file large bodies were in the same case and only certain fractions were of purely Irish recruitment, the Revolutionary feeling against it was far stronger than had been the feeling against those who served the King in England.

The moral situation on the opposing side, Royalist and Native, was of that confused sort which has been present in all Irish affairs since the success of the Reformation in Britain. It was not even clear-cut into three divisions, of sympathy with Puritanism, sympathy with (or service of) the Royalist cause, and sympathy with the traditions of Irish nationhood. For within the last two of these categories there were bewildering subdivisions. In the diminished and ill-equipped Royalist force were many among the rank and file ready enough to join an English Army of any kind rather than fight for a cause which was in part Irish. Between the officers of that body also there was the gulf of religion, Catholics and anti-Catholics commanding side by side; while in the third element, which of course as far as numbers went was the vast majority

(I mean the Nationalist body), there was every degree of feeling from indifference to intense nationalism, from passionate attachment to the national religion to the rare cases of those who, though not Catholic, had begun to hold nationalist feelings. There was also a gradation in the sacrifices which men were prepared to make; townsmen of the old corporations who could not hold office as Catholics, townsmen of the new who feared to see their commerce destroyed and their wealth looted, and the great bulk of people who lay outside the towns and lived by pasture and tillage were prepared for very different degrees of resistance. There was present, therefore, that fatal element of feud.

Add to all this the fact that upon the Irish side of the coming struggle there was the overshadowing sense of military inferiority; the feeling that comes upon numbers who can depend only upon their numbers and know their weakness in equipment. There you have roughly the balance between the spirits of the forces now about to engage. Upon the one side unity, a common intensity of feeling, an undoubted military genius in command, but difficult communications by sea, distance from their base, fear of the coming winter, but a sense of presumable victory: upon the other side numbers, but ill equipped; the memory of a recent successful rising, but no one common purpose; and yet, running through and inspiring a sufficient majority, fierce civil and religious determination. Such being the moral factors in the antagonists, let us consider the material.

On the material side the Irish suffered from numerical inferiority in trained men. Next, an absence of sufficient medium and heavy mobile artillery; next, a dispersion of such force as was available into a number of garrisons. Lastly, a lack of instruction and training in the rapidly developing art of fortification.

This—the lack of instruction in fortification—we have seen at work in England, where preparation to receive bombardment from heavy artillery by the proper use of earth was not yet understood, as it was already understood on the Continent. But if this was true of England it was far more true of Ireland; all the work of the Cromwellian army in Ireland consisted in breaking down stone walls, and the breaking down of such defences by the use of a siege train such as Cromwell had with him was a matter of course. They were certain to be destroyed, most of them at once, all of them in the long run.

Cromwell's heavy guns, though not numerous, were the only thing of the kind apparent in that field. His opponents had nothing to set against them. He could set up his batteries in security, certain that they would not be silenced by enemy fire nor even seriously molested, for they had the superior range. The war in Ireland was bound to be a war of sieges, and such sieges must inevitably turn against the besieged.

The dispersion of garrisons was necessary as an original arrangement because the issue was not clear-cut between the invaders and the invaded, but was, even at its simplest, a triple quarrel between the invader, the Royal forces, and the Irish themselves, whom the Royal forces had been occupied in subjecting to an alien will. As against these material disadvantages the defensive in the coming campaign had two things in its favour: First, the peril for the invaders, under canvas, of campaigning in the bad season; secondly, the individual fighting qualities of Irishmen. It was due to the second of these that after a breach had been effected the defenders were to be found holding that breach with sufficient vigour to prevent the immediate storming of the town, and under cover of such defence putting up new obstacles behind the gap in the wall. But a mere defensive is always defeated; the other favourable factor—that of weather—was of more serious importance.

Cromwell's army would have difficulty in living upon the country. It was not, as it had been during the Civil Wars at home, provided with ample civilian resources at every turn; its morale was affected by the sense of distance from Eng-

[ 241 ]

land, by memories of the difficulty of the journey, and by the interruption of supplies: therefore Cromwell, who had already begun operations too late in the year, felt himself anxiously pressed by time.

## II

### DROGHEDA

The first task before Cromwell was that of getting elbow-room along the coast opposite England, and the first step in this must be the reduction of Drogheda, a walled and garrisoned town commanding the crossing of the obstacle of the Boyne on the road leading to the north out of Dublin, and itself two long days' march from that capital (twenty-nine miles). He could not leave Dublin to use his army elsewhere until Drogheda was reduced.

There was some question at first on the side of the Royalist army and the Irish Confederation whether the place should be held or no; at a council of war just before the appearance of Oliver it was decided to hold it. Ormonde therefore left within its walls a garrison of 2,500 men under Aston, an English Catholic. The officers of this garrison were divided in religion and in race, some Catholic and some Protestant, some English, some Irish. But the bulk of the rank and file were of Irish recruitment and Catholic, as we know from Ormonde's own testimony. It is important to remember this in reading what follows for two reasons: first, that the contrary is often asserted from a general but erroneous idea that the King's army in Ireland, being organised for an English cause, was itself English in recruitment; second, because it helps to account for what followed on the taking of the City. The artillery within Drogheda was insignificant; Aston commanded three gunners and their mates, while even within a week of the siege they had no round-shot at all.

It was on the Monday, the 3rd of September (and the date

is to be noted) that the throwing up of earth for two batteries was begun to the south-east of the town walls, that is, on the side towards the sea and against that part of Drogheda which lay beyond the river Boyne—for the bulk of the town lay to the north of the Boyne. The heavy guns had to be landed from the ships which had brought them up and it took some days to emplace them. The first shots were fired on Sunday the 9th. It was not till the batteries had thus opened that, on Monday, the 10th, Cromwell summoned the town. The guns made two breaches in the course of that day, and by the afternoon, about five o'clock, the assault began. It was somewhat hampered by the fact that the breaches were not complete, but the lower courses of the stone walls, six foot thick, still standing. The garrison put up a very fine defence against the foot (for the horse could not be used), but before dusk an entry was forced and heavy fighting in the streets began.

It is here that the chief question concerning Cromwell in connection with this business appears. Everyone has heard of the massacre of Drogheda; it is one of the outstanding dates in the history of England. Not only were the whole garrison put to the sword, but all the civilian population as well save for some insignificant remnant. The unarmed men and women and children who took refuge in the great Church of St. Mary had it burnt above their heads, Cromwell's soldiers picked up children and held them before their bodies as a protection, and the Catholic clergy were (to use Cromwell's own phrase) "knocked on the head promiscuously." There was a general murder of men, women and children on every side. The more horrible details, although they would emphasise the character of that day, and therefore Cromwell's own responsibility, I omit—such as the ghastly story told by Wood of the murder of a wealthy young woman pleading for her life, and the burning—amid shrieks and oaths of agony—of the man on the steeple of the church, which Cromwell himself notes with curious particularity.

The massacre went on for five days, such a prolongation being due presumably to the fact that there was a continuous seeking out of men and women still in hiding. The whole place was, of course, pillaged, and the Church plate—a rich reward— went with the rest, stuff peculiarly suited to the loot, for it came from the polluted altars of Baal.

But the matter for examination in a study of Cromwell is not all this, but the following three points:

First, the excesses of cruelty, compared with anything that had happened in the English Civil War; secondly, the personal responsibility of Cromwell; and thirdly—what is really the gravest point of all—whether the bulk of the murders were not committed after the victims had been promised their lives by him?

As to the first point, we can be quite clear. Drogheda was the earliest opportunity that Cromwell found in this war of giving free rein to his religion. He was dealing for the first time not with an isolated post such as Basing House, but with a whole population that was Catholic. It was to him what I have already called it, a crusading action, and counts with the extermination of religious opponents in religious wars throughout the ages. The feeling was here exasperated, of course, by the memory of the rebellion eight years before, but the horror had its root in the feeling that the Catholic was of another world: of the Pit: a thing to be destroyed. No incident in all Cromwell's life illustrates this passion of his more clearly.

On the second point, that Cromwell was personally responsible is also certain. He openly said this himself. He did not even plead somewhat obscurely (as he had pleaded at Basing House) that it was the soldiers who were not to be denied. He advances the idea that things of this kind were really for the best because they would shorten the resistance of the enemy by striking terror. He alludes to it only two days after in his summoning of Dundalk, saying that the garrison of Drogheda by not accepting his summons "had brought their evil upon them," and said that if they of Dundalk "refuse this offer and that which you like not befalls you, you will know whom to blame." He writes under his own hand that those who had fled to the Church for sanctuary "to the number of near 1,000 of them were put to the sword, flying there for safety"—a misfortune which he regards as a punishment for their wickedness in having had Mass there on the Sunday before. There is really no room for dispute upon the motive and character of Cromwell's orgy of killing on this occasion. He writes with his own hand relative to Aston and his men on the mill mount, "Our men were ordered by *me* to put them all to the sword"; and again, "*I* forbade them to spare any that were in arms in the town and I think they put to the sword about 2,000 men" (this last, of course, very much less than the truth).

The massacre of Drogheda was Cromwell's; he must carry it in history as his deed, just as Tilly must carry the sack of Magdeburg.

The third point, the question of Quarter, can also be put beyond dispute, though naturally there has been more active discussion upon it, for the disgrace of a breach of faith is indelible. Everyone knows that there was an indiscriminate slaughter on the first day and that nearly all human beings within Drogheda were murdered, some of them in cold blood, four or five days after the first storming. But had the lives of the defeated been promised to them on surrender? The evidence is clear enough. The affirmative is asserted by those who speak for the victims, and there is no contemporary denial of it upon the other side. "All the officers and soldiers were promised quarter to such as laid down their arms, and performed it as long as any place held out, which encouraged others to yield. But when they once had all in their power and feared no hurt, the word 'No Quarter' went round and the soldiers were forced, many of them against their will, to kill the prisoners." That is Ormonde. Arthur Aston, the commander, was killed, according to Inchiquin, after quarter given;

and Inchiquin, it must be remembered, was not at all a partisan of the side upon which he happened to be serving for the moment—rather the other way.

The estimate of the total number of victims varies of course, as is always the case in scenes of this kind; but there is plenty of contemporary evidence to show that it came very near to extermination. The contemporary anti-Catholic print of Cork, the "Mercury," tells us that only thirty were saved; the same figure is given by an independent witness, Ludlow, in his Memoirs, while Clarendon talks of "the universal massacre of the whole population." On the other hand there is evidence that two small bodies of men who surrendered in certain "towers" were only decimated and not slaughtered wholesale. Yet it matters little whether a hundred or two hundred or less than fifty were allowed to live; the whole mass of the place, soldiers, civilians, men, women and children alike disappeared. And the attempt to cast doubt on so plain an historical truth is mere advocacy. "The glory" (it need hardly be added) was given by Cromwell "to God alone." It is a phrase of his with which we shall become familiar.

## III

### WEXFORD

After the destruction of Drogheda to the north of Dublin the next place to destroy was Wexford to the south. When Wexford should be reduced, it would afford the most direct communication with England on the east coast, the base; further, Wexford was the harbour through which, as they had not been able to hold Dublin, the Royalists in Ireland still precariously obtained supplies. Seeing the superiority of the siege train, the reduction of Wexford, like the reduction of Drogheda, was more or less a matter of course, but what is to be remarked about the destruction of Wexford is the repetition of massacre.

[ 246 ]

Cromwell allowed a fortnight for settling affairs before he began this second expedition. For a man of his celerity that was a considerable interval, and it is not easy to understand why there was such delay. It was full autumn, and the better season had not many weeks to run.

It was not until the 23rd of September that the force set out, 4,000 foot and 1,600 mounted men, of whom a quarter were dragoons. He took with him a siege train of four guns, one a very large cannon firing a shot of over forty pounds, another a demi-cannon of more than the average size, and two smaller pieces. The march was along the coast, to reduce everything on the way so as to make the approach from England secure; the fleet followed alongside, as on the march to Drogheda. Cromwell rode forward previously towards Wexford, announcing his arrival, and promising every advantage for submission; he lived on the country, getting plenty of provisions, for he kept a strict discipline over his men and boasted there was no plunder. The whole march including the capture of Arklow took rather more than a week; the fleet was off Wexford by the 29th, and Cromwell's tents were pitched outside the walls of the town by Monday, October 1st. It had been a march not at all pressed—about ten miles a day.

Wexford had with reluctance admitted the small Royal garrison then within its walls. Ormonde, who had been reinforced, would have done what he could, but he was not trusted; the alliance with troops under English command was too recent and Ormonde's own record against the Irish national interests was too violent. As for Inchiquin, who was near by with two regiments of horse, nothing could be done with him for he was himself as unreliable as his troops, and moreover his officers prevented his giving any aid—he had a foot in the enemy's camp. Here was Wexford then with a very small garrison, and that unpopular with the townsmen, awaiting the attack, and not awaiting it in any mood of confidence; indeed it was said in Ormonde's surroundings that the citizens would have given up the town had it not been for the presence of the Royalist garrison. Cromwell, probably misunderstanding the situation rather than wilfully misrepresenting it, said that the citizens "trusted in their own strength." But that was not the reason for their refusal to accept more than these few Royalist regulars within their walls.

On Wednesday, the 3rd of October, the town was summoned, "to the use of the State of England," Cromwell adding the threat that if they did not yield the innocent might suffer with the guilty—meaning by the guilty, it may be presumed, the regular soldiery of the legitimist cause, who stood within Wexford to defend it against the Revolutionary army. He was told that he should have his answer on the morrow, by noon. Meanwhile the Mayor and Corporation sent out a present to Cromwell of white wine and whisky and strong beer, and Cromwell answered that he would wait for their reply.

Sinnott, the head of the Royalist garrison, kept his word, conferring with the Mayor and Corporation and with his own officers, and asked for a safe-conduct for his four negotiators, who were to discuss matters the next morning. Cromwell wrote back a bullying letter saying that it was not usual to have these negotiations between forces so unequal, and demanding an answer within an hour. Sinnott replied again, saying that he thought he had been civil, that he had no intention of surrendering without "capitulation or honourable terms," and that he was resolved to die honourably rather than accept Cromwell's attitude. And he reiterated his demand that negotiations should reopen at eight o'clock the next morning.

To this letter Cromwell refused a reply. But when Sinnott sent negotiators next day Cromwell allowed a safe-conduct, which was, of course, equivalent to admitting his willingness to treat. By the end of the week the town, somewhat reluctantly, admitted a certain further reinforcement from Ormonde, 1,500 more men.

All this took place while Cromwell had been unprepared

to act, because his siege train was not yet landed; but on the Saturday, October the 6th, he got his artillery and stores ashore from the ships; the four heavies were set up against the south end of the town opposite the castle, at a range of about 500 yards, and they opened fire early on the morning of Wednesday, the 10th, directing it against the castle, which stood just outside the walls on this side. By midday there were three great gaps in the defences, and Sinnott proposed terms of surrender.

Now from this point it behoves us to consider very carefully Cromwell's actions and motives. He appears to the one set of writers as guilty of common treason and horrible murder; to the other of course—as always—he is a bronze and marble hero. The truth is nearer the first judgment than the second, but it does not wholly coincide with that first judgment. Cromwell was guilty of treacherous conduct, and at last *condoned* wholesale murder; but though he at last *condoned* wholesale murder he did not take the initiative in it as he had at Drogheda.

It must be remembered that the conditions were quite different from those of Drogheda, since before the attack was delivered negotiations had begun and terms had been laid before the besieging General. The capitulations were in ten articles, demanding the fullest liberty and immunity for the surrendered place; but the gist of them in Cromwell's eyes consisted in the first three. These demanded (1) the uninterrupted liberty and profession of the Catholic religion, (2) the preservation of their property for the Catholic clergy including the religious of the monasteries, and (3) that the Bishop of the Catholic flock should remain in office. It is very important to note this point: on the one hand men making what seemed to them an obviously reasonable condition of surrender, and on the other hand a man receiving it to whom it was the demand of devils to continue their Covenant with Hell. Unless we are clear upon this contrast in mental condition we shall misjudge what followed.

The demand for the free exercise of their religion by the

Irish people in Wexford moved Cromwell to violence, even on paper. He talks of their "abominableness" and their "impudence." He writes to Sinnott, telling him "he had the patience" (to read the horror); that he would be brief; he would give quarter to the rank and file and their bare lives to the officers, and he promised that there should be no plunder. On all the rest he kept silent, and he gave them one hour to decide.

The garrison determined to resist. Wexford had better fortification than perhaps any other Irish walled city, for proper use had been made of earth, not indeed outside the walls as it should have been but within, and there was plenty of small artillery—no use of course against a siege train but ample to support resistance to storming parties. Ammunition was short, as it always was on the Irish side, though still sufficient for some days of action; but the townspeople were badly divided among themselves and Sinnott reported that there appeared some inclination to give way. However, what decided the issue was something more direct—it was the acceptation by Cromwell of the surrender of the castle behind the back of the negotiators and without communicating with them.

This was a particularly bad piece of business, quite indefensible. The castle was commanded by a man of doubtful loyalty, but he was one of four commissioners sent to treat by Sinnott and accepted by Cromwell as parliamentaries.

Cromwell's own account of the nasty business is quite clear, and its clarity vividly illustrates Puritan morals in such matters, for plainly he does not think he was doing anything out of the common. One of the enemy's parliamentaries being prepared to betray the castle, and therefore the city, Cromwell privately accepted his profitable treason, though he was actually in course of negotiation with the traitor's colleagues. As negotiations were proceeding the garrison was not in a posture for defence: Cromwell, in possession of the castle while negotiations were proceeding, was able to have the gates opened and his troops could pass into the town, at first without opposition, and occupy it at once.

Those within did not know what had happened until the guns of the castle were turned against them; there was confusion, during which some attempt was made—too late—to put up obstacles to the cavalry in the streets, but the garrison, thus surprised by treachery, fell back on to the market-place, far beyond the centre of the town, and there huddled together with them were a mass of the terror-stricken population, over whom hung the horror of the recent happenings at Drogheda. In that market-place a second general massacre took place. There is the usual effort of partizans to make it out if possible a little less bad than it was; all the usual pleas are put forward that some of the evidence is not actually contemporary, but, though written by eye-witnesses, was written later; that some of it is only traditional—and so on. But all these apologetics flow from a desire to escape the responsibility for the general murder, and that desire is wholly modern. It was not so with Cromwell himself. He is as straightforward here as he is about the treason and that for the same reason: he thought he was justified in anything because he was dealing with the forces of evil. "When they" (the townsmen and the garrison) "were come into the market-place, making a stiff resistance, our forces broke them and then put all to the sword that came in their way." Again, he estimates the slaughtered at "not less than 2,000," while he affirms that on his side "not twenty fell altogether." So it is pretty clear what the "stiff resistance" was like. Then he writes on with a torrent of confused words about "the Will of God to have things so," it is "an Unexpected Providence," it is the "Righteous Justice of God," they brought it on themselves, they had done the same thing in the past (as he hears) to Protestants—and so on.

Before the end of the letter he again alludes to the inhabitants of the town having been killed, and tells the Speaker of the Long Parliament (to whom the letter is written) from the very spot, there in the first hours after the universal blood-shed, that he may regard the property of the townspeople as being confiscated, and that the houses and port will make an excellent English plantation. These, remember, were the people to whom he had promised security in a treaty which was in process of negotiation, when it was secretly broken—not by them but by himself.

But remark, I repeat it, that all this fitted in with his system of morals. He ends the letter with once more giving the glory to God for the splendid achievement of Drogheda, as a pendant to which he now offers Wexford, "of which it hath pleased God to give into your hands this other mercy."

## IV

### WATERFORD

Cromwell's failure in front of Waterford illustrates all the leading features of his Irish War. It shows how justified was his anxiety about the winter campaign; it shows in the clearest fashion the weakness of the Irish through division, and it shows how the debate between resistance and surrender in each Irish city depended upon the doubtful attitude of the propertied townsmen. And the next phase of the campaign shows how great a part the English command of the sea played through the effect of reinforcement which Cromwell received.

The episode was simple enough. Cromwell's available force in the field was heavily diminished; it was now less than 7,000 men. He had some 4,000 foot, 2,000 horse, and 500 dragoons. The passage of the Suir at Carrick had been seized for him by his subordinates, he crossed the river, marched along the south bank and appeared before Waterford on the 24th of November, drawing up on the north-west of the town. Waterford had one advantage over most of the walled cities which Cromwell had to face in Ireland, it was well provisioned with artillery. It even possessed, it seems, a certain proportion of heavy guns. Ormonde's comparatively large force in the neighbour-hood, had it come fully into play, would of course have prevented any question of the siege, at any rate until Cromwell should have been reinforced. But the townsmen hampered Ormonde in every way. They refused his help; later, when his appearance on the north bank finally decided Cromwell to break camp and be off, they would not send Ormonde boats for the crossing of the water, and when he proposed to recapture the fort at Passage which Cromwell had taken and which commanded the entry into the harbour, they would not allow the passage of Ormonde's troops through the town. Amid all the examples of the ruin brought upon Ireland by her lack of unity during these two fatal years, Waterford, though it stands for an example of successful resistance, is the most lamentable. Ormonde represented an alien and obstructive power; he had been, and was still, the head of that alien power's forces; but there was a common cause against the English revolutionary army, and it was an elementary piece of military as of general policy to have seen the large lines of the thing and to have established a common front here at Waterford, as everywhere else. It was imperative for men to decide which were the more important, to compromise with the Royalist bodies though alien in command and acting for a foreign government—or complete subjection. But the thing was not seen on its large lines either here at Waterford or anywhere else; the Cromwellian conquest had not yet been achieved, and how inevitable it was if a common front were not made was not yet realised either.

When the town was summoned thoughts of surrender were entertained. The terms offered were favourable and seemed to argue haste on the part of Cromwell, and his anxiety to conclude the business, winter being now full upon him and his men falling sick at a great rate, a thousand of them off the roll and reinforcement not yet come. He even gave a promise of freedom in religion; but here came in ambiguity. For quite recently at Ross he had offered the same thing, and then said that he meant permission to believe what one liked and keep quiet about it, but emphatically *not* the right to perform or assist at an idolatrous Mass. Indeed, the conception of Cromwell's permitting that is not conceivable; for even if he had promised it verbally he could not have got himself to keep such a pact with the Scarlet Woman and the Beast.

Anyhow, the offers were refused, but only after that considerable hesitation characteristic of divisions to be found in every Irish community during that crisis. Hardly a week had passed—eight days—when on the 2nd of December the citizens saw the camp of the besiegers struck and Cromwell's command filing off in weather so abominable that he himself noticed it as the worst marching day he had known in his life. That is the end of the first effort at Waterford.

Cromwell had failed, and what had finally determined him to accept failure was the presence of Ormonde in force upon the north bank opposite to him. He was in such haste to get off that he abandoned two of his precious heavy guns in the soaked soil, wherein their broad wheels were stuck fast.

## V

### KILKENNY

Cromwell's operation at Kilkenny illustrates, conversely to that of Waterford, the effect of division of opinion among the Irish when it was sufficiently strong to destroy a defence. At Waterford, in spite of division, the town held and the siege was raised; at Kilkenny on account of division the town was surrendered.

In between the two operations Cromwell had gone into winter quarters. His troops were in grave need of repose and he himself still more of recruitment. Such recruitment had come to him from England, and also from units left in Dublin at the time when he had marched south on Wexford. These last were led by Hewson. He took certain places on the way, massacred certain monks, and was joined by Ireton at the indicated point of general concentration, Gowran, seven miles south of Kilkenny; in which place (Gowran) he reduced with his siege pieces the castle, commanded by a Kentish gentleman of the name of Hammond. When this commander asked for a parley it was refused him; the common soldiers were spared, but the officers, including Hammond, were shot, and as there were Catholics in the regiment their Chaplain Priest was hanged. The treason of a Lieutenant, however, who had helped to the surrender of the place, was rewarded by the sparing of his life.

It is to be remembered that when Cromwell found himself thus in front of Kilkenny it was for the second time. He had already come forward to take it earlier in the year, relying upon a traitor; but the correspondence was interrupted and that effort failed. This time Cromwell halted a mile outside the town (after taking a castle on the way and massacring all the inhabitants) and on the 22nd of March he summoned the town, of which Sir Walter Butler was the Governor.

The garrison was Royalist, not Irish, and Cromwell was answered that Butler would maintain the city for His Majesty (meaning of course young Charles II, far overseas, but, as we shall see later on, being urgently begged to come over to Ireland). Cromwell put his siege artillery, three heavy pieces, two twenty-pounders and another, on to the tower of St. Patrick's Church, which stood to the south of the town, and he put forces blocking the exit of the place. He again summoned the town on the 25th, when his guns were planted, and met with a second refusal; then opened fire on the town and made a breach.

An eastern part of the city beyond the river, Bregagh, called "the Irish town," was occupied by the besiegers, having only townsmen to garrison it and they unwilling to fight. But the wall of the main town ran outside Bregagh so that the loss of this outlying part did not effect the fate of Kilkenny. At the breach it was the same story which we have heard over and over again in Cromwell's attack on the Irish garrisons: the breach was defended so well that the storming parties were thrown back, thirty or forty of the assaulters were killed and apparently some hundreds wounded, including Hewson, who got a shot in the back which did him little damage, no more than bruising him through his buff coat. On receiving orders for a third assault the troops refused to obey, which mutiny Cromwell very decently veiled by saying that it would have been a pity if he had tried to get in, for the resistance was too strong for him.

Now it was with Kilkenny as with every other town: *sooner or later* it was bound to go, unless, through some accident, whether of mutiny or disease, the invading force should prove ultimately insufficient for its general task of conquering the country. As far as the mere taking of garrisons was concerned the siege train was bound to have its way in the long run and the garrisons or their defence were bound to be exhausted of ammunition. Ireland could not produce enough powder and shot for the war as a whole, and, in many places, could produce none.

Cromwell asked for a second parley with the Governor, who answered with a demand for complete immunity for all the inhabitants, their goods and estates, and the right to arm the town; promising that the garrison would march out if it should be promised immunity.

It seemed probable or certain that at this moment Cromwell might have to raise the siege as he did that of Waterford. He would come back of course; Kilkenny would have fallen at last as Waterford did to Ireton, a little later in this same year, since a defensive never lasts for ever; but at the moment the Mayor of the town, *speaking in the name of the townsmen,* offered surrender, being in dread of the ruin of trade and expecting that the resistance would command fairly good conditions.

This offer of surrender was made *by the civilians* on the 26th of March. Cromwell welcomed it, naturally, his moral position much strengthened by this division among his opponents. He wrote to the military Governor refusing to treat on the conditions of the garrison's having a right to go away free with their arms. The Governor had also asked for the immunity of the clergy in the town, and Cromwell took the opportunity to insult him by talking of "your clergymen, as you call them." He only promised that they might march away free on this occasion, but added, "If they fall otherwise into my hands I believe they know what to expect from me"—which indeed they did, for what happened to Catholic priests when they met Cromwell was by this time common knowledge throughout Ireland.

A new effort at negotiation by Cromwell in the evening of the 26th was followed by a further attack on the 27th, when another breach was made. The townsmen again broke down, and the garrison again beat off Cromwell's men. But seeing the temper of the townsmen, the defence could not last much longer; and Kilkenny was surrendered on Thursday, the 28th of March, 1650, upon terms. There was to be no loot; the garrison were to be allowed to withdraw, and Kilkenny was to pay an indemnity of £2,000. Cromwell, according to Ormonde's testimony, respected the courage of Butler and his garrison and congratulated them on their defence: according to the same authority he said he could not have taken the town save for its betrayal by the citizens.

The taking of Kilkenny was another very heavy blow to the dwindling Irish defence, because it was in the heart of the country, "in the bowels of it" as Cromwell said; and also, morally, because it was from Kilkenny that the national Catholic organisation had worked and had had its headquarters. The fear of the plague, which had something to do with Cromwell's anxiety during the siege, made him withdraw his army at once; he left only the regiment of Axtell, the man who had threatened to shoot at Lady Fairfax during the trial of the King. As for the Cathedral, "They have thrown down the great roof of it, taken away five great bells, broken all the windows and all the doors, that the hogs may come in there and root and dogs gnaw the bones of the dead." The glass was that glorious stained glass of the Middle Ages which the earlier iconoclasts had spared, and which was famous throughout the country.

## VI

### CLONMEL

The last of Cromwell's own operations in Ireland was that of Clonmel, just over a month after the taking of Kilkenny. It was defended by Hugh O'Neil, with a garrison quite inadequate. Here again there was division; to the fifteen or sixteen hundred, almost entirely foot, whom O'Neil commanded, nearly as many again might have been added by Ormonde's orders, but the commissioners refused them.

The town was summoned, and the summons refused in the regular fashion; the heavy guns were planted and the usual story of these Irish fights proceeded. There was the same prolonged courage in defence, the same efforts at corruption and the same beginnings of treason; a breach was made when night fell, and once again the breach not being sufficiently low, part of the wall remained standing near the ground.

One incident of the siege was most remarkable. A sort of trap was laid, so that the passage in through the breach became a blind alley leading to fortifications raised some way back, parallel to where the wall had been. Musketeers were placed aiong the sides of this "lane with a dead end" and two guns were concealed enfilading the whole length of it; and behind the final wall O'Neil in his lack of armament put men with pikes and scythes.

[ 258 ]

When the assault was launched at eight o'clock in the morning, to the strange sound of hymns, there was no check until they were well within the trap. Most of the force so packed and pressed forward was mounted, and it received an unexpected check at this new inner obstacle that had been raised, those behind rushing on and pressing the van more closely. The muskets from left and right opened upon this packed mass of men, and Cromwell himself saw the welter as he rode up behind the column, expecting the town to be rushed. It was thought that about 1,000 fell in that "pound," as they called it.

For some time it was impossible to make a second attack, the men would not face it; but at last another party was got together, all on foot this time, and this further determined effort went on far into the day, lasting till well past noon. It was defeated in its turn, with double the loss of the first attack; the invasion had lost on that one day more men than had fallen in every other action since Cromwell had landed. So much for the "moral effect" of Drogheda. The effort at storming was abandoned; and Cromwell sat down to the longer business of blockade. Whether he knew that the ammunition of the defence was failing we cannot be certain; there is a rather romantic story telling us how he got wind of it, or perhaps the nature of the fighting with so many of the defenders armed haphazard, with scythes and what-not, was enough to inform him.

Hugh O'Neil, when all ammunition had failed and his provisions as well, left the townsmen free to surrender if they would, but not until he should have marched his men out of the town by night, sufficiently far to be safe from attack. It was about ten o'clock at night, or a little earlier, that the small force filed out on its first stage to Ballynasack, a dozen miles away. Not till this was fully accomplished did the Mayor send to Cromwell for a parley. It was the 10th of May, 1650.

For a long while past the danger from Scotland had urged

the Parliament to send for Cromwell; it was five months since they had first moved towards that end. He sailed on the 29th of May from Youghal, handing over his command to his son-in-law, Ireton. He had his usual bad luck with the weather at sea, but was in London by the last day of the month. He was received in triumph, took his seat again in Parliament on the 4th of June, and a week later gave his account to the House of his conquest. He had left in Ireland three main places to be reduced: Waterford, Limerick and Galway—and their end was certain.

.        .        .        .        .        .        .

It is often said that Cromwell, for all the brilliance of his brief career, left nothing permanent: that he built up nothing; that he has no monument. There is no code of laws, and there are no great public buildings, there is not even a military organisation or tradition proceeding from him as its creator.

The accusation is not wholly true. If glory consist in making or destroying something great, then the ghost of Cromwell can point to a ruined Ireland. It was the blows *he* struck, it was *his* programme, complete and ruthless, which reduced Ireland to a condition from which she did not re-arise—from which, indeed, her resurrections seemed for long impossible.

That monument is material as well as moral; and those who mark in Ireland the roofless houses, the deserted lands, the diminished harbours which still make it a desolate exception in all western Europe, are gazing on Cromwell's monument; in direct succession from the massacres and plunder of 1649-52 runs the whole story of decay.

When Cromwell landed, the Irish Catholics still possessed nearly one-half their native land. When this work was accomplished they possessed but one-twentieth of it, and were reduced to servitude under an alien religion, which meant also in some part an alien race. On the soil which had been theirs since days older than Christendom, when they were already something of a nation while as yet no other nation was, they were now doomed to labour, increasingly impoverished, for the enrichment of others. Their natural leaders were cut off, exiles or renegades; their instruction was destroyed, as was all the organisation of their former life. So that it might appear in the mid-nineteenth century, two hundred years after the mad slaughter, that Ireland was passing at last. The wise man, who can see beneath the surface of things and reviews the whole story from Cromwell's time to our own, sees it to have been a contest less of races than of religions; some years ago he might have concluded that the contest was over and the issue determined.

But that conclusion would have been erroneous. Had Cromwell succeeded in his intention—beyond the powers of his simple intense energy—of destroying the nationhood of the Irish and its essential religion, then indeed he would have left behind him a monument of the most permanent sort. All these islands would be one. But he did not succeed in that task. He therefore cannot be said to have even one enduring monument, unless we give that name to a modern statue in the ditch outside the House of Commons—unveiled by the late Lord Rosebery.

# I

## PRESTON

Cromwell's campaigns as distinguished from particular actions—that is the operations in which his genius in tactics and defects in strategy have room to appear, are those undertaken against the Scotch and the one undertaken in Ireland. The Irish campaign I have dealt with separately; it gave little scope for strategy and was almost wholly a campaign of sieges. With the three Scotch campaigns it is otherwise.

They involve long approaches against a concentrated foreign enemy force and therefore give strategical opportunity. They all end in victories and decisive actions which vividly illustrate tactical principles.

They are three in number. The first of them is that in which he defeated the Scottish invasion under Hamilton of 1648, undertaken as an effort to save the life of King Charles. The decision was reached at Preston and the campaign takes its name from that town. The second campaign is that undertaken as an invasion of Scotland in 1650. It concluded in the most remarkable of all his victories, that of Dunbar, and should therefore be called the campaign of Dunbar. The third and last campaign was undertaken against the final Scottish invasion of England in 1651 and was decided by the battle of Worcester.

I will now deal with these in their order:

The campaign of Preston is the most difficult to judge because Cromwell's talents were pitted therein against unworthy opponents. The approach, though blind, was aided by the ineptitude of the quarry he sought. The final tactical success,

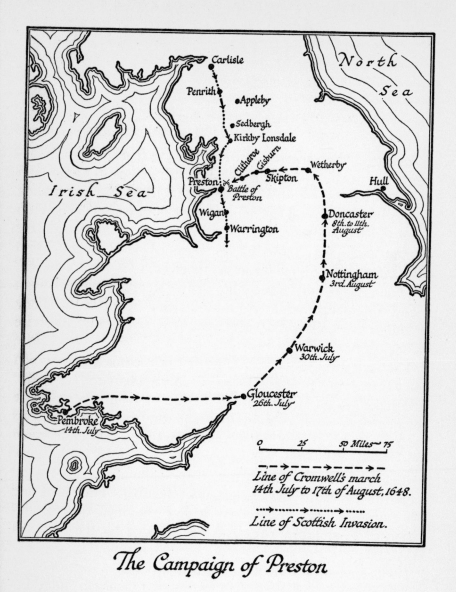

The Campaign of Preston

though it was immediate and complete, does not sufficiently illustrate the victor because the vanquished were a detached body, less than half their opponents in number and abandoned through the incapacity of Hamilton, their Commander-in-Chief. Preston was an operation in which a commander far inferior to Cromwell in technical sense and cavalry work might well have obtained the same results.

When the mere numbers of the affairs are first set down the results might astonish the reader even more than those of Dunbar. The total of the Scottish invading force against which Cromwell was called to act was *three* times as great as that which he could bring against it at the moment; such enormous odds, if they were all that we knew upon the matter, would make the victory seem miraculous. But that huge disproportion was much more than compensated for by the action and conduct of the invaders. Their forces were not homogeneous, they were dispirited from the beginning, ill-led, and hopelessly disorganised before there was any issue to be decided in the field. Cromwell in this affair marches 369 miles in thirty-three marching days. With a rest of one full day * in the middle, giving a total of thirty-four days—July 14th-August 16th inclusive —this is only average going. Nothing like his later achievement of the march from the Forth to Worcester. The one is an average of eleven and a quarter miles a day, with a break in the middle; the other was to be, as we shall see, a continuous effort of sixteen miles a day.

Hamilton's command, as we may call it, covered at a critical moment 120 miles in forty days, an average of three miles a day. Cromwell's command was a compact body mostly composed of long-trained and now veteran professional soldiers;

* The halt at Doncaster is usually put at three *days,* because Cromwell *arrived* on August 8th and left on August 11th. But the interval of repose for Cromwell himself was only two days (9th and 10th) and for his infantry only one day (the 9th). The infantry reached Weatherby, thirty-one miles from Doncaster, on the 12th. They could not, in their then condition, have covered thirty-one miles in two days. They must have started on the 20th, even though the train started next day.

it could strike one blow in one place like a clenched fist. Hamilton's was a long disjointed line of stragglers. At the critical moment the van of the forward part was approaching Wigan, the middle part lay east of Preston, while the very last units of that grotesque advance had just left Kirkby Lonsdale, the whole column nearly fifty miles by the roads altogether and certainly not less than forty-two as the crow flies. Cromwell, coming upon this contemptible disposition, which had hardly the right to call itself a disposition at all, cut it in two by striking at the middle part. He would not have done so if that middle part had been supported, as it should have been, by the forward part. The middle and forward parts combined, even without the rear which had been left so far behind, outnumbered Cromwell by at least two to one and should easily have defeated him. But the middle part, left to itself, was outnumbered in the same proportion.

Even after Cromwell had destroyed the middle part, the forward half remained much larger than his own force numerically; but it was utterly broken in *morale*, and not only began to be defeated in detail but expected nothing save further and final defeat—or dissolution. Its fate, in a countryside where the invaders were detested by all parties as aliens (and at once detected by their accent—many by their Gaelic speech), scattered without provision, and under no effective orders. At last there was disintegration.

But allowing for all this, what Cromwell did was memorable. The alarm of invasion came at a moment when he was occupied in reducing Pembroke Castle by siege, that stronghold being held against the Parliament through the effect of a recent rebellion. The field-guns and munitions which he would need in his decisive action against the invasion were at Hull, in Yorkshire, a point 245 miles away as the crow flies, and at least 260-70 miles away by road, at the other end of England and on the other side of the island. Having collected these, he would have to swerve round an angle of about 120° to pass over a chain of barren hills, with only one indifferent road across them, in order to reach some point where he might strike the Scotch invading force. There was in all this a celerity of movement which was sufficient—especially as all his footsoldiers were at first ill-shod and many shoeless. But there was no strategy except that which was dictated by obvious necessity; to get results he had to meet the Scottish force whereever it happened to be at the moment and in what disposition he would find it he could have no idea. Luckily for Cromwell there was on the other side a sluggishness unexampled in all the story of this war—and of strategy not a sign.

. . . . . . .

The political position was grave though not desperate. All winter and spring England was growing angry, and a general rising was to be feared. This keeping of the King a prisoner and the exclusion of the mass of the people from any voice in government was exasperating opinion. It is true that public opinion was not a strong factor, though it counted for more than it does now, but there was enough of it to exercise a negative effect.

The English people were not republican; a large number of them, perhaps a majority (of those who were politically conscious at least) had at one moment been prepared to resist the King out of annoyance against the new taxation; the small freeholders, still, perhaps, half of an overwhelming agricultural population, had followed the greater landowners in resistance —but an England without a King was not conceivable to them. As for taxation, the burden put upon them by the victorious revolution had become enormously heavier than anything they had had to bear under Charles.

There must be added that other element I have mentioned— the prolonged exclusion of the mass of Englishmen from having any say in their own affairs. It is not negligible, though it did not count nearly as much as the taxes. The importance of this factor must not be exaggerated; no very large number of people spread over a great territory are ever anxious for any length of time to mix themselves with government, and in England this idea of interfering with those in power was especially weak in the lower ranks of society. But still, for now six years of heavy strain, Englishmen had been able to apply no pressure either upon the outworn remnant of the politicians or upon the victorious and increasingly powerful army. Hence the rising spirit of resistance which might in the early part of 1648 have undone the revolution—and with it Cromwell.

It had been arranged that a general Royalist rising in England should coincide with the Scottish invasion. The whole thing was badly done. The beginnings of the second Civil War in England were premature. Hamilton had difficulties in recruitment. The Calvinist clergy of Scotland tried to prevent his using godless men. The Godly were less keen to march and he could not cross the Border until the 8th of July and even then he had to leave half his army behind him, still drilling and mustering. He only went over the Border as early as he did in order to put more heart into the Northern English Royalists. By that time (July 8th) the siege of Pembroke was drawing to an end. Colchester, though it was able to hold out longer, was encircled. Still, Cromwell must be victorious, and that rapidly, or he and the whole cause which supported him might perish.

On paper the odds were heavily against Oliver. There would be present in the north of England a hostile army composed of three sections, the main Scottish force under Hamilton himself, a body of English cavalry under Langdale and a body of Scottish soldiers recently come over from Ireland under Munro. The total force, before it suffered losses by disease, desertion or in action, might be reckoned at something between 25,000 and 30,000 men; of which Hamilton's Scotch were two-thirds at full strength, Munro's and Langdale's each about a sixth. Cromwell would not have at his disposal, even when he should have effected his junction with Parliamentary forces in the north, as many as 10,000. That under such conditions he should have achieved the success he did—and it was complete—is due to two complementary factors, the cohesion of his own command and the imbecile dispersion of his foes.

Pembroke surrendered from hunger on the 11th of July, Hamilton having, as we saw, already crossed the Border with 10,000 men three days before, leaving another 10,000 behind, whom he would wait for in England.

This move of Hamilton's, advancing half his men before the other half was ready, was the result of a dilemma. If he waited too long before moving, the Royalists in England would be crushed before he could come to help them—as it was that premature effort was already three-quarters beaten. On the other hand, if he started even thus late on the 8th of July, he could only bring 10,000 men with him, the other 10,000 were still being assembled in Scotland, trained and armed. It would be some time before he could hope to be at the head of the whole force. So he invaded England with half his total to begin with, in the hope that such invasion would hearten the Royalist rebellion and procure large English recruitment for him. But having invaded, he was unable to go forward until his remaining half, the other 10,000, could join him.

Langdale was awaiting him in Cumberland with Carlisle as his centre. He had around him a body of English loyalists—at first mostly mounted—who were expected to grow to seven or even eight thousand, but who never reached any such number. When the day of action came, nearly five weeks later, he certainly had not 4,000 under his command; his own account gives 3,600.

It must further be noted that with Langdale were the guides who knew the mountain districts, through which all had to pass, and that his force alone was native. All the Scottish troops were foreigners to the Englishmen of that day, and the hostility of the average Englishman to the Scotch as a nation, let alone as invaders, had much to do with the result.

A week after Hamilton had crossed the Border, Lambert, with a Parliamentary force, was at Penrith. He marched north towards Carlisle and offered battle, but Langdale was too weak to engage until the whole Scotch force was assembled. Moreover that half of the Scotch who had already crossed the Border was without a train as yet, and without artillery. Lambert was too weak to meet the *combined* forces of Hamilton and Langdale, so, when Hamilton appeared, he fell back somewhat eastward into the hills, leaving the road into England and the south through Lancaster open.

That his presence thus upon the flank of the invaders' advance represented a piece of calculated strategy designed to hold that advance and delay it until Cromwell could come up from the south is a theory reading modern ideas into the facts of 300 years ago. It is to make Lambert even more of a strategist than were the Piedmontese generals acting under the young Napoleon in 1796. He had no such science. He simply held on until Cromwell should arrive.

Lambert thus hung on to the flanks of the invasion (relying especially upon Appleby Castle), because it was the only task present to him; the delay in the advance of the invading force was not due to Lambert's presence but to the necessity of waiting for the train and for the other half of Hamilton's command, which was still north of the Border.

In those same days, on the 14th of July, Cromwell, released by the fall of Pembroke, began his advance eastward and northward to effect a junction with Lambert, in order to deal, if it should prove possible, with the greatly superior numbers of the invaders.

We must appreciate exactly the nature of that march, in order to take the measure of Cromwell's ability without exaggerating its value, as do his enthusiasts, or judging it by modern standards. It was a respectable achievement. If one merely goes by the map and by dates the beginning of it may seem much too slow. His infantry was not at Gloucester till the 26th of July; 138 miles in thirteen days, only just over ten and a half miles a day. But this infantry was ill shod, many of the men being actually barefoot; and he could not get proper supplies until he was well into England. He sent a considerable mounted force forward—thirty troops (all he had except one regiment), who joined Lambert at Barnard Castle. Meanwhile he was urgently calling for foot-gear to be ready in the Midlands for his forces when they should arrive. He was in Warwick on the 30th of July; and on the 3rd of August, his men now all well shod and everything in order, he was at Nottingham.

He was making for Doncaster, where he expected, and did in fact obtain, two things necessary to him: pay for his men (some part of it, at least, for it was months in arrear) and guns and powder and shot from the magazines of Hull. Meanwhile he had sent orders forward to Lambert to hold on in the north until he, Cromwell, could effect a junction.

It was on the 8th of August that Cromwell reached Doncaster with his men. At that point let us sum up the nature of his advance so far. He had marched from Pembroke, a distance of 290 miles. This advance had taken him and his men twenty-six days. Such figures, of course, give no impression of rapidity. It is nearly 50 per cent. slower than the Grand Army on its way to Ulm. But we must remember the conditions. Oliver had to get what he could out of soldiers ill equipped and many of them at first without shoes; after the shoes came his average jumped from ten and a half to twelve miles a day. He was dealing with a force the temper of which was doubtful in spite of the excellence of their commander's discipline; for the long arrears of pay exasperated them. It is an error to describe the advance to Doncaster from Pembroke as something worth special notice in the history of marching; the French in the Lombard campaign of 1796 were just as badly equipped, or worse, and yet there were days when they covered over thirty miles, notably in the dash on Mantua. On the other hand the earlier part of Cromwell's march had been through very ill-provided country.

But no matter; it is not the first part of the effort which best illustrates Cromwell's genius, it is the second. Though he had arrived at Doncaster by the 8th, he was compelled to wait till the 11th before he got his guns from Hull, sending his foot forward, after a day's rest, on the 10th. When the guns had arrived it would be his business to veer north-east and make for the invading column, which by the time of his arrival would presumably have reached central Lancashire.

Now let us turn and see what the invaders were doing during these same days. Hamilton's second half, the reinforcements from Scotland with the train, joined up in the last two days of July, Appleby Castle on his flank having surrendered on the 29th. That was the moment when Cromwell had already reached Warwick on his way to Nottingham, and was there receiving supplies and, what was so essential to him, leather for his foot. On the 2nd of August, just before Cromwell marched into Nottingham, the head of the Scottish column was at Kendal, and the cavalry had been sent forward as far as Sedburgh.

At Kendal there was another halt; part of the large Scotch force lay to the south of the town, most of it in the town itself and behind it Langdale. The delay which followed was not due to mere incompetence on Hamilton's part, though incompetent he was; he was waiting for Munro and his troops from Ireland. These had got across the sea without interference from the Parliamentary ships. They did not join up, but continued the line, standing up to the northward of Langdale's body.

At this point, in the first week of August, while Cromwell was waiting for his guns at Doncaster, Hamilton and his Council were debating whether to take the invading force down through Yorkshire, driving Lambert before them, and attack Cromwell and Lambert when they should join and stand, or whether they should strike back southward to the main road through Lancashire into middle England. This second policy was decided upon. What turned the scale in favour of it was the illusion that there would be enough Royalist feeling in Lancashire to overcome the hatred of the foreigner and rally recruitment even to a Scottish invasion. The presence of Langdale's English cavalry (they thought) *might* do that; but Hamilton himself also put special reliance upon the strong Royalist feeling in Manchester and the district. At this point, when the invaders decided on following the main road again through Lancashire, they are in total numbers, counting Munro, Langdale and Hamilton, with the mass of the forces, something about 24,000 to 25,000 men. They had lost the balance by desertion and sickness. Of this 24,000 to 25,000 Munro at the extreme northern end, the rear, had some 4,000, Langdale still had, over on the east flank in the Yorkshire hills, 4,000—but dwindling—and Hamilton had 16,000 to 17,000 or a little more.

But we must not think of these three contingents as one army. They were not that, either in situation or in homogeneity. They were three separate bodies, stretched out over an intolerable length of country. There was jealousy between the Scottish and English contingents, and the country being poor, provisionment was most difficult. The three bodies were compelled to march separately for these several causes, but even so their lack of co-ordination and their sluggishness were excessive. Langdale came in belatedly eastward from the Yorkshire hills towards the main Lancashire road, so as to take up his place between Munro in the north and Hamilton to the south of him.

From the invaders let us now turn again to Cromwell, who was about to undertake his more rapid advance, with forces now concentrated in Yorkshire but still far inferior to the enemy in Lancashire.

On leaving Doncaster his foot made three marches to Weatherby, thirty-one miles. There he turned east and was joined shortly after, at Otley, by Lambert. By this time he

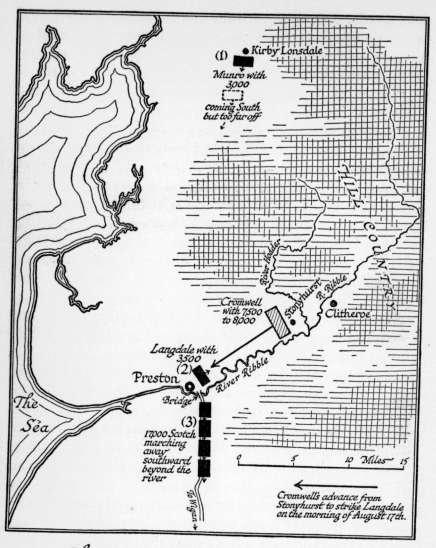

(1) ● Kirby Lonsdale

Munro with
3000

coming South
but too far off

HILL COUNTRY

River Hodder

Cromwell
– with 7500
to 8000

Stonyhurst

R. Ribble

● Clitheroe

Langdale with
3500

(2)

Preston

River Ribble

Bridge

(3)

17000 Scotch
marching
away
southward
beyond the
river

To Wigan

0          5          10  Miles  15

Cromwell's advance from
Stonyhurst to strike Langdale
on the morning of August 17th.

The
Sea

## The Elements of the Decision at Preston

Showing the isolation of Langdale's force near Preston and its consequent destruction
at the hands of Cromwell with double Langdale's numbers. The Royalist forces are
cut in two. Munro, too far off to help, goes back North. Hamilton's large force to the
South, loses its ammunition, falls into disorder and is routed.

and Lambert had between them more than ten but less than twelve thousand men; not the whole of that force would be available for battle, and as a fact when the shock came the whole of Cromwell's command was probably under 9,000. In his letter to the Speaker after the event he even put it as low as 8,600; he would naturally make out his victorious force to be as small as possible, though there is no reason to think that he diminished the total unduly. We must regard him as having less than 9,000 men actually engaged during the struggle which was about to follow, and he had a good deal more than 20,000 against him. He abandoned his heavy train and guns, which he had been at such pains to rally at Doncaster. He did so for the sake of rapidity, now that he had to take the steep gradients of the Pennines, but it argues ill for his strategical sense. If he could not use them he should not have delayed for them. On the 14th of August he was nearing Skipton, which he reached at the end of that day. On the evening of the 15th he was over the crest of the Pennines and down in the Ribble valley at Gisburn; the crisis of the campaign was at hand.

Let us summarise the situation. Langdale had learned, somewhat tardily, that Lambert and Cromwell had affected their junction and were now within a long day of him or say a day and a half. The head of Hamilton's foot on the same day, the 15th, had reached Preston; Munro was right away back at Kirkby Lonsdale, two pressed marches behind. Cromwell knew that, even disregarding Munro (who was quite out of the picture, and must so remain for at least two and probably three days more, however much he hurried), his enemy *could* concentrate round Clitheroe a force more than double his own.

But to talk of "concentration" in connection with bodies such as Hamilton nominally commanded is to use a precise term for a situation which was in fact chaotic. So far from any "concentration" to meet the coming blow Hamilton continued his march southward across the Ribble at Preston. He sent his main body of sixteen or seventeen thousand down the road towards Wigan, refusing to believe that any considerable Parliamentary force was at hand. Langdale was falling back upon Preston alone with his small command, by this time already less than 4,000; and there was coming against him at top speed Cromwell with something between eight and nine thousand men. The invaders were stretched out in a broken chain, the great mass of them, Hamilton's Scotchmen, were already separated by a river, the Ribble, from their centre; and still marching off south. Munro, as we have seen, was so far off to the north that he might as well not have existed. Poor Langdale, without assistance, save a small contingent which Hamilton gave him when he woke up too late to the situation, was isolated. Such was the situation on the 16th of August, at evening.

As may be imagined from this mere outline of the situation, the staff work on the Royalist side had been abominable. Langdale assures us that he told Hamilton of Cromwell's proximity and of the danger of immediate attack upon himself, and begged for assistance; those round Hamilton are equally positive that they received no such information. Whether they did or did not it is clear that Hamilton had no conception of the true state of affairs and even Langdale, who on this day (the 16th) *did* know that Cromwell was almost upon him, seems to have believed the rumour that so great a commander had committed the folly of separating his forces, advancing with one column north of the river Ribble and the other south of it.*

Cromwell of course had done nothing of the sort. On that day (the 16th) he crossed the Hodder (by exactly what bridge is still disputed) and bivouacked in the park of Stonyhurst. Langdale on that fatal morning was standing just to the west of him, outside Preston. By the account which he himself, or his subordinates give us, his total remaining force with which

* It is true that Cromwell had hesitated whether to advance down the right or left bank of the Ribble. But not by both!

[ 275 ]

he had to meet the shock was some 3,000 foot and now only 600 horse. On that day therefore, the 17th, whereon the issue was to be decided, more than 8,000 men were attacking less than 4,000 at this critical point just outside Preston. The great mass of the Royalists were beyond the Ribble still marching south and heedless of the danger immediately to their rear; even on this last day, the 16th, Langdale could not make Hamilton believe that the crisis had come.

Hamilton himself returned indeed over the bridge, but too late. The blow fell, and it was a crushing one.

Langdale's command fought admirably; they defended the narrow lanes one against two—but their destruction was inevitable; and when Hamilton came up with his few horse it was only to attempt by one or two rearguard charges to check Cromwell's triumph. Langdale's broken command was flying through the streets of Preston.

Cromwell seized the bridge; Langdale himself and Hamilton barely saved themselves by swimming the river. The centre of the hopelessly protracted invading column had been scattered and had disappeared. The rearguard was days of marching away, to the north, and the van, the bulk of the force, was straggling off southwards with its head already in Wigan. The Parliamentary army after its triumph in Preston pressed down over the bridge after the Scotch and southward along the Wigan road.

Even so it might seem as though during the morrow and the day after the Scotch might have rallied, halted their column, and deployed. They were still greatly superior in numbers, and if they could have formed and faced north quickly enough to meet the pressure of the victors hurrying after them from Preston they might have saved their army. But Hamilton himself and his now distracted men were incapable of any such effort. Cromwell was actively alive to the opportunity and urged on his victorious but weary cavalry in ceaseless pursuit. Most of Hamilton's train seems to have been already lost. The ammunition had gone; the fugitives—for they can hardly be called by a better name—were already thoroughly disorganised; a desperate effort was made to recall the horse from Wigan; but it did not arrive in time.

One gallant rear action was fought on Wigan Moor by Turner, with troops now only half the number in organised formation which they would have been if the army had held together. The retreat became a rout, the Scotch were dispersed over a countryside which hated them, and all that prevented their immediate and total destruction was the exhaustion of the pursuers. Hamilton himself was finally captured at Uttoxeter as he wandered aimlessly on, and was later condemned to death and beheaded, under this new theory that, since the victory of the Revolution in the First Civil War, all armed opposition to it was to be treated as treason.

The surrender of the last organised force among the Scotch had for its date the 19th of August; meanwhile far away at Colchester the last stronghold of the revolt against the victorious Revolution had surrendered, and two of its gallant defenders had suffered execution also.

That was what happened at Preston. After a most critical month during which the whole struggle lay in the balance, Cromwell by his precision, energy and the cohesion of his men but also by good fortune had determined history. He ran a great risk. He could not tell that Hamilton would fail to concentrate against him and Hamilton, had he done so, could, with his much larger forces disciplined and united, have destroyed his opponents. Oliver's gamble came off—but it was a gamble. On the other hand it would not have come off had not Oliver been the chief he was, getting the last ounce out of his command. The most heavily tried of his troops had marched without a halt during eight and a half days, at the average rate of over fifteen miles a day, wherein of course must be counted the extra rapidity of the mounted forces, who accounted for the end of the mopping up. In that brief time they had fought one major action, stubbornly contested; and a second, somewhat severe, though on a smaller scale.

The heavy risk had proved worth while, and those who legitimately give him so much glory in our modern writings for the campaign and the decisive victory at its close, though they exaggerate the clarity of his strategy, and see in it more of a plan than could have been present in his own mind, do not exaggerate those factors in the success which proceeded from his military talents alone. Had he not been able to create that force and to hold it in hand as he did, to demand of it the effort which he not only demanded but obtained, Preston would have had a different ending.

## II

### DUNBAR

Meanwhile, during the summer of 1649, some months after his father's death, Charles II, in exile, discussed his fortunes with his mother at St. Germain (an unwelcome guest for the French Government) hesitating between the fronts upon which the recovery of his kingdom might be attempted.

Scotland would receive him of course. The Stuarts were their national dynasty, and under himself he might unite their factions. Either of the two groups in Ireland—the much larger Catholic group and the smaller but organised group of Ormonde with his remnants of the Royal army—would accept him. The Scotch would only receive him on terms of establishing the national religion and himself taking the Covenant, pretending to accept the (to him) odious creed of Calvin and explicitly denouncing his own mother and condoning his father's murder. Yet against an attempt through Ireland there were to be said these things:

A yielding to the demand for the toleration of the Catholic Church in Ireland would throw all the Covenanting organisation of Scotland into violent hostility against him; it would

[ 278 ]

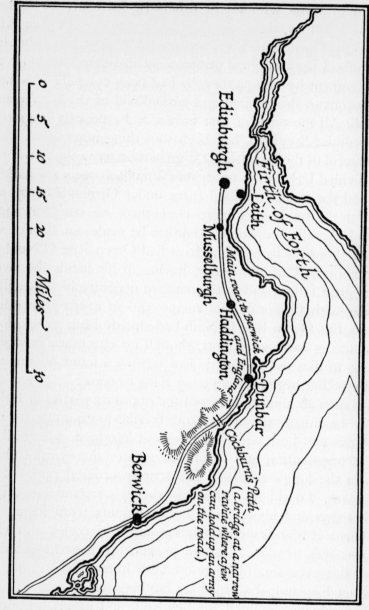

APPROACHES TO AND FROM DUNBAR

Firth of Forth

Edinburgh
Leith

Musselburgh

Haddington

Main road to Berwick
and England

Dunbar

Cockburn's Path
(a bridge at a narrow
ravine where a few
can hold up an army
on the road.)

Berwick

0  5  10  15  20  *Miles*  40

rouse hostility in the majority of Englishmen and in a great portion of those who might otherwise be ready to support him; and further, the loyalty of Ireland to any English King must always be doubtful. He was not their King. His father had never stood for a national government in Ireland but only for a government by conquerors; he had been compelled to make concessions to the religion and nationhood of the Irish against his will. All the reign of that father, and especially the strong action under Strafford, had been something imposed of force, and hateful to the Irish people. Further, between the two forces that divided Ireland the unorganised millions upon the national side and the small organised force under Ormonde, there was —so far as the leaders were concerned—no common moral ground. An alliance would doubtless be made—an alliance was indeed almost in being. The Irish had Owen Roe O'Neill for their national Catholic leader, having in his hands the sword of his great father; and in the national necessity he was willing to join with Ormonde, his enemy and in every way odious to him. But Owen Roe O'Neill had already been struck down by illness as early as August, though no one knew how soon he was to die; and Ormonde had written a letter on the 27th of September begging the young King to come.

But such an alliance between the opposing parties in Ireland would be unnatural and therefore fragile: more unnatural than an agreement between the factions of Scotland, where all the active organisation and much the greater numerical strength was in the long-established and strictly ordered ranks of the Covenant. To aid him in acting through Ireland Rupert lay with a fleet at Kinsale, and Charles, coming from Jersey (for the Channel Islands were the last atoms of his own realm where he was free to move), would presumably have been able to land. But even should he re-establish himself in Ireland, that was not England; the broad sea lay between.

The schemes inclined for Scotland, and meanwhile during the hesitation, there had swept over Ireland the storm of Cromwell's conquest. The King was King again in Scotland. A Scotch army was again being summoned and *might* invade England under David Leslie. If it came in support of an acknowledged King what might not follow?

The Revolutionary Parliament ordered a new campaign to meet the danger. They would forestall it by themselves landing an invasion of Scotland. They offered the command to Fairfax —still nominally Commander-in-Chief.

He refused to go. *He* was not guilty of the last King's blood. *He* would not—presumably—suffer death if the new King should succeed; and he had scruples about breaking an oath. After all, the Scotch and English were bound by one Covenant and the Scotch had not denounced the alliance.

Cromwell was in a different position. With him it was life and death. All Europe knew and all England and Scotland that upon him lay the blood guiltiness. He was the chief regicide, and if a Stuart should reign again he would be hanged— probably butchered as well, as the Priests and poor young Burley had been butchered. He protested that he would rather serve under Fairfax than lead the greatest army in Europe, and, having so protested, took Fairfax's place and accepted the Commandership-in-Chief.

Cromwell thus remained—to his great good fortune—the single figure in this summer of 1650, at the head of the host. It profited him greatly, because what seemed at first a doubtful adventure, what soon became a perilous one, was turned by his own genius, by the full exercise of his high powers in the field into a miraculous victory: miraculous, as miracles should be, sudden and complete. For the episode that followed is the campaign of Dunbar, and of all Cromwell's military affairs the tactical work at Dunbar, though following on a thoroughly muddled piece of strategy, was mainly Oliver's own, a conspicuous triumph of special ability against circumstance.

Marston Moor had established him, Naseby had confirmed

him, Worcester was to be final and determinant: but at Marston Moor the result was only partly his, he would not have done what he did had he not been succoured by others at the critical moment; at Naseby, though there also success might have been doubtful, he was backed by great superiority in numbers, and to some degree in arms; at Worcester the thing was, as we shall see, a matter of course; Worcester could not have had any other end unless there had appeared before the final action a political element, which as a fact was lacking—Royalist support for the invaders; but Dunbar stands by itself as something quite different from all these. It was a special unexpected glory, and though Lambert and others had grasped the opportunity, the final blow was Cromwell's: a success against very great odds and one of crushing political effect.

We begin with the date the 19th of July. On that date the General finds himself at the Border, near Berwick. He has under him as chiefs Fleetwood, Lambert and Monk; he commands 11,000 foot and some 6,000 horse; with these 17,000 he goes up northward and westward by the coast road against the capital of Scotland, and the enemy's army. On the 30th of July he has concentrated at Musselburgh, and the campaign proper opens.

It is important to understand the nature of the Scotch policy at this point, and his reason for that policy, and the elements of strength and weakness of Cromwell's opponents. Leven and Leslie commanded a larger force than did Cromwell. The total numbers voted to the Scottish command by the civilian power was 30,000; of whom, as we shall see, some 20,000 to 22,000 were present in the final action of Dunbar. But of those 30,000 only 5,500 belonged to that old and experienced and excellent Scottish army which had saved the Parliamentary cause during the recent Civil War in England. The remainder were new levies. Among these of course were a number who had already served, but the majority appear to have been trained only after incorporation in early July. They had therefore only seen eight weeks' training when the shock came. But they were in their own country on their own recruiting ground, near their own supplies, while the English were dependent for supply upon the sea.

The Scottish commanders had fallen back, not attempting to check the invaders' advance, but denuding the country on either side of the road through which those invaders had to pass so that they might be more and more hampered as that advance proceeded. There were two reasons for this attitude on the part of the Scottish commanders; in the first place their army, though it had a fine fighting record behind it, had had no continuous training as their opponents had had; it had largely been disbanded and reassembled again.

So long as the numbers were nearly equal—seventeen English to twenty Scotch or even sixteen to twenty—Leslie might reasonably fear superiority in real strength on the English side when the clash should come: for one thing, the English had better artillery and more of it ready in mobile form. Another reason was that, other things being equal, it was obviously to the advantage of the native force to wear down the invader; it is nearly always so in such a contrast between a better-trained and better-equipped invasion and a defending force which retires before it. There were only a little over two months to run before the campaign would fall under winter conditions, and every day that passed tried the invader more and more, especially with his supplies at the mercy of the sea. It was for all these reasons wise for the Scotch to retreat. Nevertheless Leslie did not propose that Edinburgh should fall into the hands of the English, or that its port of Leith should be used by them as an avenue of supply from the sea; he fortified lines to the east of the capital and he fortified Leith.

In the first week of August, Cromwell was already anxious about his position. He had planned badly. He had left no communications, no detached bodies to hold essential points if he should be forced to retreat. He clearly had no idea of what might happen if his enemy played for time. In a fortnight of dwindling strength he had gained no advantage; there seemed no prospect of his gaining any against the Fabian tactics of his enemy; and all the while that intensity of religious feeling which was the moral motive force throughout all these conflicts was stronger in the Scottish than in his own command. The ministers of the Kirk were thundering prophecies of victory, and living in an inspired world. They were not in the real Scotland of a rainy late summer; they were all in Palestine, their trust was in Jehovah, and Oliver's regiments were accursed Semitic tribes with strange Oriental names. It was grief to Oliver to find his own phraseology, the Hebrew terms which were so sacred to him, thus turned against himself; and it was in these days (upon the 3rd of August) he wrote that letter which is too often quoted, beseeching the ministers in the opposing camp "in the bowels of Christ" to think that they might possibly be mistaken.

He laboured to inform them that though they had a Covenant indeed, it might be a Covenant with Death and Hell—for remember that these enthusiasts had now a King among them, the son of a man whom Oliver had killed, and this would never do. No wonder he felt strongly; for with a King among them, even a King who was only a boy and bound by that strange Covenant to those who had sold his father, their victory would have undone him. He remembered that his enemy's ranks had among them (their best fighting men) Highlanders wholly indifferent to the Contract with Jehovah, some of them even openly Papist; Cromwell denounced such an unnatural alliance with "wicked and carnal men."

But argument would not save him. The situation was getting worse and worse. He had thought at one moment of attempting to seize Queensferry and so threatening the Scotch with a turning movement from north of the Clyde—the very thing he was to do so successfully the next year. But his force rapidly weakened, his campaign was hampered by an increasing number of sick men, and the prospect of success, even of a compromise and a draw, weakened daily, as that cold, wet August of wind and rain drew out its miserable length. Dysentery, insufficient and irregular food, mud all about, lack of shelter (for the English general had not even tents until after the first week of August) made it necessary at last to act in a fashion the opposite of victorious. He must retire. He must get him back somehow—he and that well-trained force of which he had been so rightly proud—into an England that would mock at his discipline, and think him a failure, as it had found Charles a failure, when he had fallen back before the Scottish rebellion years before. But retreat he must. He put his sick on board ship at Musselburgh and at the end of the month his retreat was begun. He had been guilty of as bad a bit of strategy as the wars had seen.

In the night between Friday and Saturday, August the 30th and 31st, a Council of War sat at Musselburgh round Cromwell. The determination was taken at last to fall back upon Dunbar. That might have to be followed by a further retirement to the Border; the English strength was greatly diminished, the retirement would be harried and might not be successfully carried out; a halt at Dunbar in the midst of it might be impossible. But if possible, for a moment at least, such a halt at Dunbar was to be their aim. They would fortify Dunbar if they could, house their men, putting again on ship-board such further numbers as had fallen sick, and stand there for new supplies by sea. But if in practice all this could not be done under the pressure of a following and now inspirited enemy, why, they must continue desperately from Dunbar on towards England with what remained of their force and cut their way through if they could.

Now Leslie, great as his superiority in numbers had by this time become, dreaded an English fortification of Dunbar. Cromwell might or might not be able to achieve that task under the menace of a pursuing foe, but if he did, it would be a jump-ing-off place for further operations, even if these had to be postponed until after the winter. Dunbar would be a gate of entry for supply to the English army from the sea, which the English ships held. Therefore Leslie determined to pursue vigorously.

On Saturday, the 31st of August, the first march of Cromwell's retreat was undertaken, the stage ending at Haddington, a total distance of between nine and ten miles. Leslie harassed the rear of the column perpetually, but could not yet engage; he could not out-march the English at a sufficient rate to menace their column while it was still stretched out along the main road. Moreover, though Leslie was so anxious to prevent the fortification of Dunbar, time was still on his side for twenty-four hours at least and perhaps forty-eight; also he had had reinforcement, three regiments reaching him in these days, so that his numerical superiority was now greater than ever. Though he would not engage, he never left the retiring English in peace, and on the midnight between Saturday and Sunday he beat up their quarters at the west end of Haddington, where the head of his column touched on the last of theirs.

On Sunday, the 1st of September, Cromwell thought it wise, perhaps by way of demonstration, to threaten, in spite of his inferior numbers, an engagement. He drew up in line perpendicular to the retreat, thus covering the road, and so awaited attack for four hours. Such an action certainly displayed continued confidence in the *morale* of his hardly-tried but long-trained and excellent soldiery. No attack was delivered, but during the delay the train was sent forward ahead of the column and it neared Dunbar before evening. As the English column massed in the neighbourhood of the town the head of the Scotch one in pursuit was but half a mile from the last of their men.

At this point in the affair Leslie acted with wisdom and a soldierly eye. Had he had not had against him certain civilian

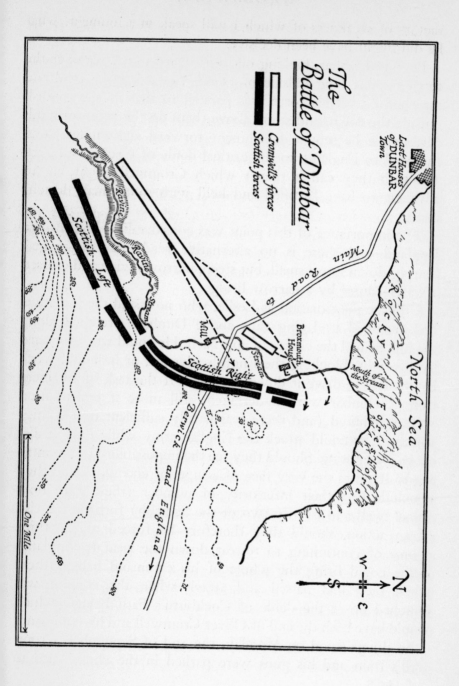

The
Battle of Dunbar

▭ Cromwell's forces
■ Scottish forces

Last Houses
of DUNBAR
Town

Main Road

Ravine

Ravine & Stream

Scottish Left

Mill

Stream

Scottish Right

Broxmouth
House

Mouth of
the Stream

North Sea

Rocks and Foreshore

Berwick and England

One Mile

N
W  E
S

factors of weakness of which I will speak in a moment, what he did might have been decisive.

Beyond Dunbar, looking out northward to the sea over the town lies the long hillside of Doon. Leslie left the road and marched on till his force was parallel to that of the English outside the town, and stood above them on the rising ground. Meanwhile he sent a detachment forward eight miles along the road to England, to the critical defile of Cockburn's Path (Co'path they call it there) which Cromwell ought, in his advance, to have fortified and held with some small detachment.

The importance of this point was considerable. The road to England—and there is no alternative road—here zig-zagged sharply down into a small, but steep, narrow ravine and crossed a water-course by a narrow bridge.

Observe the situation as Leslie, who possessed the initiative, had arranged it. Lying thus above Dunbar, stretched along the hill, he had the choice of approach. He could work forward by his right, blocking the English advance, or he could work by his left to drive it down the road. If the task of fortification at Dunbar were undertaken, still more if embarkation were attempted (and there was hardly sufficient opportunity for that) he could attack the English army while thus in disarray for fighting. Should they see the impossibility of attempting to stand in the very face of a superior enemy, should they conclude that their inferiority of number (they were now about twelve to twenty-two of the Scottish) forbade the risk of an action, should they therefore be forced to the third course of continuing to retreat down the road to England, Leslie could bring the whole of his command behind them when they had passed and attack when the column was bunched up at the defile of Cockburn's Path Bridge—which would have been the end of Oliver Cromwell and his command.

So things stood on Monday, the 2nd of September. Cromwell's train and his guns were parked in the churchyard to the east of and just outside the town; he kept his army deployed in the fields outside, to be ready in case of attack, and all day long under a gusty gale the rain fell in cold, driving showers. The late harvest of that wet and wretched summer lay cut but not garnered, the sheaves piled into their stooks on the fields, with water dripping from the ears of corn; and the grey sky raced overhead above the storm.

By all calculation it would seem that Cromwell's command was doomed. But there were those factors of weakness on his enemy's side of which I have already spoken, and which I will now describe. First of all—a minor point, but to be remembered—Leslie's artillery was insufficient in quality. He had only nine guns that really counted out of a total of thirty-two, the remaining twenty-three being a hotch-potch of small pieces, some of them made of leather. But what mattered much more than this and was in the end to prove fatal was the power of the civilians—and they civilian fanatics. Enthusiasm, invaluable for the animating of soldiers, works disaster in the mechanism of handling them. The ministers of the Kirk in the midst of their frenzied denunciations of Baal, and Midianites and Amalekites, and I know not what other strange beasts, had determined to purge their own host of whatever might offend the Lord God of Israel. This effort was directed chiefly upon the body of officers; it was among these, of course, that you would find gentlemen indifferent to the religious fervour of the preachers, and some of them even sunk in the abominations of Rome. Their places were taken by new men, often the sons or relatives of the ministers themselves. An eye-witness and contemporary mourns most legitimately the effect of such a transfer; men will follow officers who know them and whom they feel to be soldiers like themselves, but ministers' sons quite new to them, even if full of fervour, were not quite the same thing when it came to holding men together against a charge or rallying them in a night surprise.

And there was another action of the clerical civilians even

more dangerous than this; they insisted upon interfering with Leslie's plan. He had intended, we may presume, after considering the advantage of the double approach (which his dispositions gave him) to work for compelling the English to continue their march down the road south, calculating rightly that they could be forced to take this course. Indeed, during that very afternoon the council of English officers, after dining in Dunbar, met in Broxmouth House under Cromwell's directions just outside the town; it was concluded that it would be impossible in the face of the enemy to embark any sufficient numbers, or with the diminished remnant to cut their way back to England—for it was known that the defile of Cockburn's Path was held. There was nothing for it but to continue the retreat, trusting to their full assembled strength to force their way through; but how doubtfully could this be done!

The civilian masters of the Scottish commander here came to the aid of Cromwell. They insisted upon Leslie's not waiting to follow up the retreat and pin it between the main Scottish army and the Cockburn's Path Bridge, but to move at once by his right, stand a-straddle across the road to England and, trusting in his superiority of numbers, thence attack upon the following day—the Tuesday—and in a general frontal action destroy the whole English army.

Leslie had to obey. In the last hours of full daylight, from five to seven o'clock in the evening, Cromwell grasped at once the opportunity this move might give him. The enemy was, as he said, "shogging" to his right (that is, shifting his line from the hillside round so that it should lie with one end towards the sea). They would thus, for reasons which will be seen in a moment, put themselves in a position whence they could only move with difficulty if they were attacked suddenly, early, and by surprise before they had formed.

This move on the part of the Scotch having been noticed, the last of the light beginning to fade under that continuous rain and wind, Cromwell rode up and down the field upon a little Scottish nag, his nervous tension greater than ever, biting his lower lip till it bled, considering the desperation of his position—but remembering the new hope which the false move of his far superior enemy had given him.

And here it is necessary to describe the field, that we may understand what followed.

To the east of the last houses of Dunbar, as they were then, or rather of the Church and churchyard there, skirting the town, a little stream called the Broxburn runs into the sea. It is everywhere easily fordable, even in very wet weather such as that which had preceded the present action. Eight hundred yards up its course from the mouth stood the house and gardens called Broxmouth. Five hundred yards above this again the main road to England crossed it; and 400 yards above that crossing was a mill. A little higher up from this mill the stream issuing from the hills forms a difficult military obstacle; it runs through a sort of trench rather than a ravine, steep on either bank but between them a flat, the sides of which were somewhat marshy. There could be no rapid advance across this part of the water, which higher up still becomes insignificant as the ground rises. Any advance across the stream either way, either eastward or westward, was easy whether to cavalry or infantry in the flat country below Broxmouth House, fairly easy at the road and easy also at the mill.

The first positions in the course of Monday afternoon— when Leslie, under the fatal pressure of his civilian masters, was "shogging" (that is, "shuffling") forward his extreme right towards the sea, were as follows: Cromwell's 12,000 (some 7,000 to 8,000 foot and 3,500 to 4,000 horse) stood in front of the town; sixteen regimental field pieces (two to each regiment) were parked in the churchyard, as were also the few heavies which accompanied the army. Meanwhile, by the end of the day the enemy line lay beyond the brook and making to extend across the road which led to England.

To conform to the dispositions of the enemy, Cromwell

wheeled his line round from in front of Dunbar so that by the fall of darkness, or perhaps shortly afterwards, it stood parallel to and behind that water-course. He occupied Broxmouth House and gardens, he put apparently the greater part of his guns along the western side of the ravine, in a position to play upon the Scottish left when the action should open. Then he awaited the early morning.

At this point it is essential for a comprehension of the battle, that all turned upon which force should cross the stream first in the small hours and so surprise the other.

It had been Leslie's intention to cross the water-course with his right just before dawn and strike with superior numbers upon the English left, which he hoped to break under the sudden pressure; for the Scottish right towards the sea had been reinforced all during the day from the depleted Scottish left. Cromwell effected a corresponding strengthening on his left, but apparently somewhat later and under the cover of darkness. During the night pouring rain continued in gusts and a high storm wind.

These conditions of weather led the Scottish commander to the singular conclusion that nothing would be done by the English until daylight, and he himself had prepared and given the orders to advance his right before it should be day—say something like 4.30 a.m.

An English prisoner who had been captured the day before had been interrogated, by way of making certain, as to what chance Cromwell thought he had considering that he was embarking his men and guns; but the prisoner told his captors that they would find a sufficient force in front of them, there would be plenty of men for them to deal with.

Under that pitiless rain and gale the Scotch army took what shelter it could beneath the stooks of corn, though some of the new and untried officers on the left had abandoned the line to take better cover. Meanwhile on that Scottish left also, that is, along the south-eastern bank of the ravine, Holbourne had given orders that the matches should be extinguished.

The firearms of the Scottish infantry were of two kinds: muskets with wheel-locks, whereby a spark was struck from a flint upon the powder, and muskets in which the powder was exploded by the application of a burning match to the touch-hole. The greater part of the Scottish equipment was of this latter kind. But their supply of matches was insufficient, and Holbourne may well have ordered the matches to be put out lest the smouldering of them during the whole night should exhaust that supply. There is no need to accuse him of treason, but he was none the less suspected of it, for the infantry was useless and disarmed until its matches should be alight, and to light them again in such weather and especially under conditions of surprise would be difficult.

So the first hours of the night passed, up to one, to two, to three in the morning. It was then, somewhere about three o'clock, that a stealthy advance was ordered to begin upon the English right, units of which, coming round above or across the ravine, appeared in the darkness amid the Scottish, taking what uneasy sleep they could upon the sodden ground, dispersed under the shelter of the corn stooks and with matches extinguished. Disorder at once followed; and while the Scottish left was in this confusion Cromwell moved the English left against the Scottish right, *before* the hour at which Leslie had planned to attack. Leslie, as we have seen, had proposed to deliver his blow against Cromwell's left along the stream towards the sea, and probably to use the great Scottish superiority in numbers for curling round the flank of the English between Broxmouth House and the coast, proposing to attack between 4 and 4.30 in the morning, the object being a shock of surprise. Under the weight of his larger body, the English left should break down. The idea was to have the first effect of the blow achieved just as it became broad day, so that the subsequent movements could be driven home under full observation.

But Cromwell anticipated him. He had got many of his men across the water-course long before 4 o'clock in the morning, and such early action alone would explain what followed.

The effect of this move of Cromwell's anticipating the Scottish attack and getting while it was yet dark upon the flank of his enemy must be carefully appreciated, for it determined all that was to follow.

So long as the darkness lasted the streaming of the English up eastward across the brook and between the right flank of the Scottish army and the sea did not immediately affect the enemy. In daylight, of course, the thing would have been seen and dispositions would at once have been taken. Indeed, by daylight Cromwell's manœuvre could not probably have been accomplished, for there would have been a counter-attack by the numerically superior forces of the Scottish side. But evidently a sufficient number of English got over before the significance of the movement had been appreciated, and it was too late for the enemy commanders to rouse and order their men to take up formation. There is a glimmering of daylight very early upon the 3rd of September so far north as the latitude of Dunbar (exactly 56° north), before 4 o'clock in open weather. It is true that the sky of that night was obscured by hurrying clouds, but the movement must have been perceived shortly after it had taken form. We may note by the way an example here of that attention to necessary detail which is the mark of a great Captain: Cromwell's move must have been exactly timed; it came just early enough to be executed under the cover of darkness but late enough to be marked by the enemy when it was completed and so to make the Scotch hurriedly fall back at right angles so as to meet the unexpected threat upon their flank.

It was just past the full moon and the tides were high upon that rocky coast under the storm. There was light therefore

## 1st. Position
*before dawn*

Guns

Ravine     Stream

Sea

Hill
Steep toward the Stream
less steep towards the Sea

▬ The Scotch, not yet in formation, extend their right towards the sea, giving their left a narrow flattish strip pinned between a steep hillside and the ravine below, while their right is dispersed on a shelving slope towards the coast. They are double in numbers Cromwell's command, and intend to cross the stream and attack at dawn.

▢ Cromwell's command forestalls the Scotch and gets across the stream *before* dawn, and so compels the Scotch right to form hurriedly and more and more "refused" at right angles to their left.

## 2nd. Position
*between dawn and sunrise*

Guns

A

The Scotch right hurriedly forming in the half light under pressure of the English who unexpectedly appear across the stream, are compelled to draw up at right angles to their left, which cannot give assistance to this right wing (A), being penned between the ravine and the hill. The right alone therefore (A), has to take the shock of nearly all the English army and is routed at sunrise. The left is rolled up and the Scotch army goes to pieces.

# The Elements of Dunbar

under the flying clouds, to the noise of the waves upon the shore, as the troops filed out before that dawn on to the flats, to turn the flank of the Scottish army. But the moon was already very low upon the western horizon, and shrouded by the rain-cloud above the hills.

As the light broadened round about four o'clock the Scottish commanders perceived that they had increasing enemy forces upon their exposed flank; there was immediate necessity for making there a change of front, they had to bend their line backwards, and began to order it on this part of the field more or less at right angles to its original positions, which had been parallel to the water-course. By the time they were ready to counter-attack and attempt to throw the English back the whole of this right part of the line, from just above the brook eastward was bent back and ran east and west, while the rest of the line continued to lie north and south, and here it was that the difficulty of manœuvre, which Lambert and Cromwell had foreseen, hampered the Scottish command. The configuration of the hill is such that the Scotch left could not readily communicate with the hastily reformed right bent back behind the hill. One may almost say that Dunbar was won because Cromwell was thus attacking a divided army: it was an army not divided by a gap but hampered by an unforeseen crook or elbow in its hastily formed array.

The more the English extended eastward in this manœuvre the more the Scottish were bound to throw back their new right front; and it is in this imposition of the hostile will upon their formation that the root of their subsequent defeat lay.

The whole Scottish right was now—in the first light—bent perpendicular to its original line, and so thrust back upon Doon Hill that there was little opportunity for manœuvre; it found in front of it English bodies still inferior in number but having the advantage of freedom of movement, because the ground behind them was clear—and across this ground, between the Scotch right and the sea, Cromwell was pouring his reserves

[ 296 ]

of men, principally by the passage of the water-course over the flat ground near the coast.

It was full dawn, though not yet full daylight, when the first shock took place and the Scottish commander ordered the charge; it pressed hard upon the as yet insufficient English line in front of it. The Scottish lances, obsolete though these weapons were, proved effective enough; but during this brief first encounter (it can hardly have lasted over fifteen minutes) the English line both rallied and was reinforced. Oliver himself was coming up with three regiments of foot and one of horse: Pride's Regiment, Lambert's and his own, and the mounted men whom the General himself commanded were not only strengthening the line but extending it further and further towards the east and round the Scottish right.

Leslie's command was already so packed, as the result of these first moves, that it found itself ill able to manœuvre; and as the light broadened Cromwell had got his horse well round the Scottish flank, and prepared to charge. The English guns opposite the far Scottish left up the ravine had begun to play, pinning their opponents to that part of the line and cutting off all chance of further reinforcement towards them right in front of the sea.

There was already confusion appearing in the numerically superior (greatly superior) but now disordered bulk of the Scottish forces between the centre and the right; into that confusion a charge of the English foot was ordered. It succeeded fully. Leslie's men in greater and greater tumult were pushed back three-quarters of a mile when, at the critical moment— exactly chosen for its fullest effect—Cromwell's trumpets sounded for his horse to charge and all that body of cavalry whereof he was the soul, which he had formed and informed, came sweeping like the turn of a sickle round the flank of the dense enemy masses, whose formation had already almost gone. They began to disintegrate; those further from the immediate blow had begun to join in the flight, and Cromwell, perceiving how in this short three-quarters of an hour of the first light the thing had been decided, cried out loudly, "They fly! I profess they fly!" The impossible had been accomplished: twelve had routed twenty-two.

Looking over his right shoulder, as he halted for a moment to re-form the line, he saw under the shade of the storm-clouds, in a belt of clear sky, the sun rising; its first rays met him from over the sea-line beyond St. Abb's Head; and one near him heard him shouting the Psalm, "Let God arise and let His enemies be scattered, let them also that hate Him flee before Him."

Under the new full day the last effort at resistance failed. It was a very fine one; two Scottish "battails"—that is two lines still in full formation and facing the English charges—held their ground in spite of the rout and did not break until they were cut in pieces. But for the rest, all had gone, and in the place of Leslie's army was a mob of individuals, each running with what speed he could after the woeful fatigue of those night hours and the collapse at the end. The whole great body of the Scottish force became a torrent of flying men, save for the cavalry on the far left which had easily escaped; and the English pursued without pause, after such a night and morning, all the way back to Haddington—killing, capturing, cutting off—till the full fruit of the victory was reaped.

When the pursuit was halted after the horse at least had covered eight miles, the results could be counted. All the Scottish guns were, of course, in Cromwell's hands; so were 10,000 of foot taken prisoner, and of killed (lying on the field there, stripped and robbed) 3,000 at least were counted. The English could also stack for trophies scores of colours and 15,000 stand of arms. Such was the work of that Tuesday morning, the 3rd of September, 1650, the fullest of all Cromwell's deeds in the saddle, the most absolute, and finally accomplished by his tactical sense alone.

.     .     .     .     .     .     .

In Haddington a minister was preaching to his congregation in a fine fervour of revelation from on high, was thundering out to them that his Jehovah had triumphed and the sectaries were undone. But even as he paused a fugitive from the battle staggered in breathless and fainting with fatigue. He brought other news. The two Jehovahs had indeed met, but it was the English one who had triumphed.

### III

#### WORCESTER

The campaign of Worcester was the last of those operations upon the study of which our judgment of Cromwell as a soldier depends. It was that campaign in which he had the army nearing its perfection and in the best discipline; after long consecutive service it had been becoming for some time past a true professional army, probably superior to any contemporary force in quality.

Worcester was also the campaign in which, especially at its conclusion and decision, he was pitted against the least formidable of the opponent forces he had had to meet. For even at Naseby, where the revolutionaries had nearly double the numbers of the King, the Royal remaining force still possessed Rupert, and the cavalry there defeated was still good. But at Worcester the army of Charles's son, again at the most but half its enemy in number, was hopeless as a military machine for the effecting of a decision. It contained elements of the highest value as fighting men, full of fire and tenacity in the actual conflict, notably the Highlanders, but it was not homogeneous; much of it was untrained, nearly all of it ill armed; it was weakened by a long march through hostile country, despairing of success, and weakened morally even more than numerically by perpetual desertion during the advance.

None the less, in spite of the disparity of forces in the campaign of Worcester, we can there perceive the talents of Oliver

[ 299 ]

Cromwell to have been at their summit. He was acting with undivided authority for the first time, and his power of command, the moral effect he had upon his soldiery, the energy of his movement, were never more conspicuous.

He never fought again. After the day of that victory he had exactly seven years to live; he was to die upon its anniversary; and during those seven years Cromwell was still the Army and nothing but the Army. But his function was no longer to fight; it was to attempt the art of government—an art to him uncongenial and one at which he therefore failed.

.    .    .    .    .    .    .

The main lines of the campaign at Worcester are these:

Oliver Cromwell maintained himself in South Scotland and about the Scottish capital after the unexpected triumph of Dunbar. He was best supplied (not without difficulty) by sea, and he had facing him in the following year, 1651, a renewed Scottish army, of necessarily inferior quality though not yet inferior numbers.

Its leaders relied once more upon the Fabian policy of wearing down the invader, avoiding a general engagement, relying upon the impregnability of Stirling, while Edinburgh and the coast of the Forth remained in Oliver's hands. This insufficient national force in and around Stirling depended for further recruitment and for munitionment and supply from the North; notably was it expecting a further contingent of men from that direction. It was the first task of Cromwell, the obvious and only task before him, to get this Scottish army out of the position at Stirling and manœuvre it into the open. This could only be done by getting round to the north of it and cutting off its chance of further supply. That done, Cromwell's opponents would have to surrender from exhaustion, or engage.

The first phase of the campaign therefore is the throwing by Oliver of a force which operates along the north of the Forth and gets between Stirling and its enemy's northern supply.

[ 300 ]

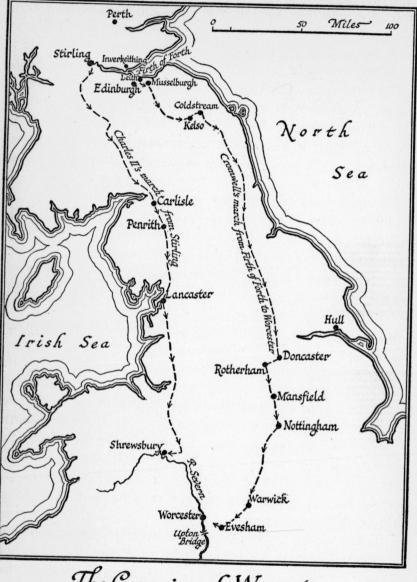

The Campaign of Worcester

This done, Cromwell himself proceeds to occupy a further portion of Scotland beyond the Forth. The centre of this is the town of Perth which he sets out to reduce.

The second phase consists in the decision of the Scotch to take the open by way of a march southward into England. They feel themselves unequal to meeting Cromwell directly in the field. Still less will they be equal to meeting him when they shall have crossed the Border and invaded; for they will inevitably, the further they advance, lose more and more of such strength as they have. Yet they will be compelled sooner or later to meet Cromwell himself in force, coming after them, and increasing bodies drawn from the English garrisons or further levied by the English government.

Of the two military policies therefore, the desperate one of meeting the English in the open upon Scottish soil, or bolting south to cross the Border, the latter would seem even more hopeless than the former, *unless* one new factor, political rather than military, should appear. *If, after crossing the Border, Royalist recruitment should be found in England, sufficient in amount and quality, then Charles may, when the clash comes, be in a posture to meet his opponent.* If such recruitment fails, his army is doomed.

Everyone sees this, friend and foe alike. After the Border is crossed there is no strategy to speak of upon either side, only an advance by the hunted and a pursuit by the hunter—*with the one chance for the hunted that sufficient English strength will come to his aid.*

The third phase then is the bolt southward, the hunted followed by the hunter. Each performs an astonishing feat, each accomplishes one of the most rapid marches in history. And of the two feats that of the hunter, Cromwell, will be seen to be the more remarkable. Each covers a distance of some third of a thousand miles in just over three weeks. It is during this third phase that the issue is decided, for the only thing that could possibly have saved Charles, failed him. He obtained no appreciable English Royalist recruitment.

The fourth phase, therefore, the battle itself, the only engagement and the end of the campaign, was a foregone conclusion. Charles and his men, exhausted and diminished, reached Worcester and halted there; Cromwell, reaching the English midlands just after, surrounded and encircled his enemy with his vastly superior numbers, and the Scotch army as a military force was wiped out.

## The First Phase: The Forcing Manœuvre

To make his enemy bolt from cover Cromwell must come in between Stirling and its northern avenue of supply. With this object he had thrown across the Forth at Queensferry a body now totalling some 4,000 to 5,000 men under Lambert, which force occupied, in the third week of July, 1651, the promontory opposite Queensferry (now attached to the southern bank by the Forth Railway Bridge).

This promontory has at its mouth the position remembered under the name of the village of Inverkeithing. Thither the Scottish command sent a body nearly equal in number to the invaders—something over 4,000—certainly not equal in training, but containing in its Highland contingent and particularly in the MacLeans, some of the best fighting material in these islands. The clash came upon the position of Inverkeithing on Sunday, July the 20th, and resulted in the almost complete destruction of the native force. Some two-thirds were put out of action, killed, wounded or taken, mainly killed and wounded. Lambert's own losses were very much less; how much less we shall never know, for he lied about it, in true warlike "propaganda" fashion, pretending they were but a handful—which, from the nature of the struggle, largely hand to hand and dealing with such troops, could not have been the case. At any rate, his victory was complete, and after that victory the cutting off of Stirling from the north was certain to come.

## The Second Phase

The Royalist army had lost at Inverkeithing an appreciable fraction—perhaps fifteen per cent.—of its numbers and had given proof of its lack of training as well; nothing could prevent an English advance westward till the roads leading to Stirling from the north should be blocked, and the help that was arriving to Charles from the Gordons cut off. Cromwell himself had crossed the Forth, and gone north with a main force, to sit down before Perth.

The Scotch army, entrenched and depending upon the impregnability of Stirling, was now forced to move. Because Stirling could now no longer be supplied, some policy of action in the field was alone open to the Scotch Royal army. Either they must do at last what they had successfully avoided for so long and challenge Cromwell upon Scottish soil close at hand (and to do so was to meet immediate and final defeat, for their enemy was their superior in every way), or there remained the alternative of attempting that doubtful gamble (so soon to prove a forlorn adventure) the invasion of England in the hope of a general Royalist rising. The young King and Leslie, his chief soldier, determined upon this alternative—desperate, as I have said, but the less desperate of the two—they would break south; and on Thursday, July the 31st, eleven days after the affair at Inverkeithing, the disparate force, Kirk-governed, Covenant-dominated, yet mixed with the Highland fire, faced towards the Border and began its march.

Its numbers have been variously estimated; at the highest they have been put at 20,000; at the lowest at 14,000. Political passion is still so strong that the enemies of the Monarchy prefer the larger estimate, the enemies of Puritanism the lower. In favour of the higher estimate is the fact that in spite of the

[ 304 ]

losses on the long and very rapid march there seem to have been at Worcester something like 16,000 in the Scottish command; some of these were due to the very slight recruitment obtained on the way, but most of them must have been men who had crossed the Border. In favour of the lower estimate is the fact that it is that of an experienced eye-witness (Turner) accustomed to estimate numbers of soldiery. He judged the number of men marching on foot at the beginning of the enterprise who passed before his eyes as somewhat over 9,000; the mounted men perhaps 4,000; but there was some addition between the beginning of the march and the Border.

## The Third Phase

Cromwell had seen, of course, for it was patent to anyone, that this decision to march southward into England might be taken. Nevertheless, when the news reached him in front of Perth, it had something of the effect of surprise, for he had as yet made no preparation against it. Perhaps he thought that if it did come it would come later, for Stirling was not yet in bad straits, though its ultimate fate if Leslie had stayed there was certain. Perhaps he thought that the Scotch would engage him in the open in spite of their sense of inferiority in the field; here again his reason for not warning the authorities in London may have been that he did not want to frighten them until it was necessary. It was clear that if the Scotch did decide to go south he must be after them with the utmost rapidity, for everything turned upon whether they would or would not get English recruitment, and Cromwell's own presence in England with his army, even though the Scotch had thus slipped ahead of him, would make a great difference to that decisive factor. Such measure of strategic surprise as Charles and Leslie had gained, therefore, was only one of date; Cromwell knew the march south was possible, but was perhaps not expecting it so soon. Harrison was warned to make for the Border when or if such a move on the part of the Scotch should take place, Monk to remain in Scotland, Lambert to follow south and ultimately join with Harrison.

The very day after Cromwell heard the news, that is, on August the 2nd, any doubts he might have had as to what to do next were resolved for him by the surrender of Perth. He at once began to concentrate for the southward march in pursuit of Charles, and made his dispositions as follows:

Monk with some 5,000 to 6,000 men to deal with the small Scotch garrison left behind in Stirling; Lambert was to follow as best he could on the heels of the Scotch army with his 3,000 to 4,000 men; Harrison, with much the same number, was to make for the Border, obtain additional force and effect, ultimately, a junction with Lambert. Though the two between them would not have sufficient strength to engage, at any rate they could harass the advance of Charles's army and hope to keep it in play till Cromwell should arrive. As for the main force under his own command, Cromwell had to wait—though he must have chafed at the delay—one or two days. He had to break camp, to concentrate certain outlying bodies, and then transfer these considerable forces over a broad sheet of water at Queensferry. It was not until Monday, August the 4th, that he wrote to the Speaker of the House of Commons telling him that the Scotch were on the march for England, and admitting that it might cause "some inconvenience," but begging the Parliament not to be frightened. At last, on the morning of Wednesday, August the 6th, he started out, six days after his enemy. It was his to get down southward as quickly as possible by the roads along the eastern edges of the Pennines, parallel to Charles, who was marching by the western road, making for the Moffat Pass, and aiming to advance to Carlisle and Penrith through Lancashire. So did the race begin.

## Fourth Phase

During this race down Britain, the Scotch by the western road and the English by the eastern, one who should be able to watch the two bodies would have noticed the contrast. The first ill-equipped, for the most part ill-mounted, marching light, half armed, with no known provision awaiting them nor power of establishing advanced bases; the other an army at the zenith of its organisation, fully equipped, coming back to their own territory, where they would find all that was needful to them, and succour and reinforcements more and more available with every day's march beyond the frontier.

Each proceeded at a pace exceptional in military history. I have already alluded to that character in this chase, it is the moment to give it in some detail because, for some reason which escapes me, it has not as a rule been emphasised. So far as it is possible to identify the roads of the period, it would seem that the Scottish under Charles II marched at an average of at least 15 miles a day, probably slightly more; in the earlier part of the advance certainly more. The performance is the finer because the first half of it was in barren, mountainous country, and the last half of it hampered by attack.

Cromwell's achievement was as remarkable, though in a different way. His troops were, of course, for the most part highly trained men, whose organisation was matured and tested; he had only one pass of any height to cross, and this was lower than either of the two which the Scottish army had to scale (Shap and Moffat); on the other hand, Charles's army, after Carlisle, was following one of the main trunk roads of England —at least, until within the last three marches of Worcester— while Cromwell, judging that shortness of trajectory would be even more valuable to him than excellence of road surface, did not follow the corresponding main road through York, but hugged the edges of the Pennines. For instance, he takes the cut-off of the Roman road from near Brauncepath for more than a hundred miles, which gives him a direct line; but the surface could not have been in good condition for it was not a main artery in those days.

The total mileage from the Forth to Warwick I make to be 320 miles. Cromwell himself, at any rate with his advanced unit, covered these 320 miles in the equivalent of nineteen days, or very few hours more; August the 6th to August the 24th, allowing for the first and last days not being full marches —an average of nearly seventeen miles a day. Even if we count the final march to Evesham, twenty-two miles on from Warwick (by way of Stratford) the arrival of the last units at Evesham on the 27th (and among these first units we must allow for concentration) we still get an average of more than sixteen and a quarter miles a day. Cromwell's advance, therefore, was slightly more rapid than that of Leslie and Charles, and that although his men marched heavy where the Scottish marched light. But when all is considered and cancelling out the respective advantages and disadvantages, both forces could boast of a great achievement. There have been short individual marches, of course, of far greater speed, but a continuous three weeks kept up upon this average is extraordinary. It is further to be remarked in the case of Cromwell that the junctions he effected with his reinforcements were exact, so that he suffered therefrom no delay. Those reinforcements (Lambert and Harrison) had started earlier, but they had had a certain amount of skirmishing to do, and it is to be noted that the Scottish force, which might also have been delayed by such diversions, maintained its average none the less.

Here then we have Cromwell at Evesham on August the 27th, 1651, with 28,000 men in hand. Shortly afterwards there came in 3,000 of militia from the east counties, Essex and Suffolk, raising the total force for the day of the decision to 31,000 men.

The Royalist force awaiting the attack at Worcester was by this time probably somewhat under 16,000 men, say half the power concentrating against it, and, of course, far less well equipped and with a far smaller proportion of well-trained men. The thing was already settled, for the prime "unknown quantity"—Royalist recruitment on the way—had failed altogether. Derby had made a gallant attempt to bring in a Lancashire contingent, but Lilburne had cut it off, and Derby only came in, wounded, with a handful.

There were several reasons for this lack of support. The first was that the Royalist sympathisers had been largely dispersed and almost wholly disarmed; even had they joined Charles's column he had no muskets or pikes to give them. The second was that they were not only disarmed but cowed; it is true that sympathisers with Catholicism, who to a man were loyalist, were more numerous in Lancashire than any other county; it is also true that the counties along the North Welsh Border as Charles approached it down Severn were largely Loyalist in sympathy also: but it was now more than six years since the last considerable decisive action had ended in the destruction of the last appreciable Royalist army. The two attempts at restoring the situation—sometimes called "The Second Civil War"—had since failed. To aid Charles now would have been an overt act of rebellion against the *de facto* Government. The leaders would be treated not as enemies but as traitors. Derby was actually so treated; after having been made prisoner in battle, he was later put to death. Another reason for this lack of support was the fact that this invading army was alien. The Scotch were, to all Englishmen of that day, a national enemy. Our judgment of this must not be confused by the political and military alliance made under necessity through the genius of Pym with the original Scottish enemies of their common King; the Scottish invaders of 1651 were, to the average Englishman, odious and aggressive foreigners whom he detested. A violent religious sympathy might artificially unite them for a time with a fanatical minority of English, but there was no substance in this union; it was no true friendship; Scotland was still, and was long to remain, not only an alien but a hostile country. Other things being equal, it would have gone against the grain even for the loyal Englishman of the north-west to find himself marching alongside of Scotchmen invading his country.

Yet another reason was that a victory of Charles's army under these circumstances would have meant the imposing of the Covenant—an idea increasingly offensive to the mass of Englishmen as time went on. Even such a proportion of Englishmen as would have followed the politicians and accepted that unnatural instrument for the sake of saving a political cause in arms, had now no such incentive; to the rest the Covenant was intolerable.

All these things combined are amply sufficient to account for the absence of support and recruitment. Charles and Leslie in Worcester must fight their hopeless battle with their own resources and nothing more.

A bad blunder (though a very unlikely one) on the part of their enemy, the throwing over of bridges in the wrong place, the breaking of a bridge once formed, bad timing in the crossing and deploying, *might* give them an opportunity of defeating Cromwell's great host in detail when it should come down to Worcester later. But, of course, no such blunders were to be feared under Cromwell's command. He was about to use his overwhelming numerical superiority in a manœuvre of encirclement. He proposed to surround the enemy in Worcester so that no one fighting unit of them could escape.

With that object he opened the ball by sending Fleetwood round with nearly half his command to Upton, eight miles downstream. A central arch of the bridge at Upton had been broken, but Fleetwood's men threw a plank across the gap, the breach was temporarily repaired, and the whole of that part of the army crossed. Meanwhile Cromwell threw a bridge of boats across the Severn just above the point where the

Teame comes in and another bridge across the Teame itself from the northern to the southern bank.

These works were not completed until the early afternoon of the 3rd of September, but when all was ready Fleetwood

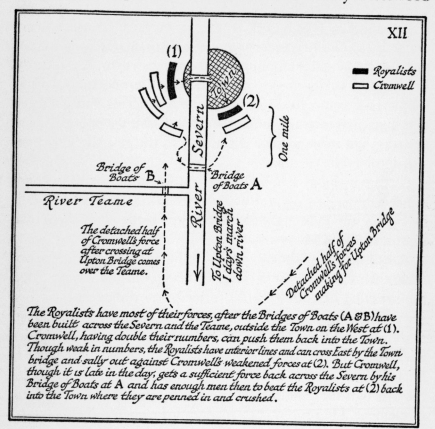

THE ELEMENTS OF WORCESTER

crossed by the bridge over the Teame and deployed in front of the Scottish army, which thus lay between him and the bridge over the Severn in Worcester town itself. When the first shots were fired there remained rather more than four hours daylight at the most in which to complete the business; but even if it should not have been completed when darkness fell there would hardly be hope left on the morrow for the enemy, contained within this circle of superior strength.

Fleetwood found the beginning of the task in that afternoon harder than he had perhaps imagined; it was blind country with small patches of field and hedgerow and it was contested with great tenacity.

Cromwell brought over by the Severn bridge of boats a contingent in aid, with which reinforcement Fleetwood and he began driving the enemy over the bridge into the town. Meanwhile, the King, watching from the top of the Cathedral tower, estimated rightly enough that the depletion of Cromwell's main force on the eastern side of the city was such that a sudden attack upon it might prove successful. There was here, at the south-eastern angle of the walls, a work called "the fort royal," and the fire from it would help the King's sally. Charles therefore sent out a column by the southern gate (the Sidbury gate) and did there obtain a temporary success. But Cromwell at once led back sufficient forces to the eastern bank across his bridge of boats, counter-attacked and drove back the sortie into Worcester. The fort was stormed, as was the gate itself, and meanwhile the survivors from beyond the river had all crowded into the town above the bridge, and the last of the light and the beginning of dusk were filled with a violent hand-to-hand struggle in the narrow streets of the city.

It could have only one end: some few of the mounted forces cut their way out, Charles himself having the good fortune to be among them, but the mass of the army he commanded was killed or wounded or had laid down their arms before it was fully dark. It was a complete decision, which is frequently and justly compared in character to that of Sedan. The last Royalist army had ceased to be. And it was September the 3rd, the anniversary of Dunbar.

# RELUCTANT POWER

In the morning of Wednesday, the 20th of April, 1653, Cromwell swept away the last dregs of the old Revolutionary Parliament.

The scene is too famous to need repetition. He rose in his place from the left of the Speaker's Chair just as the question was to be put, interrupted the proceedings by an indictment which turned into passionate (and well-deserved!) abuse of individuals, called in the handful of his soldiers who were waiting outside, and drove out the Members, their Speaker, and the last symbol of their authority. It was the beginning of the last phase, five and a half years long, which ended only with his death.

Those five and a half years were years in which the international repute of England rose high as such repute of any country will rise during a despotism, before the bill has to be paid. The power of her government at home and its means of action abroad were so strong that this nation of something over five millions appeared as the equal ally or enemy of great monarchs, each commanding many times her numbers and apparent resources. England in those years mastered and passed her rival, the Protestant commercial oligarchy in Holland, and proved herself everywhere possessed upon the ocean and the narrow seas of instruments adequate to her claims. To such an episode every patriot looks back with pride, and on it is mainly founded the great place which Cromwell occupies in the national mind.

But for the inward man himself those five years were a confused burden of reluctant power. He was not made for absolute control; he did not desire it and he would not willingly maintain it; it was not consonant with his nature. Yet in spite of every effort to share and to delegate responsibility, such power was thrust upon him, and has warped history by founding those false views of him, each of which in turn has had a long and vigorous life; the legend, which represented him, until modern times, as a hypocrite and a schemer possessed by ambition; the later legend of a mighty figure, almost majestic, inspired to autocracy by zeal for the public good, himself throughout not only of an iron integrity but of an iron will, imposing rule.

He was neither the one nor the other. He was a man who could not but take on the task which his own immediate past, and the past of that society wherein he found himself the chief, imposed upon him. But it remained a task and a grievous one: ungrateful, distasteful, in moments abhorrent. Over and over again he would have relieved the pressure of it from his own shoulders—and death caught him, too suddenly, still anxiously conceiving yet another scheme whereby he might escape from carrying a weight for which he was unfitted.

First, then, let us ask how such a situation arose.

After the battle of Worcester, after he had returned in that final triumph to London, he was certainly already, whether he would or no, the master. He had under his hand an army now largely veteran, all of it in good training, fully equipped, controlling the disarmed people of three kingdoms. That army was, for the mass of it, devoted to him and he was the incarnation of it. It and he together were invincible; therefore to him of necessity turned all that confused but clamorous demand for a settlement and a true peace. Saving the few in theory (and with zeal) republican and the many, who, among the millions, clung to the old traditions of the nation, and were not exhausted by the absolute defeat of their leaders, men could only think of Oliver Cromwell as the man from whom a solution must come.

And, indeed, a solution was acutely needed. There was everywhere a hunger for it, which, in the great masses of the people was a passion, a physical necessity. Such a solution was not to be found in a single aim. The demand for relief and for repose, for justice and quietude, took a hundred forms, according to the classes and interests, sufferings, temperaments and recent fate of the intertwining groups. Throughout that congeries of unorganised demands there were contradictions, but throughout there also ran a universal clamour, for adjustment, security and the refoundation of normal English life—even if the return to normal had to take the form of strange innovations.

But a main contradiction lay between the power to which all turned and the bitter public grievance against that power. The power was the organised armed force; the grievance was the inhuman strain upon men's fortunes and labour, without which that power could not exist. Most who petitioned for or expected redress laid their pleas at the feet of Cromwell, almost as though he were already an acknowledged monarch; their attitude was nourished by the ever-deeper obeisance which foreign opinion makes to him. But what was Cromwell, to whom they thus turned?

Cromwell was the Army: but what was the necessary condition without which the army could not exist? Ruinous levies on all fixed wealth; confiscation of estates; sale of men's lands; distraint. The cost of the armed forces in special levies alone was much more than had been demanded by Charles for *all* activities of his peaceful and prosperous government combined. Where Charles Stuart had required less than 20/- for *all* the business of the State, the Commonwealth was asking nearly 30/- in extraordinary levies for its armed forces alone, and much more than 40/- for the full business of the nation. Charles's demand had led to the active revolt of the larger taxpayers, the great landowners and the merchants of the City, largely supported by the lesser freeholders and the smaller owners of businesses and crafts. The King's levies had seemed too burdensome; what had been suffered seemed monstrous.

And yet it was not enough. It had to be supplemented by heavily increased duties at the ports, by confiscations right and left, by the sale of public estates, by every ruinous expedient—and still the debt piled up.

That was the main problem, urgent and crying of necessity for a solution. But there was, of course, much more. There was tithe still levied from every farmer in England and going to support a Church Establishment which no one could define, which was in chaos and which in its entirety pleased no one. There was the standing religious quarrel between the various sects. There was the hated anomaly, the old battered fragment still calling itself the House of Commons and still asserting its sovereign power over the community. It was now but a quarter of its due numbers at the most; its original members had sat there unchanged through nearly a dozen years of catastrophic change; it had in part renewed itself by filling vacancies with men of its own choosing—for it could and did reject whom it willed—it had suffered every indignity without exhibiting the strength to defend itself, it had been forcibly lopped down to what it was by the strength of the sword; it obviously was no true master, it obviously lived on the toleration of that which was really master—but it proceeded as though it were master indeed. The thing calling itself Parliament was at once impotent, hated and arrogant. *That* situation urgently and clamorously demanded liquidation.

It is in the nature of Parliaments, especially when they have been some years in existence, to misunderstand their true position. Every Parliament is a clique; but soon the clique becomes a corrupt oligarchy which, from the reiteration of verbal forms calling it "The People," thinks itself immune. But the manifest and real power of the sword hung over it like a shadow and the Parliamentarians must now use all their skill in twisting and turning to save themselves.

Yes: they would dissolve. But on conditions. They needed time—they even needed three years! There must be special privilege for themselves. Whatever new body was to take their place as representatives, *they* must have the right to choose who should be admitted and who not; and whatever new men came in, in whatever numbers, *they* at least must remain.

Cromwell in that same autumn after Worcester already insisted upon some declaration of their conditions. He insisted, and he had behind him the whole army for so insisting, that they should fix a time-limit after which a new Parliament should be called. They dragged out debate on this, although the wretched body often sank to little over fifty men. They remembered their power of patronage. To be a Parliamentarian was already a lucrative thing, and the shadow of power smelt like the substance of it.

And still the demands arose. For what had the war been fought? What fruit had it borne? Was not justice still bought and sold by the lawyers so that a plain Englishman found it beyond his means (petitions called it "a Norman bondage"): and there came from various counties the cry which Westminster feared most—they told Cromwell that the Lord had not put the sword into his hand in vain.

A conference was summoned by Cromwell to meet at the house of the Speaker, Lenthall. It was a sort of mixed committee of the Parliament and the Army; we do not know the names of all those who came, we only have nine, but among those nine, five are directly connected with Oliver either by great friendship or by blood. This conference was to discuss what form of government would best suit the state of affairs. Cromwell himself inclined vaguely to some form of "monarchical power" as against "an absolute republic." But it was remarked that those who were closest to him and most under his influence were against an overt monarchy.

We can only guess what was passing in the minds of men all of whom were occupied with thoughts which were not allowed to appear on the surface, but it is certain from all we know of Oliver's actions and from the lucidity of his mind that he would allow no return of a Stuart. How far he was already thinking of taking monarchical power himself no man can tell, possibly he himself could hardly have told you: a soldier is accustomed to undivided command, it recommends itself to him instinctively, after years of military experience, and Cromwell was doubtless quite sincere in speaking generally in favour of rule by one man. He must have known that if such was to come, that one man could hardly be any other than himself: even if he were only called the Viceroy or Minister of a nominal King.

The conference broke up, of course, without result; but it is to be remembered that he summoned it and that he picked its members, and that its general effect was to block the return of any Stuart.

Meanwhile the House continued, during the following year (1652) to spin out its deliberations concerning its own dissolution and the type of Parliament that was to follow it. And the friction between the so-called House of Commons and the higher officers (of whom Cromwell was in their own eyes, no more than the chief) increased.

The House had already of its own authority made a bid for the popularity which it so sorely needed by reducing the Army to three-quarters of its existing force, and the enormous county assessments by one-third. From having to find for the support of the soldiers a good deal more than half a million pounds of our money in a month, the unfortunate owners of property were in future to pay no more than £400,000—or at any rate a good deal under half a million. This was enough in all conscience for the little England of that day—but it was *some* relief and therefore did give the Parliament some passing glimmer of support.

This was in the autumn of 1651, contemporary with the negotiations just spoken of. By the middle of 1652 yet another proposal for a reduction of the Army was made; and that date, the late spring and early summer of the year, marks the point after which the survival of the unfortunate Commons, already precarious, became impossible.

In almost any political crisis you must look for economic motives, and here they are quite clear. The officers cashiered lost money; the Parliamentarians on their side were filling their pockets steadily, as they had been doing from the beginning of their revolutionary action. Private gain is always one of the chief activities of any Parliamentary system. Threatened with further reduction, the Army protested; the Council of Superior Officers presented a petition at the Bar of the House, and Oliver's cousin, the ubiquitous "cousin Whalley," the man who had worked with him the plan for destroying the King, was at its head. This Petition, though the terms of it were respectful, was an indictment of the Parliament; it demanded a strict half-yearly account of the money received by that body, it asked for a religious settlement, it attacked the severity of the Excise, and, most important of all, it insisted on the hastening of the Dissolution, and a Bill framing the regulations for the election of the assembly that was to replace them.

By this motion Parliament was alarmed, but not quickened. They gave involuntary proof of their own inferiority by appealing to Cromwell to prevent such petitions in the future, thereby admitting that it was for Cromwell himself to decide in person on the most important political matters.

It is possible that the reduction of expenditure proposed by Parliament if it could have been brought into effect would have given the politicians a rather longer lease of life, for the measure was obviously popular. But here came in another economic factor: the rivalry between the City of London and the Dutch Merchants. This had caused the Parliament as early as the autumn of '51 to pass the Navigation Act, which forbade merchandise other than that of the country of origin to come into English ports save in English ships. The Dutch had been, for all that generation, the carriers of the world, and a policy of this kind certainly meant war sooner or later. A Dutch ship could no longer carry goods to England unless those goods were of Dutch origin, though it is true that such origin included the goods of the great Dutch possessions in Asia. The maritime war which resulted from this policy (the first shots were fired before the Petition of the Officers to the Parliament and an admitted state of war followed not long after it) created a necessity for more revenue, more revenue meant more taxation, and whatever slight popularity the Parliament might have got by its first measures of retrenchment was undone. It was compelled to pursue the war vigorously, right on to the end of 1652; and beyond—to late February, 1653. But to make war was saying good-bye to all efforts at economy.

During these months, one fine day in the course of November, 1652, perhaps the 8th of that month, the lawyer Whitelock was strolling in St. James's Park and there met the Lord General, Oliver Cromwell. That they had a long conversation on the coming and necessary settlement is almost certain, for even in memoirs people do not usually invent the whole of an interview from beginning to end. That the words spoken were exactly those remembered by Whitelock may be doubted, for they were not published until after the Restoration; but here again it may be presumed that they do represent a substance of what passed. They have a ring of actuality and truth about them, and they are just what we should expect from Cromwell's habit of suffering sudden nervous impulses.

It seems, then, that Cromwell said to Whitelock, "What if a man should take on him to be King?" It is not so certain (though also probable) that Whitelock's reply represents something he said, for he assures us that he proposed as an alternative that Cromwell should act as Chief Minister under Prince Charles—the said Prince Charles being restored to the throne, but with only nominal power. He adds that Cromwell showed no enthusiasm for such a solution; and that also sounds probable enough, for if there was one thing on which his limited, but clear mind was fixed, it was the danger which he himself would run from any Stuart.

Thus through the early days of 1653 and on into the spring the opposing interests raced towards collision. Yet another conference was held, the last session of which was on Tuesday, the 19th of April, 1653, in Cromwell's own rooms at White-hall. With his officers surrounding him, a petition from the Commons asked plainly for the final views of the Army, Cromwell answering by asking as plainly for a full description of the Parliament's plan for the calling of a new House. They answered that continuity between the new House and the present group of professional politicians of which they had so long been members was essential to the good of the nation, that England could not be safe without them. In other words, they intended to pursue their original plan of delay, and the renewal of their membership under their own supervision, and of affirming their private privilege to sit continuously in the new House as in the old—so that something like a quarter of the new, or rather more, would be formed of that same remnant which they themselves composed.

The officers must have continued to discuss the matter with Cromwell till a late hour, for the last of those present did not go home till the midnight of that Tuesday. It shows the temper of that moment that they met again early the next morning. They were given news that the House would do their will and dissolve. But just after this, a false rumour had got abroad. Colonel Ingoldsby, yet another of Cromwell's cousins, came in to tell them that the Parliamentarians were determined to rush their Bill through before there could be any interference from the Army; that the republicans (headed by Vane) proposed to make it law that very morning. Now if, or when, it should be law, any undoing of it by the soldiers would be technically rebellion. A shock of that kind acted on Cromwell like a spur. It was then that he ordered a few musketeers to be in readiness, and walked down the quarter of a mile to St. Stephen's.

We know what followed. It was just as the Speaker was rising to call the Division which would have made the Parliamentarians' Bill law that Cromwell interrupted him, and that the famous scene was played out which ended by the Speaker himself being handed from the Chair and the Mace removed.

· · · · · · ·

That same afternoon Oliver turned up at the Council of State, the members of which, under the chairmanship of Bradshaw, had met as usual, as though nothing had happened. He informed them that as private gentlemen he was glad to see them, but that they were no longer a Council of State, seeing what he had himself done but a few hours before in the way of dissolving the Parliament. To whom Bradshaw himself answered that they were all well aware of what had been done, that all England would know it soon, but that Cromwell was mistaken if he thought the Parliament were dissolved, for no earthly power could dissolve it until it had dissolved itself.

It was a courageous speech on the part of the bullet-proof-hatted regicide, but if he thought that there was going to be any general support for him and his kind he was mistaken. Amid a mass of evils the broken, unhappy, confused people of England thought that the Parliament had been upon the whole the worst.

But (alas!) Cromwell did not think so. He was not of the calibre that can govern single-handed—or, if a kinder expression be preferred, he had not the vices of a tyrant. Immediately after turning out the dregs of the Long Parliament, Oliver, working with his chief military officers, published an appeal to the country to justify what had happened. But he dared not undertake (or rather could not undertake) full personal responsibility. Another Council was to be summoned to take the place of that former Council of State which he had got rid of at the same time as the Long Parliament. The size of that

CROMWELL DISSOLVING THE LONG PARLIAMENT
FROM A CONTEMPORARY DUTCH PRINT

Council was, for the moment, unsettled. Finally it was settled that the Twelve Apostles were an even better model than the Sanhedrin. Some had wanted no more than a Council of ten, a reasonable number. True to the strange atmosphere of their faction, the zealots bethought themselves of the Jews and pleaded for a membership of seventy, upon the model of that ancient House of Advice in Israel. But the model of the Apostolic College finally prevailed, and since there could be no question of Peter, it was natural, and even in their eyes beautiful, that, as Our Lord was admittedly at the head of the Twelve Apostles, Cromwell should be at the head of these twelve.

So there he sat, as Lord President, with eight of his major officers about him, to whom were added four civilians.

The orders given out immediately after this singular and hasty arrangement, though they were weighty, were not co-related to any recognised and definite authority. Judges were dismissed and others put in their places, the Treasury and the Admiralty were secured in the hands of new men; the enormous levy for the Army was openly authorised to continue; but you could not say that all these important orders flowed from one source; the Council of War decided some, the Council of State others, others again Oliver himself. In the confusion some believed that the King would come into his own again; there were petitions for the old and legitimate Constitution of England, others for a new Parliament, others for the recalling of the Long Parliament that it might dissolve itself and so remove the reproach of illegality. As for Cromwell, he consulted the spirit of the Lord and his chief soldiers, and the fruit of this double consultation was his determination to share responsibility with a new experimental Parliament.

It was summoned by Cromwell in his military capacity, as "Captain General of all the Forces," and 156 "Persons fearing God" got their writs sent to them on the 6th of June, with orders to assemble with full responsibility for the national

[ 323 ]

affairs on the projected date, the 4th of July. It was wondered by some why they accepted such a charge; Cromwell assured them their commission was from God; they were not displeased with such an assurance. Round a great table in Whitehall these 120 were gathered, a somewhat lesser number than the total of those who had been called.

Cromwell inspired them by telling them that they were called to make war in alliance with the Lamb against his enemies; he pointed out that God shook mountains and had a high hill which was the hill of Bashan, and that the chariots of God were 20,000, even 20,000 of Angels, and that God would dwell upon that hill for ever. He then delivered to them supreme authority for fifteen months, that is, until October, 1654.

The Assembly was not badly chosen; they represented the various factions from left to right who would support the Government; they included many Presbyterians, and there sat among them the great Blake, fresh from his victories at sea. It is one of the lamentable myths of history that this body should pass as something ridiculous because one of its worthy members (the junior member for the City, who had a leather business in Fleet Street) was called "Praise-God-Barebones." The name was originally "Barbone"—posterity has made "Barebones" to satisfy the comic taste.

This crutch which Oliver had had fashioned to rid him of responsibility set to work to do so with some independence, and not without judgment. Of those summoned, all came in but two, raising the total numbers to 154. Above them Cromwell and his Council continued their executive action, and it is worth remarking that when a new Council had to be elected, though the vote was by ballot, all men present voted for Cromwell; the nearest to him, Pickering, had nearly as many votes, and the next nearest, more than seven-tenths of the total.

This odd Parliament, however, the first of Cromwell's experiments in sharing responsibility and removing the full burden from himself, failed disastrously, as every other similar experiment of his was to fail. It failed for the very simple reason that one cannot divide the supreme authority of the State. If it does not reside in one man it must reside in an aristocracy, or if the State be very small in a democratic assembly of the citizens. To attempt any other thing is to ride two horses— or more.

The assembly being an assembly, and not one man with the personal responsibilities of one man, nor a gentry with the class responsibilities of a gentry, nor an assembly of the people responsible to themselves, attempted collectively what no one with full responsibility could attempt, that is universal and wholesale reform, particularly of the iniquities of the law. They found themselves opposed by the formidable organisation of the Lawyers' Guild, and it was that more than anything else which broke them down. Their collapse was aided by the extravagance of religious mania, and it was only a question, when December came, of how, after these few months, the unfortunate makeshift should disappear.

On Monday, the 12th of December, 1653, Cromwell's personal supporters in the assembly determined the issue. Sydenham, the soldier, one of his Colonels, moved that they should go off to Whitehall and put their resignation into the hands of the man who had created them. An attempt at debate was settled by all Cromwell's adherents marching off, their Speaker among them. All this was done quickly, before the bulk of the House had met, and as the Opposition drifted in they knew not which way to turn. They sought God in prayer, whereupon two officers coming in bade them be off. They asked to be shown his warrant, and were presented instead with a company of soldiers who cleared the House and locked it up.

Cromwell thought it best to leave the document of resignation on a table in his Palace to receive further signatures; on the day after the morrow there were eighty of these all told. And that was more than a clear majority.

[ 325 ]

So ended in a final and satisfactory fashion the first absurdity. On the very next day Cromwell determined upon a new and very important step. There could be no doubt that he had been persuaded to it by the peril of anarchy, for during these days of the "Little Parliament" (as the Barebones affair had come to be called) dangerous symptoms of breakdown had appeared. To the attacks of Lilburne were added the lunacies of certain raving enthusiasts, by name Powell and Feakes.

It had become clear, as it always becomes clear in revolutions before they have proceeded far, that the choice lay between anarchy and arbitrary rule; for it is only custom, the effect of time, and that sanctity wherewith time clothes institutions which make rational and orderly government possible. Unrooted novelties can depend at first on nothing but force.

Here then was Cromwell, compelled to adopt, I will not say despotism, for a man without love of rule could no more be an efficient despot than a man without an ear can be an efficient poet—but at any rate personal rule; he had to take on full power. But it was indeed to be what I have called it, Reluctant Power, and all the years during which he fumbled with it were marked by a sort of bewilderment which fatigued and oppressed him, till, with the debt that was its natural result, it drove him to his death.

It was "The Soldier Out of Place" over again. He was asked as one individual to produce policies for home government and for foreign affairs. In home government his sole resource was to try over and over again to share responsibility and to shift the weight from his own shoulders. Hence the futile series of efforts to be supported by all sorts of new-fangled Senates which worked absurdly, and each of which had to be dismissed in turn.

It is only fair to repeat here what will be insisted upon at the end—the way in which he was pursued the whole time by acute necessity for money. Since grants for money were associated in his own mind and in the minds of his contemporaries with Parliaments, Parliaments he must have. But what a welter! What a series of futilities!

As for foreign policy—there was none. Cromwell had only one guide in that: his violent religious emotion. Now to let religion underlie foreign policy is a high piece of wisdom, for nations clash through differences of culture and difference in culture derives from difference in religion. It is apparent today as much as ever that the true line of cleavage running through Europe is the line of cleavage between the three religious cultures—Protestant, Catholic and Orthodox; just as the lines of cleavage between our civilisation as a whole and what is external to it runs between Christendom and Paganism, Christendom and Islam. But it is one thing to recognise this profound general truth, and another to let it interfere with detail. One may hold to such a guide as a general informing principle, but with Cromwell it acted upon the details, everything he did in his relations with Europe, and therefore pushed him hither and thither at random.

He had of course no knowledge of the world through foreign travel; but he was a gentleman of good birth (three generations of great wealth) and he had met dozens of men who knew their Europe; yet he was never properly advised, and the picture of the Continent which he had formed in his own mind was quite unreal and out of proportion.

Although these years which I have called those of "Reluctant Power" are the best documented in his life and must, in any chronicle of his activities, fill more space than all the rest put together, they teach us little with regard to the man himself save these lessons I have pointed out: his fundamental unwillingness for, and therefore incapacity in, civilian rule.

There never was a man less of a statesman than Oliver. It is somewhat to his honour, because his inability to govern at home or to direct the forces of England abroad proceeded from good qualities in him; his is an excellent case for asking the question, "Can the good man govern others?" as also for asking that other question, more to the point, "Does the good man ever desire to govern others?" Not that Cromwell was a man especially good, but it was the good in him which made him unfitted for this wearisome task under which he succumbed.

I will take the domestic and foreign affairs in their order, beginning with the domestic.

The first thing to grasp here is that in the interval of five and a half years between the suspension of Parliament and poor Oliver's death *there was no strong personal rule*. That sounds paradoxical, of course, if we are considering only externals; but when you are judging a man the last thing you must consider is the external—a man is to be judged from within. There was in those years no persistent tenacious emanation of authority proceeding from an appetite for authority. Cromwell did not "inform" the State, still less mould it, as he had so magnificently informed and moulded his troop, his regiment, his cavalry and at last his whole army. He was of that already mature English upper class—an aristocracy, the type of government which proceeded from the Reformation and the remains of which are still precariously in control today. Now you do not get despots out of an aristocracy any more than you get aristocrats under a despotism. A gentry is not the material from which your master of men is drawn; they can well be masters in the plural, indeed that is their very nature, but they cannot be masters in the singular. At heart such an idea is detestable to the gentleman.

Cromwell's effort at shifting the burden from his own shoulders and sharing it with some kind of Senate or clique or public body included four experiments—each of them a total failure. With the first, the "Little" or "Barebones" Parliamentary of nominees, we have already dealt. It met on the 4th of July, 1653, not much more than two months after he had turned out the Long Parliament. He had intended it to last till the 3rd of November of the following year; it had burst ignominiously (as we have seen) on the 12th of December, after little more than five months' existence. And it had burst through the action of his friends and himself.

There had been drawn up just before the end of the phase an elaborate document of which Lambert seems to have been the main author, called "The Instrument of Government." It was in forty-two clauses, elaborate but mechanical and neat, as are all paper constitutions when they appear fresh from the void, as yet untouched by reality. There was to be a personal Head of the State, to be called, by ancient precedent, "Protector"; and he, of course, was to be Oliver. There was to be at his side a powerful Council of fifteen members, to whom he could (with their assent) add another six. They indeed only advised him, but he had to act by their advice, especially in matters of peace and war. What was more, this powerful Senate was to sit for life. Whenever there should be a vacancy Parliament itself should nominate six candidates, from whom the Council should choose two, and of those two Cromwell was to pick out one. The Parliament was to be of 460 members, 400 from England, thirty from Scotland and thirty from Ireland. It was to consist virtually of Puritans, or at any rate of people who were not in opposition to the conquering faction. It had a high franchise, a man must have an assessment of a good deal more than 1,000 modern pounds, generally in land, before he could vote. The Instrument provided for a revenue of a million and a quarter (that is in our money near eight millions), of which only one-sixth was to be used for civilian administration; the rest of what was, for that time, a crushing burden, was to go to the armed forces.

Cromwell professed to treat the whole thing as a great surprise, but he acted promptly enough. The Instrument of Government was all ready at the moment when the Little Parliament broke up on the 12th of December; it was acted upon at top speed on the 16th. Cromwell was named Protector in Westminster Hall, grandly dressed with a gold band round his hat. He hesitated a little as he gave his consent, the Instrument was read, he swore to its observance, and went back to Whitehall in the same state in which he had come. The New Parliament, the second of his experiments, called also "The First Parliament of the Protectorate," was ordered to meet on Cromwell's lucky day—the 3rd of September following, in this year 1654. It is another of the more amiable points in Cromwell's character that he was thus superstitious.

It duly met, and was to sit for five months. The 3rd of September, 1654, was a Sunday, so no profane business was done, but the Protector treated the members to a solemn sermon the next day in Westminster Abbey, and after that in the Painted Chamber he made them a sort of "Speech from the Throne."

The inevitable happened. The Parliament treated itself seriously, and was therefore incompatible with direct government. It was very disconcerting and annoying and exasperating. It seemed silly to fail again. But the strain on Cromwell's nerves was more than he could stand. Those who read into his action an ambition that was not there thought him particularly annoyed by a vote of more than two to one passed in the Parliament in spite of Lambert, and forbidding the Protectorship to be hereditary. He may already have desired it to be hereditary, because he certainly desired things to be stable, but the intractability of the Parliament was the real cause of what was so soon to follow. On the 22nd of January, 1655, he summoned them to the Painted Chamber and told them he had had enough of them. As for the five months, he regarded them as being over, for he chose to count them as lunar months and not as calendar months. After all he was a soldier, and a soldier's wage was paid—when it was paid—by lunar months; and when it was in arrears—which it usually was—the arrears were also counted by weeks, in lunar months of four weeks each. Cromwell told them he was the more ashamed of them because they were neither Papist, nor next door to Papistry; not "strangers to the works of God, but men in-

THE JEWS' FIRST PETITION TO CROMWELL
FROM THE ORIGINAL DOCUMENT IN THE PUBLIC RECORD OFFICE

structed by God's spirit." This habit into which they had fallen of ascribing to man what had really been done by the Creator was more than God Himself could bear—and so he would tell them.

Whereupon he declared the Parliament dissolved. Armed men were at hand, of course, to support God's decision. And so ended Oliver's second experiment at relief.

He next attempted a long spell of unsupported personal ordering. It lasted for over nineteen months, that is through all the last months of 1655 and most of 1656. It was during those months that the question of his taking the Crown, which we shall turn to in a moment, was first seriously broached. He organised this experiment as a purely military thing—for that was the one kind of Government he understood. He divided the territory of England into military districts,* each under a Major-General. And he put among these officials his chief officers, Lambert, and his cousin Whalley, Fleetwood, etc. But his foreign policy had brought the finances of the country into a desperate condition, and there was nothing for it but to try to get another Parliamentary experiment. It would be a great relief to him anyhow, for nearly two years of unshared responsibility had become intolerable.

The Council also pressed, so in this summer of 1656 he counselled that there should be elections, the new Parliament to meet on the 17th of September. It had a longer life than its two elder brothers; Cromwell again launched it with a sermon, taking the form this time of a dissertation on the 85th Psalm; but even at the outset there was trouble, the Council excluded something like a third from the new House; no one could sit unless he had the written authority of the Council to do so, and the Council had decided that 150 of the 460 members were not sufficiently godly.

Then this new Parliament began to take on airs as the other had, and particularly distinguished itself by reviving the old

---

* There were ten to begin with, later increased to eleven.

claim of the House to be a Court of Justice. In that capacity it savagely punished a poor lunatic in whom (so he said) the Saviour was incarnate. To disabuse him of this idea these Puritans had him flogged all the way from Westminster to the heart of the City, put in the pillory, branded, and then his tongue bored with a red-hot iron. They had him sent back to his native Bristol and flogged there again. Then they put him into solitary confinement.

It was a new irritation. Cromwell was all against violence of this sort, especially against men with revelations; moreover it was a duplication of the executive power. Further there came protests against the military government of the country under these Major-Generals, the most prominent of whom were Lambert, hitherto his right-hand man; son-in-law Fleetwood, brother-in-law Desborough, and cousin Whalley. Again must Cromwell order of necessity a relief to his executive power. Therefore what may properly be called "The Fourth Experiment" was prepared.

Not that there was a regular dissolution, but that the Parliament was re-formed. There was to be added to it a new House of Peers, chosen principally from the Protector's chief supporters: the idea was to start the Constitution again something on the old lines, with Cromwell in the place of King but without the title. On the 26th of June, 1657, a second inauguration of him as Protector, with far more pomp than the first time, took place. He had all the ceremony of a Royal establishment, the trumpets sounding, the foreign Ambassadors standing to his right and left, and the Sword borne before him. He established a bodyguard—and all the rest of the furniture. The newly modelled Parliament was adjourned to meet in the following January. In that month therefore, on the 20th, the fourth of these ephemeral experiments assembled.

Within a fortnight it burst in its turn. The Commons quarrelled with the Lords, and though Cromwell read them all a sermon, calling God to witness (what was very true) that he

THE HOUSE OF COMMONS AS IN 1656

had not sought the office he held, and tried the impossible—to wit to make a Parliament obey one man—he was once more at the end of his patience.

He was caught in a triple tangle: debt was piling up through his own unbalanced foreign policy; he owed five months' arrears of pay to the soldiers in England and seven to the garrison in Ireland, on top of which he heard that a petition was being circulated supported by some of the great names in the Army, protesting against government by one man and against a House of Lords.

The explosion which followed upon Cromwell's part was wholly unpremeditated. It was mere impulse, even more certainly than so many of his other acts had been. He did not even send for a state coach, but got into a hackney carriage which plied for hire at the gate of the Palace and, ordering only half a dozen of his guards to follow, he drove down the quarter mile to the House of Commons.

He raved at them. He had not sought the situation in which he was! God knows he would rather have lived under a woodside and tended a flock of sheep! Surely he had a right to be supported? Yet there they were, "as God is my witness," breaking their oaths, dividing the Army, some of them trifling with Royalist conspirators, others threatening a riot in the City! He was bound in his duty to God to prevent anarchy, therefore he ends, "I do dissolve this Parliament—and let God judge between me and you." Whereat his chief opponents in the unfortunate assembly answered loudly, not without irony, "Amen."

That was the last of these gimcrack, "jury," "ersatz" Parliaments. But it would not have been the last had not Cromwell been destined to die that very year. He was, before his death, setting out once again to summon yet another such thing! That fifth misjudgment would have been followed by a fifth breakdown, and a sixth by a seventh, no doubt, had fate allowed him some few more years. But he was not allowed them.

Here then was Oliver without a Parliament to help him, and faced with the apparent necessity of finding money: for getting it somehow from an exasperated people who protested that they could bear no more.

But why had he fallen into such intolerable financial straits? In part because the very nature of his government was such that it could not have carried on without huge expenditure, even in peace time, for the Army. But he had, also, from political incapacity, chosen the very time to launch upon the most expensive of all luxuries—an inconsequent and useless foreign war.

For the original war with the Dutch which he had inherited from the Long Parliament there had been excuse enough, that Dutch were commercial rivals, and had moreover a fleet which must either be the superior or the inferior of the British—and would only be the inferior if it were defeated. In that duel which Cromwell's sailors won, with the fine instrument of war, the fleet the Revolution had inherited from Charles, English seamanship proved itself. But Cromwell, having such a weapon to hand, began to use it without any fixed policy or considered object. His alliance was wooed by the two great rival powers, France and Spain, precisely because he had such a fleet in being and so great and well-trained a professional body of troops by land; an Army which could provide an excellent expeditionary force to work in alliance with either against the other.

There was no reason why Cromwell should have joined either France or Spain; there was no reason why he should have still further added to the rapidly accumulating debt which was ultimately to destroy him. The only motive at work was that simple religious emotion of which I have spoken. Spain seemed to him on the whole the worse of the two because she was the more Papist; therefore would he wantonly attack

Spain. At the same time he hoped to raid Spanish possessions in the West Indies, while pretending firm friendship with the Court of Spain in Europe. It was the most extraordinary policy —or lack of policy—conceivable. It landed him into the disgraceful defeat suffered by the expedition against Hispaniola. His ships did indeed occupy the undefended Jamaica, with its 500 Spaniards or so, who took to the woods when the invasion came; but neither Cromwell himself nor anyone else at the time thought Jamaica much worth having. He could not get colonists for it, and the expedition was thrown away.

Blake raised the prestige of English seamanship to a great height by his personal powers of command, and especially by his success against land batteries. The English sailors captured and looted convoys of Spanish bullion.

But to the Protectorate it was of little service, for the most of what was taken was embezzled by the captors. That the fine fighting and fine seamanship of a fleet in full training, and now so manifestly superior to the Spaniards, should have been to the glory of England was excellent: but glory without a policy advanced is politically a very empty thing. Cromwell had satisfied a religious impulse; but on balance he had weakened his country. It was from an impulse even wilder, but one which had the same root, that he had conceived some years before the fantastic project of uniting England and Holland in one republic. It was the same impulse which now made him undertake that singular piece of extravagance—his interference in favour of the Vaudois. Here again the incident speaks loudly of Cromwell's sincerity and simplicity: but as statesmanship it was deplorable.

The Vaudois were mountaineers of an upper Alpine valley under the Dutchy of Savoy. The Duchess Regent was the daughter of the French King. These mountaineers of the upper valley professed a simple heresy, inclining them (though they had held it for centuries) to the Protestant side of Europe from the Lutheran movement onwards. They had been tolerated; but as mountaineers will, especially those of the upper valleys, they had raided their neighbours of the lower and richer part, downstream; these being nearer civilisation were Catholic. The victims appealed to their lord, and the Regency established order with brutality, massacring the highlanders and their families, raiding and killing in their villages.

Cromwell proposed to interfere. Heaven knows what he could have done! There was some talk of bombarding Nice, which was the port of Savoy; he could hardly have hoped to annex any part of Piedmont! Anyhow, this generous extravagance played straight into the hands of Mazarin. That great statesman, the successor of Richelieu, decided to get as cheaply as possible the aid of Cromwell's professional cavalry and foot in the French struggle against the Spaniard. The English forces were close at hand, for the field of the Franco-Spanish war lay just beyond the Straits of Dover on the borders of Flanders, around Dunkirk. It was easy for Mazarin to settle the Vaudois business, seeing that Savoy, under its French Regent, was virtually a dependency of the French Crown; he saw to it that the Vaudois should be more mildly treated; further, he could promise Cromwell the later possession of Dunkirk—which was not his to give, for it was a Spanish town, belonging to the Spanish Netherlands. His success was a score for the Protestant cause and a very great personal satisfaction to Cromwell. He had come to the aid of the slaughtered Saints whose bones had, before his intervention, lain scattered upon the Alpine mountains cold; and it was the more gratifying when he remembered that they had kept the Faith of Jehovah so pure of old when all his own forebears had worshipped stocks and stones. And once more England was to have a bastion beyond the Straits of Dover—when all need for such a thing had long passed. Dunkirk was to be English, or at least to be held by an English garrison—and it was to cost fantastic sums, adding hugely to the debt and bringing in not a penny.

During these years of Reluctant Power used to so little purpose the question of Kingship had been debated by Cromwell's Parliaments and within his own mind. He had thought of it as early as the November of 1652, before the end of the Long Parliament. His conversation with Whitelock on the 8th of that month will be remembered. The day was fine and the air pure, the scene St. James's Park—a situation suited to thoughts of a crown.

Now, four years later, at the height of his power, that power which he had so little desired and could only so awkwardly use, the question arose again. Cromwell came very near indeed to accepting the name—he already had the position—of King. There were many advantages in such a course. It would make regular every act of obedience rendered to the Revolution with Cromwell at its head, for there was a Law on the Statute Book nearly two centuries old forbidding an accusation of treason against anyone who should obey a King *de facto*. It would regularise all legal enactments and forms. The Crown was an integral part of the English Constitution, and though the usurpation would be violent, time would soon remedy *that*. It would settle that difficult question of the succession to his power which he could never get himself to tackle on his own responsibility. It had openly been proposed in Parliament early in the year that the Crown should be offered to him in his own Palace at Whitehall.

From the 8th of May, 1657, to the 27th of the month the thing hung in the balance. No one knew on which side Oliver's decision would fall. He did not know himself. But at last he came down on the republican (or rather, Protec-torate) side of the hedge. He put it characteristically, saying that if he were to accept the Crown he could only do it doubt-fully, that if he did it doubtfully it would not be of Faith, and that if it were not of Faith it would be a sin, "wherefore I cannot undertake this Government with the title of King, and this is mine answer to this great and weighty business."

He had said that for himself he valued the name King no

more than a feather in his hat—and he was certainly telling the truth; but what decided him in spite of the arguments in favour of his coronation was the ominous growling of the soldiers.

It was a month later that he was all but enthroned in a solemn second inauguration; but enthroned he was not, and King he was not. It is perhaps the better for his memory, and his instinct was sound. But little else he did or half did during those five years was as sound as this refusal of a crown his family could not have retained.

Take that phase of reluctant power as a whole, the last of his life, and see it as it was, judged by the only tests applicable to policy, domestic and foreign results, and the answer is bankruptcy. Political bankruptcy—for there was nothing to show for all his expense save Jamaica, which no one at the time could guess would have any future, and Dunkirk, which was not an asset but a ruinous liability; literal bankruptcy as well—for all this wanton waging of war only made more desperate a financial situation already at breaking-point. He had worn himself out, it is true, through many and intense soldierly efforts, years in the saddle in all weathers, no rest, long toil on insufficient sleep—and all the rest of it. But the money worry did most. That grinding menace of debt never left him, and the burden grew heavier with every week that passed.

# CROMWELL IN THE PRESENCE OF DEATH

IT is only in the presence of Death that we can understand Life; let us keep Oliver in view as he approaches the Narrows.

His passing was—like that of most of us—to be troubled by a clouding and confusion of the spirit, like that of all of us by a breakdown of the body; but it exemplifies him, revealing finally what was in him and what was not.

At the time of his fourth failure—the dismissal of his fourth clumsy experiment in political construction—a decline in his full powers had been proceeding for over seven years. As early as Dunbar he had begun to feel the beginnings of age. His wife was told it on the very morrow of the battle; he writes to her from the town round which they were burying the rifled and naked Scottish dead in the sodden ground, to his "well beloved wife, Elizabeth Cromwell" far off in the south, in the Cockpit rooms of Whitehall purlieus:

"My Dearest,

I have not leisure to write much . . . Truly if I love you not too well I think I err not on the other hand much. Thou art dearer to me than any creature . . . The Lord hath showed us an exceeding great mercy . . . who can tell how great it is! My weak faith has been upheld. I have been in my inward man marvellously supported; though I assure thee I grow an old man and feel infirmities of age marvellously stealing upon me. Would my corruptions did as fast decrease! Pray on my behalf . . . I rest thine."

A life lived through the wars in all weathers for eight years had done its work—and the gift he had got from Ireland, the ague. Camps pitched in marshland, riding under sheets of rain for days, meals got at random and at all hours, the shocks of how many charges, the extenuation of long vigils after long marches, the shaking roar of the sieges, had all worn him slowly down—and such things had come on him when he was already past forty-three. The far sound of the invisible enemy approaching, "the distant hosts of death that march with muffled drum" had hitherto but warned him—no more. But he had heard the warning.

He was still at full capacity when he wrote thus from Dunbar; within the twelvemonth he was to conduct and himself to endure the finest, the most pressed, of his advances, the swoop from the Forth to Worcester, and to crown it with the rapid concentration at Evesham, with the double stroke on either bank of the Severn, with the counter-manœuvre back across the river—which clinched the action. But he had heard the muffled drums, and after Worcester the succeeding most uncertain peace was to confirm that first beckoning.

His rasping voice was still at its loudest when, eighteen months later, he denounced and drove forth the last wretched Parliamentarians; and he yet maintained, year after year, the soldier's ceaseless attention to affairs—civilian affairs which distracted him. To such unsuitable cares were added the constant, the increasing strain of plot and threatened assassination; a whole people to be kept under by the sword and, worst of all, the accumulating, the insoluble, problem of finance.

To keep men under by the sword had become custom with him. He had said that, though nine men out of ten were against him: "What if I put a sword in this hand of the tenth man?" But debt was a new thing, with no issue, and piling up at eight per cent. The usurer was upon him.

This still accelerated the decline. It pushed him down the slope until he staggered under his burden. It never left him and was to break him at last.

His power, which tortured him, must yet be upheld. The fine fleet with its triumphs, the now perfect regiments, all depended upon supply, and supply was not to be maintained.

Such payments were beyond the powers of the nation to whom they gave glory—but glory without fruit, and it was strained to breaking-point by the toppling weight of this debt which grew and grew, and must soon break down the public machine. Now, as the spring of 1658 approached and the fifty-ninth anniversary of his birth, he was exhausted.

His enemies believed that his perpetual change of room, his nights spent now here in the Palace, now there, was a doubling back and forth from fear of sudden attack by pistol or blade. It may be so. It was much more that symptom of dissolution slowly advancing, the loss of sleep. This, which those overcharged receive with anxious novelty, undermines the man. It strikes at the heart, diminishing its action, making irregular the blood's movement, and even sapping the will. How many conspicuous and obscure have known that grip of insomnia! Ronsard in his last progress through the fields of home, moaning for repose in the long winter nights; the unflinching Richelieu whispering on his last journey northwards, "I sleep no more."

In that same February, 1657, which had seen Oliver's querulous dismissal of the last assembly, he suffered a blow within the home, and his home had been more to him than all the rest. The youngest of his children, she whom he cherished as the belated darling of them all, was stricken; Rich, Warwick's grandson, left the impetuous girl of nineteen a widow. All the trouble of that contested marriage was wasted, and the agony of his child fell on a mind already far overladen. It was the first knock on the door, a second was to follow. The third was to be a call for the broken man himself, the last of them in that family to die so soon.

New proof that his countless enemies were still upon him followed. Some months before, that well-aimed vivid piece of writing "Killing no Murder" had appeared. Now came news of yet another rising planned. Hull was to be secretly delivered as a port of entry for Royalists; commissions had been issued in the name of the young King Charles, and Hewett, devoted to the Church of England in which he was a priest, and therefore to the Blood Royal, was working underground to raise London. In May there was a rising. It came to nothing. Hewett and his accomplices were put to death—but the feeling was omnipresent and an unceasing source of further danger.

They say that his daughter Elizabeth—she who had married Claypole and whom he loved best among his well-loved young —reproached him for such severities as Hewett's death, though she also had a lively dread of what would be her own fate and that of all this family so insecurely balanced in its unnatural position, if the people should rise. She gave thanks for the father's escape. It may be that she did so intercede for Hewett, and certainly Cromwell, never moved to bloodshed save when his religious frenzy was upon him, was the man to hesitate. It is possible that Thurloe overpersuaded him; for if examples were not made, how should power without title and so widely detested be secure? And Thurloe was a lawyer, and, one might almost say, the Government itself. If it fell, his head would fall too, as chief servant to the usurper. All information, all secrets, were in Thurloe's hands—by which advantage also he saved his life at the Restoration, knowing too much about all men for any man to touch him; so William Cecil was saved under Mary Tudor.

Whoever urged Oliver to that decision was wise. His most uncertain, unsought and undesired authority would have destroyed him if he or his watchdogs neglected the instrument of terror.

The use of that instrument was the more necessary because Cromwell himself had fallen at that very moment into the toils of Mazarin and was thus ensuring the continuance and increase of that maddening taxation which his huge army and his fleet, forever in action, required. He was led now, in this eleventh hour of his career, into sending out at last that expeditionary land force to aid the French in interests wholly theirs.

It was in the month before Hewett's head had fallen that certain of Oliver's fine regiments, promised months before, were embarked for Flanders where the Hapsburg of Spain and the Bourbon house were locked in their duel. Dunkirk was the lure, and it is pleasant to repeat that in promising Dunkirk to Cromwell, Mazarin paid for the good English contingent with what was not his to give. Dunkirk was Spanish; if Cromwell's men should help Mazarin to defeat Spain, Dunkirk should be made over to England—a white elephant costing an annual fortune for its useless keep; a liability which the King of England later wisely sold back to the French King.

Mazarin might well be proud of his stroke. The English expeditionary force, acting in such strange alliance, was vastly and justly admired. It did much to secure the fall of the port, and young Louis XIV, lying at Calais, was bidden by his great Minister to play up to his role in the comedy.

It irked that Royal boy, so recently enfranchised. Here was a man who had put his own King to death, and that King the husband of Louis's aunt, a Queen of England still living, and a daughter of France: how could he deal with such a man? But Mazarin knew substance from shadow. He had insisted, and Louis had done all required of him—save one last thing which he would not do. He had received Cromwell's son-in-law and ambassador, Fauconberg, with almost Royal honours. He had given over the keys of Dunkirk to that envoy with his own hands; he had sent Oliver a letter as from a monarch to a monarch, and the bearer was instructed, on delivering it, to flatter Cromwell with the most extravagant phrases as the greatest commander living among mortal men. But one thing Louis would not do, he would not write a *"Monsieur Mon Frère"* at the head of it; he would not call the fellow a brother as, by usage, do Kings their equals.

And on that empty point turns a singular incident which

has been read as a proof of Oliver's breakdown in nerves. It was already late in June; he was months advanced in weakness since the winter trouble. When the French King's letter was given him he looked at the address, frowned, and thrust it without ceremony into his coat—he had seen that the title "Brother" was lacking. But it was not the peevishness of breaking health that provoked so abrupt a gesture in a man; always it was national feeling. He was England when dealing with the Bourbon King, and he must be styled *"Monsieur Mon Frère."* It was due to his country—which had been proved moreover once again, and to the Frenchman's advantage, the triumphant people of his God.

Close on all this fell, within the shrine of his home, the second and far the heaviest blow. It was in the beginning of the next month that the best-beloved was stricken in her turn. His daughter, Elizabeth Claypole, must die.

Men bound up with those of their own blood can testify how, in such hours, it is the picture of the victim in childhood which returns, how living, from the past: a little child laughing in vivid light against the cloud. She had been the baby in the good quiet days before the wars had come; she had been born when he was in the full vigour of his youth, just entered into public notice, his thirtieth year. And she was still the baby during the long space intervening until her sister Mary was born, just as the peace was drawing to its end. It was so that he saw her now, his little child.

She was not only marked for death, but in great pain; he would not leave her; he saw it all pass before him and he was forespent. To his sleeplessness he now added enforced vigils by her side, and his will broke down. He could not bend himself to affairs, he left work undone and all business neglected. On Tuesday, August the 3rd, she rallied, and, to make the issue more fearful, all felt hope. Oliver slept at last profoundly. On the Friday she died.

He broke into a wild lamentation, crying aloud and sobbing

out, "I cannot bear it! . . . I cannot bear it!" Through such things had Oliver to pass on the last steep of the falling road.

When they had buried her with pomp as for a Princess he sat in the King's place, in Hampton Court, all crushed; he would listen to the Epistles. He would strengthen himself if he could with the supporting strength of the Incarnate, the upholder of mankind:

ΑΓΙΟΣ ΙΣΧΥΡΟΣ ΑΘΑΝΑΤΟΣ

It cured him not.

A fortnight after he had seen her grave closed over her his own end was upon him. They took him back to the Capital, where every aid could be found, carrying him to Whitehall and the Royal rooms above the river. It was the 26th of August, a Tuesday; there was measured out to him by his fates ten days before he should be summoned.

Now, now, on the succession to him depended all their lives and all the erratic structure which supported them. In a moment a crash might come.

There is a silly pedantic talk invented from the destruction of Monarchy that the headship of the State is, in England, elective and to be decided by nothing but the choice of the wealthier men assembled in session at Westminster. It is not so. When there was doubt the ruler was implored to name his heir. So had it been with Elizabeth, sitting there silent on the floor with her finger in her mouth, in the days when Cromwell was a child. So it was now with Cromwell; yet in all those years Cromwell had published no name. Why not?

We cannot tell. Perhaps he had thought of a Crown because by that device the burden of decision would be taken from him. Perhaps he would not decide because a known heir might weaken his own difficult hold, by turning men to seek the friendship of the power to come. Therefore Thurloe told the story that Oliver had secreted some name in a sealed paper; if that story be true the paper was never found.

[ 345 ]

And now his time was drawing very short. But they dared not approach him. He had received a revelation from on high. God had spoken to him. He would not die. "You doctors," he told them, might trust their learning; he would trust a far surer thing, the very voice of God. He bade the doctors leave him, all save one, their chief, Bates, who had been the King's physician and was his own. It is from him we have the strange picture of what followed.

All being gone save Bates and Mrs. Cromwell, who stood by, he took his wife's dear hand in his own and said to the man of science:

"I affirm to thee this: I shall not die of this sickness; of that I am secure. Do not think I am in delirium, I speak the word of Truth. God Himself has given me this answer."

Upon Friday, the 27th of August, the fits of ague grew so violent they feared he might not pass the night. Upon the morrow they redoubled. Upon the Monday a great wind rose, a tempest memorable throughout Europe from the Orkneys to Italy, shaking the wooden beams of the old Palace and roaring against the floodtide of the Thames below.

Cromwell, now in full fever, muttered and tossed through nights and days. The words he murmured were from the depths of his soul, disjointed, confused, repeated as a rhythm is repeated when the brain is at its weariest. Prayers for the nation, for England; then the renewed—but doubtful—affirmation of his Election as a chosen one of the Lord. In a lucid moment he asked of a chaplain, a man of God, whether it were possible to fall from Grace? No, he was assured, the Elect can never fall. The Saints are indefectible. Was it not in Calvin's book? The sick man sighed with some small measure of relief. "I know that once I was in Grace," he said.

But the terrors returned. In the furnace of his dissolved and failing mind he was heard to affirm, despairingly, the Divine Love; but then to mutter once and again and yet again, "It is a fearful thing to fall into the hands of the Living God!"

[ 346 ]

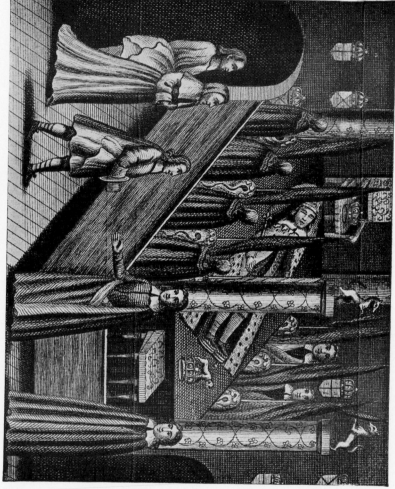

THE LORD PROTECTOR LYING IN STATE AT SOMERSET HOUSE

From an Old Print

Surely he might hope. Had he not hewed the enemies of the Lord to pieces (in Gilgal)? Surely he could claim the reward beyond conception, the supernal light, beatitude? Was he not of the Chosen? And then, with shuddering, the abyss opened —might he not wake to nameless horror, and fall shrieking into the hands of an angry God? Nor in that strong faith was there room for any surmise of mere dissolution, wherein Death is nothing but a mighty sleep.

On Thursday, the 2nd of September, he fell more quiet. Those whose main interest it was to affirm it say that as he so fluttered on the edge of life he was understood to name his eldest son. All that night he muttered perpetually the set phrases of his religion. There followed a silence prolonged for hours into the morning, and till noon. He knew no earthly thing any more, and in the afternoon he died. It was the day of Dunbar and of Worcester, and of the trumpet challenging Drogheda walls.

· · · · · · ·

When they had embalmed their Cromwell dead they placed in recumbent pomp a waxen effigy of him, royally accoutred, and on the hangings of the bed his titles and his name. There it reposed in state for the people to stare on it as they filed by. Apart and alone a few watched Cromwell where he lay.

But Cromwell was not there. He had gone to discover whether there were beatitude for his reward who had hewn to pieces the enemies of Jehovah; or whether he should fall shrieking into the hands of an angry God; or whether Death be indeed no more than a mighty sleep.

# INDEX

St. Albans, 139, 224 ; early skirmishes of, 140, 150 ; at Gainsborough, 150-2 ; calls for troops, 150-3 ; at Winceby, 155-6 ; wounded, 164-5 ; at 2nd battle of Newbury, 171, 173-6 ; and failure, 174, 251-2 ; advances in military power, 177 ; attacks Manchester, 178-80 ; and New Model army, 180-2 ; and Self-Denying Ordinance, 180-2 ; siege train of, 192, 197-99, 200, 241, 247, 249 ; at Devizes, 193-4 ; at Winchester, 194-6 ; at Basing House, 192 *et seq.* ; and the Army, 205-6, 211, 219-21, 317-8 ; and Parliament, 212, 218, 318, 321, 324, 327 ; and Monarchy, 212-3, 317 ; and Charles's escape to Isle of Wight, 213, 217 ; letters to Hammond, 223-4, 229-31 ; at trial of Charles, 234-6 ; signs death warrant, 236 ; at Drogheda, 242 *et seq.* ; at Wexford, 246 *et seq.* ; at Waterford, 252-4 ; at Kilkenny, 254-7 ; at Clonmel, 258 ; and Scottish invasion of England, 257, 262 *et seq.*, 302-4, 305-6 ; Ireland ruined by, 260-1 ; march to Preston of, 262-4, 274-5 ; at battle of Preston, 274-7 ; invades Scotland, 281 *et seq.* ; at battle of Dunbar, 281, 291-2, 312 ; letter to Scotch ministers, 284 ; retreat to Dunbar, 286-7 ; forcing manœuvre of, 294, 296-7 ; march to Worcester, 299-302 ; at battle of Worcester, 310-12 ; dissolves Parliament, 318, 322, 331, 333 ; and the Crown, 318, 320-1, 337 ; first Parliament of, 322-7, 329 ; as Lord President, 323 ; compelled to adopt personal rule, 326 ; lack of foreign policy, 327-8, 333, 338 ; second Parliament of, 331-2 ; third Parliament of, 332-3 ; fourth Parliament of, 333-4 ; war with Spain, 335-6 ; and union of England and Holland, 335 ; and Vaudois, 335-6 ; and France, 336, 342-3 ; breakdown in health of, 340-1, 345 ; and execution of Hewett, 342 ; and Louis XIV, 343 ; death of, 347 ; successor of, 345

Cromwell, Sir Oliver, 32, 37

Cromwell, Sir Richard, *see* Williams, Richard

Cromwell, Robert, 31-2, 61

Cromwell, Thomas, early life of, 23; and Wolsey, 24; and dissolution of monasteries, 23-4; fortune acquired by, 26

DALBIER, at Basing House, 157

Derby, Lord, 309

Desborough, John, 120, 332

Devizes, 191-4

Devon-Cornwall peninsula, 190

Digby family, 94

Digby, Sir Kenelm, 94

Doncaster, 264*n.*, 270-3

Donnington Castle, 171-2, 192

Doon Hill, 288, 296

Downe, John, 235

Drogheda, 242 *et seq.*

Dublin, 242, 254

Dunbar, battle of, 122, 126, 135, 184, 262, 282, 291-6; campaign before, 282-292; dispositions of forces at, 291-298

Dundalk, 244

Dunkirk, 337-8, 338

Durham, 147

Dust Hill, 186

EASTERN Counties Association, 128, 137, 142, 146, 153, 155-6

Edgehill, battle of, 125, 137-8

Edinburgh, 283, 300

Elizabeth, Queen, 29, 52, 88, 97-98

Elliot, Sir John, 107

Ely, dissolution of Priory of, 30-1; Stewards and, 30-1, 111; Cromwell in, 111, 183

England, nineteenth-century, 14-15; anti-Catholicism in, 14, 79, 89, 99, 103; Reformation in, 21-2, 84, 93; church corruption in, 25; dissolution of monasteries in, 25-8; Calvinism in, 42-3, 52, 90; Established Church of, 54; Catholic-minded men of, 79-82, 85-7; Catholicism in, 80-2, 85 *et seq.*; growth of Protestantism in, 89-90, 95, 104; number of Catholic priests in, 95; cavalry in, 137; Royalist reaction in, 212, 219, 222-3; Scottish invasion of (1648), 211, 218, 223, 228, 259 *et seq.*; Fleet of, 225-7, 334; Scottish invasion of (1651), 262, 302 *et seq.*; possibility of Royalist recruitment in, 302-3, 310-12; international repute of, 313; clamour for settlement in, 314-5; cost of Army in, 315-6; attempt to reform Law in, 325; military districts of, 331-2

# INDEX

England, Church of, establishment of, 53, 86-7, 89; Calvinism in, 53-4, 89; and Charles I, 207; tithes of, 316

Essex, 137

Essex, 3rd Earl of, 93, 129; in command of Trained Bands, 119; army of, 138, 153; relieves Gloucester, 154; at Lostwithiel, 168, 179

Evesham, 308

Fairfax, 2nd Baron, at Hull, 146; at Marston Moor, 164, 168

Fairfax, Lady, 236, 258

Fairfax, Sir Thomas, at Hull, 146, 154; at Marston Moor, 164, 168; and Cromwell, 177, 181; Commander-in-Chief, 181-183, 220; at Naseby, 186, 188; suppresses Kentish rising, 226-7; and arrest of Hammond, 231; and death of Charles, 236; refuses to command invasion of Scotland, 281

Farnham, 231

Fauconberg, Lord, 92-93, 343

Felstead, 112

Fens, drainage of, 113; enclosure of, 115

Flanders, 343

Fleet, see Navy

Fleetwood, Charles, in Dunbar engagement, 310; at Worcester, 310-12; Major-General of district, 331-2

Forth, River, 302, 303

Fowey, 168

France, Calvinism in, 34n., 41, 84; religious wars in, 84, 98; seeks alliance with Cromwell, 334, 336, 343-44

Gainsborough, 146, 150, 152

Galway, 260

Geneva, 34n., 41

Germanies, Reformation in, 24, 36, 41, 84; Catholicism in, 84

Gisburn, 274

Glenham, surrenders York, 167

Gloucester, siege of, 152-3

Goring, Lord, at Marston Moor, 163-4, 166, 168; at Langport, 190

Gowran, 255

Grantham, 140, 150

Great North Road, 28, 147

Grey, Lady Jane, 65

Gunpowder Plot, 98-99

Gustavus Adolphus, 61, 125, 137

Haddington, 286, 298

Hamilton, Duke of, leads Scottish invasion, 262, 268-72, 274-7; delayed start of, 268, 275-6; prisoner at Windsor, 233-4; incapacity of, 264-5; and battle of Preston, 275-7; capture of, 277

Hammond, Colonel, 255

Hammond, Robert, 213-4; and Charles I, 216; and Cromwell, 218, 223-4, 228-32; money granted to, 228; arrest of, 231

Hampden, William, 29, 138, 213

Hampton Court, 70, 215-6, 217n., 345

Harrison, Colonel, 235, 306, 308

Hartopp, Mrs., 51

Hatton, Sir Christopher, 203n.

"Heads of Proposals," 206-7

Henry VIII, King, 24-5, 69

Henry of Bourbon, 84

Hertfordshire, 137

Hewett, Dr., 242

Hewson, John, 233, 255-6

High Toynton, 156

Hile Sands, 154

Hinchinbrooke, 31; Elizabeth at, 29, 31; James I at, 32; sale of, 60, 62-3

Hispaniola, 335

Hodder, River, 275

Holbourne, at Dunbar, 293

Holland, see Netherlands

Holland, Lord, 94

Holmby House, 70, 203, 206

Horncastle, 155-6

Howard family, 91

Howard, Catherine, 65

Hull, 145; siege of, 145-8, 152-4; reinforcements reach, 154; munitions at, 265, 271; and Royalists, 341

Huncks, Colonel, 235

Huntingdon, and Hinchinbrooke, 28; Robert Cromwell in, 30; Town Cross of, 50; Oliver in, 57, 67, 109-10, 137, 152; Oliver returned to Parliament by, 107; Puritan "lecturers" in, 108-10; new Charter of, 110, 139; Oliver leaves, 111; Montagus and, 113

Huntingdon, county of, 137

Hurst Castle, 202, 232-3

Hyde, Edward, see Clarendon, Earl of

# INDEX

[ 353 ]

# INDEX

942.064
C 9 4 6 B

32330